https://rogerruinwriting.substack.com/

A Normie's Guide to the Dissident Right

& the Trump Era

Table of Contents

Timeline of the Internet

1991 – 2003 : Early Wild West Era
Birth of Internet - birth of 4chan and Web2.0

2004 – 2016: Late Wild West Era / 4chan Era

Birth of 4chan and Web2.0 - Big Tech Censorship

2017 - 2021 : Censorship Era

Big Tech Censorship - Elon Musk buying Twitter and establishment of Alt Tech like Rumble

2022 - Present: Modern Era

End of censorship era - ?

Timeline of the Dissident Right

Pre-2010: Offline Era

Pro-Internet groups such as American Renaissance

2010 - 2013: /pol/ or proto-Alt Right Era

Dissident Right begins to form online

2014 – 2017: Alt Right Era

Height of the Alt Right

2018 – Present: Modern Era

The Alt Right declines in popularity after Charlottesville. New groups such as America First take their place

Introduction - Who Am I, What is This, What is Dialectics, What is Dissent, What is the Internet

The Dialectic

The Millennial and Zoomer generations have lived through a time of great change and upheaval. They grew up during the peak of the post-war system, only to see it gradually deteriorate into a new and altogether different sort of system that is in many ways its opposite. The main force of this transformation was technology, in particular the Internet and information technology. However, it also follows the normal ebb and flow of history which has been described as "cyclical" or "dialectical" in nature.

"Dialectical" refers to a certain process of development. In this process, we start with a "thesis," which is the initial state or status quo. Then an "antithesis" emerges that contradicts the thesis, due to problems or contradictions that arise from the thesis. Then, after a period of time in which there is conflict between the thesis and antithesis, eventually a "synthesis" is created which incorporates parts of both the thesis and antithesis. Then this "synthesis" becomes the new "thesis." Here is an example of this process using the conflict between capitalism and communism in the 20th century:

> *Thesis: Capitalism - Due to the industrial revolution and globalization, capitalism emerged. It emphasized private ownership, free markets, and limited government intervention -- "the free market."*
>
> *Antithesis: Communism / Socialism - In response to capitalism, socialist ideologies such as communism emerged. The Soviet Union promoted communism as an alternative to capitalism. Communism advocated for state ownership of the means of production, central planning, and the abolition of private property.*

Conflict (Cold War Era) - *The clash between capitalism and communism led to the Cold War, a period of intense ideological, political, and military rivalry between the United States (representing capitalism) and the Soviet Union (representing communism). This conflict lasted for several decades and was characterized by proxy wars, espionage, and a nuclear arms race.*

Synthesis/New Thesis: Mixed Economy (Post-Cold War Era) - *The Soviet Union fell and the Eastern Block disintegrated in the late 80s and early 90s. This led to the end of the cold war, and Soviet-style communism with centrally planned economies.*

However, in the West, events such as the labor movement and the adoption of Keynesian economic theory in response to the Great Depression also transformed the economies of the "capitalist" states. The government began to closely regulate the economy. Labor unions collectively organized the workers against the capitalist business owners. And so socialist elements such as the minimum wage, the labor unions, the 40 hour work week and, in most countries, a socialized healthcare system were integrated into the capitalist system.

China, the most important remaining communist country, likewise reformed its system to incorporate more elements of capitalism and created a more liberalized market. Like in the "capitalist" countries these markets are nonetheless highly regulated by the government. As a result, China quickly rose in economic and political importance. In the end, both the "capitalist" and "communist" countries adopted a "mixed economy."

These mixed economies feature private ownership and free markets but also include government regulation and social welfare programs to address inequalities and provide a safety net for citizens.

The synthesis of mixed economies has evolved into what can be seen as the contemporary thesis. In this phase, economies around the world are interconnected through international trade, finance, and technology. Governments play a role in regulating markets and addressing social issues, but the emphasis remains on private enterprise and market-driven growth.

The rise of information technology has facilitated the dialectical process of history in ways that would be otherwise impossible as we will explore

2

shortly. Many commentators have noted this, and they seem to attribute the entire disruption of the post-war order to the technology itself. However, it's important to note that the root of the disruption is not an inevitable result of this technological advancement but is a process that will always occur, and that technology simply acts as a medium through which it is taking place. So while the advancement of technology is intimately related to this process, it is not as simple as technology = disruption = what we see now. Nor is the conflict exclusively political in nature. Rather it is a historical conflict that has always and will always take place along numerous domains, including the ideological, political, aesthetic, metaphysical, epistemological, and religious.

Take music, for one example.

> **The Thesis: Rock N Roll -** *The post-war era was dominated by rock and roll. This music is abrasive, primal, and dissonant in form. It is rebellious, virile, liberal and hedonistic in its outlook. It is a synthesis of black and white musical traditions. It is closely associated with the 60s liberal counter-culture. It is closely associated with drugs. It is social in nature -- a small, tight knit "band" of musicians who "tour," like the wandering bards of a medieval romance. "Rockstars" emerge and become rich and famous. Its lyrical content ranges from "party music" to "protest music" that contains liberal and progressive messaging.*

The Antithesis: Vaporwave - *The antithesis is electronic music, with Vaporwave being an excellent representative of this due to its association with the early "Alt Right" era of the Dissident Right. This form of music is not "primal" or "virile" at all. In fact the human element, rather than being emphasized, is totally removed. Instead, it is created by computers and synthesizers. It is inspired by "easy listening" and "elevator music" or "movie soundtracks" rather than being dissonant in nature. The music is created by a single person, in isolation, perhaps in their bedroom. The audience for the music is mostly white men. It is tonal (like white music) rather than rhythm-based (like black music, such as early rock and roll). The music is created by someone who is, more or less, a composer, rather than a travelling bard. Due to the Internet and decentralized music industry, they usually do not gain fame and fortune and may even be anonymous. It usually does not have any lyrical content whatsoever, but what little message it has is usually based on nostalgia and is directed towards the "glorious past" or "the future that was promised but never was" rather than being progressive or liberal in nature.*

It's important to emphasize again that this dialectical process is totally inevitable. It is as close as you can find to a law of gravity or law of conservation of energy in history. Therefore, what has been set in motion by the rise of the Dissident Right cannot be undone. These events that took place on the Internet immediately before, after and within 2016 have changed the course of history in ways that are unalterable, and there is no going back to the time that came before.

All that one has to do is study the events of the counter-culture of the 1960s, which propelled the last dialectical cycle of history and constructed the current thesis, to find their equivalents in the present dialectical cycle. 2016 was the summer of love. The original explosion of the antithesis that was primordial and had yet to take on a definitive form. 4channers, the Alt Right, Groypers, Proud Boys, incels...these are the hippies of our era. Sam Hyde, StoneToss, Murdoch Murdoch -- these are the artists like Henry Miller, Jack Kerouac, Lenny Bruce, George Carlin, the Grateful Dead, Monty Python were for the Boomers and their counter-culture. Charlottesville was something like the Manson murders perhaps. Taking the redpill is like when Boomers took their first hit of acid.

4

When you begin to remove yourself from the events as they take fold, and look at them from a bird's eye view, and see them not in their particular forms but as simply one instance of a more basic, platonic historical idea that has played out over and over again throughout time, it becomes difficult to argue that this is not the way that history is developing.

The influence of the hippies and their counter-culture ideas eventually permeated society and changed it in innumerable ways. Like the 4channers, they were not an exclusively political force. Many hippies were not involved in or interested in politics whatsoever, in fact an important part of their philosophy was "dropping out" of society (notice this pattern repeated again in the phenomenon of the NEET (*https://en.wikipedia.org/wiki/NEET*) in the online counter-culture). It took decades for the ethos of the counter-culture to fully transform from a fringe culture to the thesis of American culture, and it was only after this that it became the thesis of American politics. Between their inception and their ascension, they first influenced fashion, music, film, comedy, and various other aspects of American society. In a similar way, /pol/ was only one of the many boards of 4chan. Those of that generation that were interested in politics became involved in politics, and brought the new ideas of their generation with them. They gradually implemented them as they moved along in their careers, until their generation and their attitudes and values eventually dominated politics. The same effect will occur when this generation's counter-culture. Those who grew up with anime, video games, and memes, as well as with Sam Hyde and the Alt Right, will eventually be in positions of power.

The post-war Boomer generation was a reaction to the older, relatively more Right Wing generation of their parents, who created the relatively conservative culture of the 1950s, and thus brought with them a pendulum swing to the Left, by way of a Left Wing counter-culture. Thus, according to the dialectical laws of history, it is inevitable that their children would react to them and their liberal culture with a pendulum swing to the Right, by way of a Right Wing counter-culture.

Some have argued against this, saying that the majority of the Millennial and Zoomer generations are more liberal than their parents. This is a total misunderstanding of the process. It is not a switch that turns on/right and off/left. It is more like adding a tiny drop of food coloring to a glass of water, which slowly grows diluted while filling the entire glass. Or like a wave that reaches its zenith just as it crashes onto the beach and begins to recede, while another wave behind it has just reached its lowest point and begins to grow larger. It was only a small, fringe minority of Boomers that were hippies, yet eventually it permeated all of society. So it will be that a small fringe minority of the new, Right Wing counter-culture of the Millennials and Zoomers will one day permeate the society in the decades to come.

The Ultimate Conclusion of the Dialectic: Trump or Xi Jinping

There is one scenario in which this does not happen. The state can resist change, as it did in the Roman Republic, which slaughtered an entire generation of reformers such as the Gracchi Brothers. The dialectical process can be postponed in a particular place for a particular amount of time, especially by a wholly tyrannical and absolute government.

Perhaps the best example of this phenomena comes from China's "century of humiliation." When Western explorers reached China, the Chinese proclaimed that the West had nothing to offer them.

> *"I set no value on objects strange or ingenious and have no use for your country's manufactures. Our Celestial Empire possesses all things in prolific abundance and lacks no product within its own borders. Therefore, there is no need to import the manufactures of outside barbarians in exchange for our own produce"* — **Foreign Policy Research Institute. 2023. "China's early encounters with the West: A history in reverse. Foreign Policy Research Institute."** **(https://www.fpri.org/article/2023/05/chinas-early-encounters-with-the-west-a-history-in-reverse)**

The reason that this happened is that China, for thousands of years, had been the most advanced, powerful and influential civilization in East Asia, and regarded all others as barbarians. As a result of their resistance to modernize when faced by the threat of the West, China decayed socially. Its citizens became addicted to opium. Its government became corrupt, enervated and ineffectual, until warlords came to control parts of the country. Then it was colonized, first by the West and then by the Japanese (who took the opposite approach, choosing to learn from the West and rapidly modernizing). It became embroiled in decades of murderous revolutions and civil wars. It fell to the radical ideology of communism. Millions starved to death in famines. Thousands of years of that very Chinese culture that was so highly revered was destroyed through the cultural revolution. It was not until the late 1970s, under Deng Xiaoping, that China finally finished paying for its hubris, and recovered from its disastrously unwise decision.

It is possible that the West could repeat the mistake of China. For roughly 500 years, it is the West that has been the most advanced, powerful and influential civilization. It may decide that it has nothing to learn from the less liberal nations such as China, Russia, Saudi Arabia, and the other members of BRICS, that are expanding their global wealth and influence. Instead, it may choose to cling to the liberal post-war thesis as unquestionable dogma that has no room for compromise. If they go down that route, they will see their own century of humiliation, and be left behind by those nations that allow themselves to be more adaptive. In the end, the unstoppable force of the dialectic will continue, and these illiberal nations will surpass them, making the illiberal antithesis ascendant as the liberal nations fall into obscurity.

At the same time, while these nations may present as liberal, allowing for social liberalism such as homosexuality, they will have to be in reality less liberal and more tyrannical in order to stamp out any criticism of the status quo. Elections will be held, but they will be fixed so that only liberal candidates approving of the status quo will be elected. At the same time, they will venerate the importance of elections to greater and greater heights, declaring it a sacred act worthy of ever increasing reverence. Dissident political attitudes will be met with excommunication from society, imprisonment, and perhaps even torture or death. All while proclaiming the importance of free speech, so long as this "free speech" is only along conventional lines.

Hopefully, the West is not foolish enough to go down this route, and oppose the dialectic in vain. After all, it would ultimately be the worst of both worlds. But, if they do choose to make this mistake it would not be an unprecedented choice.

What Makes a Belief Dissident?

The amount of persecution that you receive for holding a belief is proof of how dissident it is. In this particular time, the most dissident beliefs are Right Wing beliefs. That also means that the Right Wing is the only side coming up with innovative new ideas that fundamentally challenge the status quo. Probably the most dissident belief is being labeled a "Nazi" or "white supremacist." In many Western cultures, professing this belief is treated like blasphemy, and it is enough to have a person become treated as less than human, and thrown in jail. Someone does not necessarily even need to be a Nazi or white supremacist. But if their beliefs are Right Wing enough, this label will be affixed to them and they will suffer the consequences.

Some Left Wing beliefs might be dissident to some degree. If you are trans, or if you are a revolutionary communist, perhaps you might be discriminated against in the workforce or receive a negative reaction from people. But nothing approaching what a "Nazi" would face. You will, at a minimum, not be censored from social media. The less you are persecuted, the more your beliefs are by definition acceptable by society and the less they fundamentally threaten the status quo.

It's also important to remember that just because a belief is dissident, that does not mean it is correct. Someone advocating for pedophilia would probably face persecution, but that does not mean that pedophilia is correct. But, you can also not say that being against pedophilia is in any way intellectually interesting or novel.\

The Internet and Its Role as the Medium of the 21st Century Dialectic

It is impossible to understand the events of the Trump Era and the history of the Dissident Right without understanding the Internet. They are totally intertwined.

Even more so than the counter-culture of the 1960s, perhaps the period most like our own is the reformation and religious wars in the 16th and 17th centuries, facilitated by the invention of the printing press. Nick Fuentes, The Alternative Hypothesis, Slate Star Codex, Mencius Moldbug, Sargon of Akkad, Keith Woods, Richard Spencer, Andrew Anglin, Alex Jones, Andrew Tate -- these are the modern equivalents of the pamphlet writers of the first days of the printing press. Like the various protestant sects, some are simply reformers, while others are extremists, much like the religious extremists that had to seek refuge in America due to their own persecution by the establishment of Europe.

Prior to the invention of the printing press, information was highly centralized. Books were expensive luxury items that were difficult and time consuming to reproduce. The Bible was also in Latin, a language which the populace did not understand. Thus, they relied on intermediaries to interpret the Bible for them. However, the printing press decentralized access to information, opening up the ability to read and write to the masses and allowing heterodox ideas to proliferate in a way that was almost impossible for a centralized authority to control. This is the same phenomenon we encounter in contemporary times. First, there was a trend of centralization of information in the 20th century, followed by an extreme decentralization via the Internet in the 21st century.

In the 20th century, the world saw the emergence of mass media such as nationally syndicated newspapers, radio, and, greatest of them all, that chief and foremost idol of the Boomers: television. As the idiom goes, "the medium is the message." The medium a message is communicated in has an enormous influence on the content of the message itself. This is an important part of understanding the contrast between the mass media of the 20th century and the Internet of the 21st century.

In the mass media of the 20th century, there is a single "transmitter" such as a radio or tv station, and many "receivers" such as a radio or television set. Therefore, the transmitters act as choke points for information. A small number of people can control these transmitters, and thus a very small number of people hold a monopoly on all information. Basically since its inception, governments have seized on this feature of mass media to control the masses through propaganda. The liberal, communist, and fascist spheres of the world all made extensive use of propaganda via mass media, to extremely great effect. The effect was heightened even more by the fact that the technology was brand new, and the public seemed to have some naïve trust in it, as if society had not developed any resistance to it. They lacked the widespread skepticism of the media that is now commonplace. (Any Millennial or Zoomer who has spoken to a Boomer at length will quickly notice this naivete). The public was also as addicted to mass media, in particular the television set, as we are to smartphones today.

This centralization led to the "monoculture" in which the small number of people that controlled the "transmitters," and thus the public's access to information, could dictate the public's tastes, fashion, beliefs and so forth. This is part of what led to each decade of the 20th century -- the 50s, the 60s, the 70s, the 80s etc. having their own distinct trends. Meanwhile, heterodox ideas were unable to proliferate due to their inability to reach the same audience as mass media such as television, and thus automatically had the majority against them (that is not to say it was impossible for heterodox ideas to proliferate at all, simply that they had the deck stacked against them, and many obstacles could be put in their path to impede their progress).

When you control access to information, you in effect control people's minds. People, after all, can only form ideas of the world based on the information that they have about the world from their 5 senses. This sense data is essentially the raw materials from which their ideas are created.

Then came the Internet, and changed all of this. The Internet is an entirely different medium by nature, and as a result went against the current of the previous 100 years. Contrary to mass media, the Internet is a medium in which every node in the network is *both* a "receiver" *and* "transmitter." Any average Joe could suddenly gain just as large of a following on YouTube as a giant media company with billions of dollars, simply from recording videos on his bedroom computer. This instantly removed virtually all of the power from the owners of the "transmitters" and gave it all back to the "receivers." No longer did a small group of people control the tastes and opinions of the masses. Now the masses were in control of the tastes and opinions of the masses. No longer were there obstacles in the way of heterodox ideas. Now these heterodox ideas were right next to the ideas of NBC or *The New York Times* on an even playing field. There did exist *some* choke points. The Network Effect (*https://en.wikipedia.org/wiki/Network_effect*) made Facebook and Twitter more important than "Joe's Politics Blog". There were certain limitations in regards to bandwidth and things of this nature. But as long as the content was user-generated and non-curated, these were minor and trivial.

To amplify this effect, the Internet, due to numerous factors, was almost entirely unregulated. The original character of the Internet was highly libertarian. Even the government seemed to share this sentiment. In the

Communications Decency Act of 1996, Congress protected free speech on the Internet on the basis that it was essential to the interests of democracy.

> *Congress wanted to encourage Internet users and services to create and find communities. Section 230's text explains how Congress wanted to protect the Internet's unique ability to provide "true diversity of political discourse" and "opportunities for cultural development, and... intellectual activity." -- **EFF, "Section 230" (https://www.eff.org/issues/cda230)***

However, this was in an era where the Left, while on the cusp of its total domination, was not quite there. Therefore, as all movements do before they achieve absolute power, it still held freedom of speech as a virtue. Much as the Bolsheviks did in 1905. Libertarianism was also well within the Overton Window of acceptable beliefs. So until somewhere around 2014, this was more or less the zeitgeist of Internet culture. It was not until 2014 when the Internet would begin to take an extreme rightward turn. At almost the same time, the Internet grew from a hobbyist medium to one that had as large of an audience as television, and was in the hands of every American at all hours of the day.

In the following chapters, we will see how the Internet changed over time as a result of the political developments that it itself was partially responsible for, and how these changes, which are ongoing as of 2023, have in turn influenced politics, which have then further influenced the Internet.

We will watch the slow formation of Right Wing ideas in the Wild West Era of the Internet, especially on 4chan's "news" and later "politically incorrect" boards. The birth of Pepe the Frog, and the proto-Alt Right. Also the rise of 4chan "ops" such as Habbo Hotel, and "hacktivist" activity by Anonymous and LulzSec. In these days, the online political sphere included the Ron Paul presidential election in 2012 and Occupy Wall Street.

We will watch the culture of the Internet suddenly explode into a far-Right environment in 2014 with GamerGate, leading to the rise of "anti-SJW" content, politically incorrect comedy such as *Million Dollar Extreme*, and the creation of the "Alt Right." Meanwhile, new advancements in technology lead to the mass adoption of the smartphone and social media, taking 4chan troll culture to critical mass.

We will watch as the Alt Right galvanized in 2015 and 2016 through the Trump Presidential Campaign. As the Internet flexes its muscles during the "Great Meme War" and trolls the world through the successful election of Donald Trump. Then in the years to follow, the Internet continues to show its potential for anonymous mass organization during "He Will Not Divide Us."

We will then watch the fall of the Alt Right in 2017 in the wake of Charlottesville, as the Dissident Right transforms from ironic politically incorrect trolling to a true dissident movement. Meanwhile, the Internet becomes further and further censored via collusion between Big Tech and the government. Also the Optics Wars and origins of the Alt Right's successors.

Then the rise of the Groypers in 2019, the Covid years of 2020 and 2021, the BLM riots, J6 Capitol Riot, and finally the end of the Censorship Era as Elon Musk buys Twitter and promises a return to free speech on the Internet, opposed at every turn by the forces of the ADL.

Finally, some final thoughts on the return of Trump in 2024 and new developments in politics and Internet culture. The rise of TikTok, and with it a return to a more passive "receiver" Internet experience than the early Internet or even the days of Twitter and Facebook.

Who Am I And Why Did I Write This

I am not really anyone noteworthy. I am simply a Millennial who has spent too long on the Internet.

I have been fascinated by the phenomenon of the online Dissident Right since before it had a name. I became aware of it in roughly 2010. In around 2008 or so I discovered 4chan, the source of most online culture, of which the Dissident Right is one descendant. Since then, I have been somewhat obsessed with it. It is at the intersection of technology, history, philosophy, and politics, and it has led to most of the bizarre and unprecedented events of the last 10 years. What other subject could be more interesting?

The Millennial generation is divided into those who grew up online and those who did not. The Zoomer generation is unaware of the things that happened before them. Boomers are completely clueless. There are many who only grasp bits and pieces of the rise of the online Dissident Right, its history, and connection to Trump.

To those who are unfamiliar with Internet culture, the rise of the Dissident Right and the online events that have bubbled up to the surface, it is inevitable that the Trump Era, which is perhaps the defining aspect of our generation, will be misunderstood. To future generations, these events will likewise be rendered incomprehensible. If the Trump revolution is defeated, and only his enemies write history, it will be even more distorted.

Therefore, I have endeavored to create this text. I intend to explain the history of the Dissident Right and the emergence of Trump from my own perspective as an extremely online person who grew up around it, with an ordinary person who is unfamiliar with it as my intended audience. It is my desire to portray the events in a way that is not explicitly ideological and to understand them simply from the viewpoint of historical analysis.

"Oldfags" (older, experienced Internet users) who are already familiar with Internet culture might cringe, or they might feel nostalgic reliving old times. I am not sure how it will be received by them. Probably with the Internet's typical hostility. But that is not my target audience. My primary audience is normies, both of the Boomer variety and of posterity.

What is a "normie?"

A "normie" or "normalfag" (adding the suffix -fag to a word to describe a type of person was typical Internet slang during the Wild West era of the Internet) is a person who is unfamiliar with the Internet and its culture. I will delve further into this Internet culture in the rest of this text.

Choice of Words

"Liberal" is often used to mean "Democrat" or "Leftist" but that is not its true meaning. Really it means something more along the lines of what we would call a "classical liberal." Throughout this text, I will use the word liberal in this true sense.

The word "libtard" is often used by people on the Internet to mean "liberal" in the opposite way. Someone who is neoliberal, Democrat, vaguely Leftist etc. So I may use the word "libtard" in this way.

I do not like the terms "racist," "misogynist," "Islamophobic," "fascist," "anti-Semite" etc. I feel that these terms are very broad and vague. Instead, I prefer to engage with the specific claim a person is making. However, I still may use these terms throughout the text to describe something that an ordinary person would consider one of these things. I will also offer context and further explanation about the specific view being expressed. When it comes to Left Wing or mainstream views, I might not be as careful or as charitable, because the purpose of this text is to explain a dissident, Right Wing perspective, not a mainstream, Left Wing perspective.

Are You in the "Alt Right"? Are You in Anonymous? Are You The Hacker Known as 4chan? Are You a Nazi? Are You Evil?

It is true that I have been influenced immensely by having interacted with online culture, including politically. I was originally something like a libertarian, and very socially liberal. But now I would consider myself to hold many political opinions that are considered fringe. I do not like the term "Alt Right" for the contemporary Dissident Right and would not use the term to describe myself. It has also become synonymous with white nationalism or some vague sort of neo-Nazism, neither of which I identify with.

I have a deep respect for other cultures. That is part of what attracts me to a more nationalist perspective. I want to preserve the unique character of the many diverse cultures that exist on Earth, and if they are all allowed to mix into one homogeneous mass through global mass migration, it will, ironically, eliminate this diversity.

I am partially Jewish. I love my Jewish family. So, I obviously hold no ill will towards the Jewish people. I also do not really think that the rise of nationalism or Right Wing ideologies will result in anything like the holocaust happening to Jews in America. I do not practice the Jewish religion. I am a Christian.

I am a Trump supporter. Although hesitant at first, I would say I had fully jumped on the Trump train by 2017 or 2018. Even if I was still a liberal, I would support Trump due to his anti-establishment status.

I don't support Hitler or the Nazis in any way. But, I am open-minded towards other leaders considered to be authoritarian such as Lee Kuan Yew, and Nayib Bukele.

I am not really active in politics, in spite of my interest in political events. I am not affiliated with any political organizations of any kind, officially or unofficially. I attended several IRL political events in the 2020s as part of Stop the Steal, and briefly considered becoming active in local politics, but quickly lost interest. For the most part I simply prefer to observe and write about it. I wanted to write a history of the Dissident Right from a more neutral perspective, rather than from the perspective of someone who thinks they are all evil Nazis.

This is not really about me or my personal experience, but I might include bits of that from time to time to add context to the history.

Chapter 1 - Before 2014: The Wild West, 4chan, /b/, /new/, Anonymous, Occupy Wall Street

The Wild West (1991 - 2016)

The years between 1991, when the Internet was first opened to the public, and 2017, when Internet censorship began following Trump's victory in the 2016 election, roughly correspond to a time known online as the "Wild West" Era of the Internet.

It is interesting to note the dates here. 1991 was also the fall of the Soviet Union. Just as the Iron Curtain fell, and the entire world became united into one global system, so too did the Internet connect this entire world into one worldwide information network ("the world wide web"). And this new world would be united under one ideology, the post-war liberal thesis. A phenomenon that Francis Fukuyama dubbed "the end of history."

In 2017, the same year that Trump rose to power, as a personification of the antithesis of the liberal thesis, history began again. And this was instigated in part by the new world wide web that had begun the year that history had ended. And so 2017 would also see an attempt to shut down the means by which history had been resurrected, from that seed planted at the very moment of its intended death. But, we are getting ahead of ourselves. Let us start by going back in time to the 1990s and 2000s.

The Internet as it existed before 2017 was in many ways an entirely different Internet than what we have today. The Internet existed alongside older forms of mass media such as television, radio and print. It was often accessed on a large and cumbersome PC, often in a family computer room. Although ubiquitous in business, entertainment and other industries, it was, for the average consumer, still an "opt-in" experience. Some people went online, while others chose not to. For the first decade or so of the Internet, the culture of the Internet was the product of a specific demographic: predominantly young, predominantly hobbyists who were interested in technology or other related industries, predominantly white, overwhelmingly male (a common meme at the time was "there are no girls on the Internet"), usually geeky and above average in IQ, and generally either from the English speaking world, parts of Europe, or Japan.

There was a clear demarcation between "the online world" and the "IRL" (in real life) world. The Internet was something that you "logged on" to. It was not omnipresent. Your various gadgets were not "smart gadgets," and they did not connect to your WiFi.

There was also a culture of anonymity to varying degrees. Most users did not post under their real names or with their real identities. In fact, one of the first things that parents would tell their children before allowing them unsupervised Internet access was to NEVER give out their real name, address, or any personal information whatsoever. Instead of their real names, users used a username (also called a screenname or "handle"). Instead of their own face, they used an "avatar." Anime and video game characters, as well as memes, were popular avatars.

Most Millennial and older Gen Z readers will probably be familiar with at least these basic aspects of early Internet culture, but it is still important to note, if for no other reason than to contrast it with the very different Internet that exists today.

In the beginning, the Internet was wholly decentralized. The first large "platforms" were search engines, such as Yahoo and Google, that connected a multitude of totally autonomous blogs, homepages, and forums. These forums, such as Usenet, Something Awful, and various phpBB boards, were the first communities online in which Internet culture proliferated. By the 2000s, social networks like Facebook and MySpace came into existence, along with the first "platforms" such as DeviantArt, LiveJournal, YouTube, and Newgrounds, where users could share original content. By the 2010s, the Internet had become more centralized, with social networks such as Twitter and YouTube gaining importance. However, these existed alongside older-style, independent forums like 4chan and Reddit.

There was above all else an ethos of complete, free and unrestricted access to information for all. A democratization of the means of information. Information anarchy. This attitude was shared by basically all Internet users no matter what community they belonged to, or what other beliefs they may hold. Copyright law was seen as something like a relic of an older, less advanced age, and piracy was rampant. Freedom of speech was unquestioned. Forums were self-moderated by their users according to the rules of that particular community. Even large platforms like Facebook were lightly moderated and adhered to the principle of "free speech absolutism." Twitter originally claimed to be "the free speech wing of the free speech party" (*https://www.theguardian.com/media/2012/mar/22/twitter-tony-wang-free-speech*). Until 2014, 4chan's /b/ board allowed basically all speech that it was not forced to take down due to law, such as child pornography.

With the exception of the attitude towards copyright law, this libertine attitude towards speech was for the most part shared by the government and corporate establishment. It was unthinkable that someone would be banned simply on the basis of their political beliefs. It was not until 2017, when Andrew Anglin and Alex Jones were banned, that this attitude was challenged. When moot banned GamerGate from 4chan in 2014, this was seen as a betrayal of the entire community, and caused alternate platforms such as 8chan to be created in protest. Until 2017, the Internet believed in a principle known as the "Streisand Effect."

The "Streisand Effect" was the idea that any attempt to censor information on the Internet would instead backfire and cause this information to proliferate even more. It was named after a case in 2003 in which Barbara Streisand sued to remove a picture of her mansion from a publicly available aerial photograph created as part of the California Coastal Records Project, a collection of 12,000 California coastline photographs documenting coastal erosion. The highly publicized lawsuit instead caused thousands more users to download the photo and share it online. (*https://en.wikipedia.org/wiki/Streisand_effect*). It was thought at the time that this was some sort of unquestionable law of the Internet, and that it was therefore impossible to censor information online. Later, during the Censorship Era of 2017-2021, this would be challenged, and censorship would prove to be more successful than previously assumed. But, in the early days of the Internet, it did bear itself out from time to time and seemed like a plausible theory (GamerGate got banned by moot? Well, we'll just carry it over to 8chan and it will proliferate even more!)

All of these various trends combined to create "Internet culture," an underground subculture that existed throughout the online world. While various sites and their communities were important sources of this Internet culture, including Something Awful, YouTube, DeviantArt, Twitter, Tumblr, Reddit, MySpace, Facebook and elsewhere, none were as impactful as 4chan.

4chan: "The Final Boss of the Interwebs"

4chan was started in 2003 by a 15 year old named Chistopher Poole, better known by his Internet alias, "moot."

Poole had been a regular participant on Something Awful's subforum "Anime Death Tentacle Rape Whorehouse" (ADTRW), where many users were familiar with the Japanese imageboard format and Futaba Channel ("2chan.net"). When creating 4chan, Poole obtained Futaba Channel's open source code and translated the Japanese text into English using AltaVista's Babel Fish online translator. After the site's creation, Poole invited users from the ADTRW subforum, many of whom were dissatisfied with the site's moderation, to visit 4chan, which he advertised as an English-language counterpart to Futaba Channel and a place for Western fans to discuss anime and manga. **-- Wikipedia (https://en.wikipedia.org/wiki/Christopher_Poole)**

4chan was originally a product of "otaku" culture -- a subculture of Japanese pop culture enthusiasts, especially of anime, manga, and Japanese video games. The first boards on 4chan were /a/ - anime /b/ - anime/random (later shortened to just random), /h/ - hentai, /c/ - cute, /d/ - hentai/alternative (the d was related to the word "deviant") and /y/ - yaoi. **(Author's note: Hentai is a term for pornographic Japanese comics and yaoi is a term for homosexual pornographic Japanese comics. In other words, all of the original boards discussed anime, manga, and Japanese culture)**

4chan contained a small number of fixed boards. Unlike other forums which would archive their threads for months or years, threads on 4chan would eventually be deleted and replaced by newer threads when people stopped posting in them or the post limit was reached for that thread, usually after a few hours or days. This gave content on 4chan an ephemeral nature. Each board was dedicated to a separate topic, and designated with one or more letters. /a/ was the board for anime, /co/ for western comics, /v/ for video games, etc. But the most infamous and popular board was /b/ - Random.

> *The stories and information posted here are artistic works of fiction and falsehood.*
>
> *Only a fool would take anything posted here as fact.*
>
> *-- **The official description of the board on the top of 4chan's /b/***

It was on /b/ that much of 4chan's unique culture originated. The posts here ranged from discussions of various topics, "drawfag threads" (artists would draw things and take requests from the users), "greentext stories" (anonymous personal anecdotes), "copypasta" (stories or short posts that were frequently reposted again and again), memes (images or phrases that served as essentially "inside jokes" in the form of templates that users could riff of, such as "advice animals" and "rage comics"), "troll posts" (users would try to invoke a response from other users with intentionally provocative posts, often pretending to be someone else, hiding their own views, or even ironically mocking the views they claimed to hold), "raids" (users would go to other parts of the Internet to troll them), and "ops" (users would work together to accomplish a task, such as a raid).

On 4chan, anonymity was taken to its furthest extreme. Unlike most forums, users on 4chan could post entirely anonymously, without having to create an account of any kind. The user could choose to enter a username for individual posts, but this would not be stored in any way. If a user did not enter a username, which was usually the case, their name would appear as "Anonymous." As a result, 4channers began to refer to one another as "anon" and to themselves collectively as "Anonymous." It's interesting to note that this was entirely a random coincidence of history. The technology was invented in Japan, not deliberately by moot, and just happened to include this anonymous aspect.

As discussed earlier, "the medium is the message." The fact that 4chan was anonymous and ephemeral had a profound effect on its culture. It encouraged the already anarchic and free speech nature of the Internet. It would not be an exaggeration to say that it created a decade in which an entirely unprecedented historical anomaly occurred, allowing for a level of free speech that has probably never existed before or since in the entirety of human history. Thousands of users could express whatever view they wished, entirely anonymously, and receive entirely anonymous feedback. Unlike typical forums such as Reddit, in which users had an online identity that was consistent from post to post, there was no online persona for anon, unless they wished to create one by "namefagging" (entering a name into the Name field of the post and continuing to use this name for subsequent posts). Unlike typical forums such as Reddit, or social media platforms such as Facebook, posts did not receive "upvotes" or "likes" based on their popularity. Unlike today, no "algorithm" chose which posts would be shown, hidden, boosted, or shadowbanned. Instead, every post was treated as equal, displayed in sequential order, and judged solely on its own content.

The sense of humor of 4chan reflected both that of the Internet as a whole, and of the times. Surreal and absurdist humor such as the Adult Swim show *Aqua Teen Hunger Force* was very popular, and "lolsorandum" humor such as *Invader Zim* was also contemporaneous with the golden age of 4chan.

> *hi every1 im new!!!!!!! *holds up spork* my name is katy but u can call me t3h PeNgU1N oF d00m!!!!!!!! lol…as u can see im very random!!!! thats why i came here, 2 meet random ppl like me ^_^… im 13 years old (im mature 4 my age tho!!) i like 2 watch invader zim w/ my girlfreind (im bi if u dont like it deal w/it) its our favorite tv show!!! bcuz its SOOOO random!!!! shes random 2 of course but i want 2 meet more random ppl =) like they say the more the merrier!!!! lol…neways i hope 2 make alot of freinds here so give me lots of commentses!!!!*
>
> *DOOOOOMMMMM!!!!!!!!!!!!!!!! <--- me bein random again ^_^ hehe… toodles!!!!!*
>
> *love and waffles,*
>
> *t3h PeNgU1N oF d00m*
>
> **-- "t3h penguin of doom," a copypasta from 4chan circa 2006 mocking the random humor popular at the time**

Irreverent "shock" humor such as South Park was also extremely popular during the 2000s. This irreverent shock humor included: violence and gore, extreme obscenity and vulgarity, extreme nudity, blasphemy and anti-religious content, and over-the-top racism/anti-Semitism/misogyny (the latter of which will play an important role in the original, less serious and more ironic, manifestation of the Alt Right). Writer and Twitter personality Paul Skallas (also known as "lindyman") has termed this type of humor "the vulgar wave" and estimated it lasted between 1991 - 2008 (https://lindynewsletter.beehiiv.com/p/vulgar-wave). Note that this timeframe roughly corresponds to the Wild West era of the Internet, starting in the same year the Internet begins and lasting until the "Great Awokening" of 2011 (a development to be covered in a later chapter, and which will lead both to the end of the "vulgar wave," the rise of the Alt Right, and the Censorship Era of the Internet).

4chan, more than anywhere else on the Internet, perhaps anywhere else period, embraced this "vulgar wave" style of edgy, irreverent humor. The culture of 4chan seemed intent to push the limits of free speech as users tried to one up each other over how offensive they could be. This soon gave 4chan its reputation as "The Final Boss of the Internet."

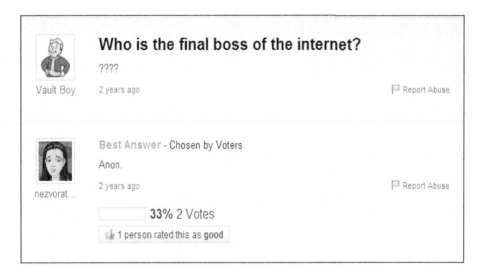

	Who is the final boss of the internet?	
Vault Boy	????	
	2 years ago	Report Abuse
	Best Answer - Chosen by Voters	
nezvorat...	Anon.	
	2 years ago	Report Abuse
	33% 2 Votes	
	👍 1 person rated this as good	

Another great example of this is from 2014, during the Tumblr-4chan raids. This was an event that occurred during the 2014 anti-SJW era, in which 4chan raided Tumblr. Tumblr was a blogging platform. It was popular with artists who would post and share digital art, but also included text content. In many ways, it was the opposite of 4chan. The stereotypical user of Tumblr was a progressive leftist female, very concerned with social justice, anti-racism, LGBT issues, belief in multiple genders, etc. (at a time when many of these positions, such as gender ideology were still somewhat fringe). 4chan, which had by now transformed into a proto-Alt Right community, raided Tumblr with racist content, gore, Nazi content, etc. Tumblr responded by trying to "counter-raid" 4chan. However, they found it difficult to do so, as no content that they could post could offend anon. This lead a Tumblr user to proclaim *"You can't troll 4chan. Trolling 4chan is like pissing in an ocean of*

piss." (Author's note: Perhaps it was actually anon who made this comment. I cannot track down a source and various versions of the story exist). (https://knowyourmeme.com/memes/events/2014-tumblr-4chan-raids).

However, we are again getting ahead of ourselves. Prior to around 2014 or so, 4chan did not have any particular political beliefs. They were, in fact, entirely nihilistic. They were only interested in "trolling" others "for the lulz" (lulz was an intentional bastardization of "lol" or "laugh out loud"). This segues nicely into another important aspect of 4chan humor, irony.

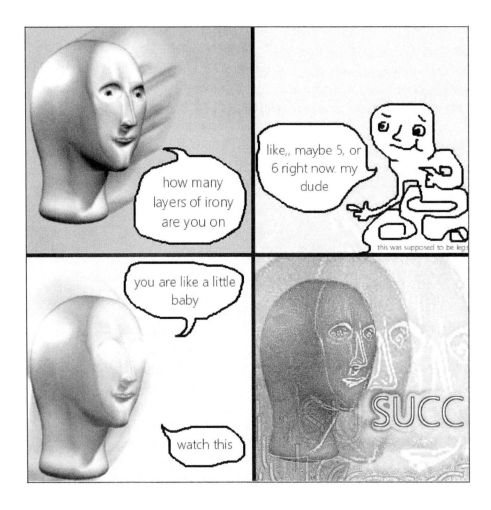

Irony was one of the most characteristic aspects of 4chan culture. Irony, along with nihilism and shock humor, was popular in the "vulgar wave" mainstream culture of the 2000s, but as with other aspects of humor, on 4chan it was taken to its extreme. Due to the anonymous nature of the board, it was impossible to tell what a poster's true background or views actually were. This was taken advantage of by "trolls," who posted content in order to intentionally provoke people, regardless of whether it was their true beliefs. A particularly skilled troll would drop subtle hints that they were a troll, using ironic humor such as pretending to genuinely hold a particular belief while making humorously intentionally poor arguments for it and making fun of the belief they claimed to be holding.

*What the fuck did you just fucking say about me, you little bitch? I'll have you know I graduated top of my class in the Navy Seals, and I've been involved in numerous secret raids on Al-Quaeda, and I have over 300 confirmed kills. I am trained in gorilla warfare and I'm the top sniper in the entire US armed forces. You are nothing to me but just another target. I will wipe you the fuck out with precision the likes of which has never been seen before on this Earth, mark my fucking words. You think you can get away with saying that shit to me over the Internet? Think again, fucker. As we speak I am contacting my secret network of spies across the USA and your IP is being traced right now so you better prepare for the storm, maggot. The storm that wipes out the pathetic little thing you call your life. You're fucking dead, kid. I can be anywhere, anytime, and I can kill you in over seven hundred ways, and that's just with my bare hands. Not only am I extensively trained in unarmed combat, but I have access to the entire arsenal of the United States Marine Corps and I will use it to its full extent to wipe your miserable ass off the face of the continent, you little shit. If only you could have known what unholy retribution your little "clever" comment was about to bring down upon you, maybe you would have held your fucking tongue. But you couldn't, you didn't, and now you're paying the price, you goddamn idiot. I will shit fury all over you and you will drown in it. You're fucking dead, kiddo. -- **This is the famous "Navy Seal Copypasta" from 4chan posted circa 2010. It uses ironic humor to make fun of "Internet tough guys." Note that the poster drops hints that the post is ironic with its over-the-top tone, ridiculous claims and comedic intentional malapropisms. A savvy Internet user is supposed to pick up on the fact that it is a troll and be in on the joke, while a naive user will take the bait and respond earnestly, resulting in them being "trolled."***

This heavy use of irony would become an important factor in the creation of the Alt Right, in which the line between an ironic stance taken to "troll" someone with shock humor, and a person's sincere belief, was intentionally blurred.

This technique, sometimes called "post-irony" or "meta-irony" would become a characteristic aspect of the humor of Sam Hyde, a comedian who adopted this from Internet culture. Sam Hyde would sometimes use irony in his humor, similar to Stephen Colbert's *Colbert Report* character, taking on a satirical persona such as an extremely cringey anime fan, annoying hipster, or anti-social Internet poster. At other times, he would take on the persona of an extremely politically incorrect Alt Right personality, pretending to do so ironically, but dropping subtle hints that this "ironic persona" was actually professing Hyde's sincere beliefs.

This type of "post-irony" or "meta-irony" evolved later, in the mid 2010s, after many years of ironic trolling on 4chan, which led to extremely complex and hard to decipher troll posts, with multiple levels of irony and possible interpretations. It seems to have become less popular during the Censorship Era, after 4chan-style Internet culture declined, and the Dissident Right stopped being ironic and slowly transformed into a genuine political movement.

Memes

4chan, especially the /b/ board, was responsible for generating the overwhelming majority of the most famous memes, copypasta, and slang in Internet culture for almost a decade. This includes, but is not limited to:

Memes: "Oh Really?" Owl, Rick Rolling, Pedobear, Advice Dog/Advice animals, the Guy Fawkes Mask and association with hackers, Rage Comics, doge, 4ever alone, Pepe the Frog, Troll face, Groyper (and other Pepe variants), shoe on head, Virgin vs the Chad, Gigachad, slenderman, caturday/lolcats, demotivationals, Wojak, Soyjak, and variants **(Author's note: technically Wojak originated from another chan board, Vichan, not 4chan)**

Vernacular: kek, lulz, vidya, sauce (instead of source), epic win, epic fail, Rule 34, /ourguy/, based, redpilled, bluepilled, blackpilled, clearpilled etc, Chads and Stacies, soyboys, normies **(Authors note: I am internally cringing at many of these)**

Social phenomena: Anonymous ("hacktivist" group), Bronies (adult male My Little Pony fans), GamerGate, the Alt Right, Q-Anon

4chan culture would then trickle down to other areas of the Internet, including Reddit (seen as 4chan's dorky tagalong little brother), YouTube or Twitter, and other nodes of Internet culture such as the lobbies of online games (Counter Strike, World of Warcraft, etc) then to the more "normie" parts of the Internet such as Facebook, and sometimes eventually into "IRL."

/b/ is not your private army: trolls, raids, ops

With the near absolute free speech on the website and the anonymity of all posters, one might believe that the website is a completely chaotic experience, and they were right most of the time. However, it also creates an environment where thousands of people can all see one person's idea, and if asked, execute an action. Thus, a culture of collective actions began on 4chan. –
culturehistoryoftheinternet.com (https://culturalhistoryoftheinternet.com /student-projects/fall-2020/4chan/)

With time, trolling grew ever more advanced. One of its many manifestations were "raids." Named after "raids" in video games, in which players would team up to fight powerful monsters or another team of players, raids were organized actions on 4chan to troll and attack another online community. For example, a raid might involve spamming another forum with extremely shocking or offensive content, or simply enough content to overwhelm the moderation (which in the early days of the Internet was done by a handful of volunteers and with no assistance from AI automatic moderation which did not yet exist).

One early memorable example of this was the "Habbo Hotel" raid of 2005. "Habbo Hotel" was a Finnish game. I personally have never played it and did not participate in the raid. But it seems to have been a game similar to Second Life or VR Chat where people would make a virtual avatar, chat and hang out. Users from 4chan raided the game, all creating an identical avatar of a black man in a suit with a huge afro. They then trolled the other users in various ways. For example, they lined up and blocked the exits and entrances to the in-game rooms, trapping the other users inside.

They lined up into the shape of a swastika. They blocked the entrance to the in-game pool, declaring to the other players "*pool's closed due to fail and AIDS.*"

"Raids" are a type of "op." The words are more or less synonymous, but have a slight difference in meaning. "Raids" are one of the most common types of "ops," but technically an "op" (short for operation) can basically be any organized collective action on the Internet, even if it does not include raiding another community. On the Dissident Right, an "op" by another organization, such as a Left Wing activist group like the ADL or a government entity like the CIA would later be called "gayops." Raids/ops would usually be coordinated in a dedicated thread.

Random users would post screenshots of the raid taking place, information about how to become involved such as a link to the site, and discuss ideas about what to do next. Other anon would curate and organize this information into copypastas and infographics. When a thread expired, a new dedicated thread would pick up where the last one left off.

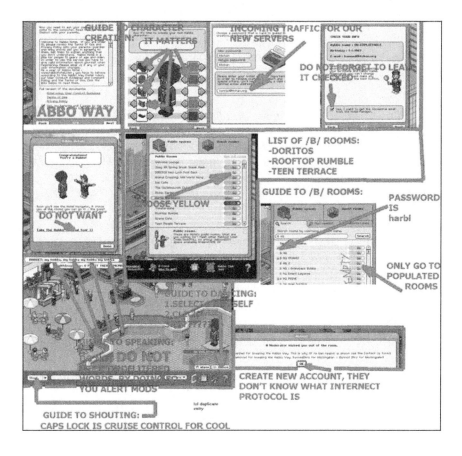

One raid I did participate in led to the meme "shoe on head." 4chan organized a raid of LiveJasmin, a sexcam site, and trolled the camwhores in various ways. Each camwhore had their own room where they livestreamed to a livechat. In one room, anon trolled a camwhore by demanding she put various random items on her head, such as pens, books, their keyboard, shoes, shoeboxes, etc. They would spam the chat with "*BOOK ON HEAD BOOK ON HEAD BOOK ON HEAD BOOK ON HEAD*" "*SHOE ON HEAD SHOE ON HEAD SHOE ON HEAD SHOE ON HEAD*" etc. over and over hundreds of times until the camwhore broke down and complied.

ht the "shoe on head" request was particularly funny. So I started going to all of the other rooms and spamming "SHOE ON HEAD" over and over again ad infinitum, causing other users to do the same. This then became the de facto method of trolling the camwhores. Apparently, it was part of the raid described here:

> *"Put Shoe on Head" is an online prank/raid coordinated by a group of YTMND users and /b/tards in 2006. Using Ventrilo as their ground of communication, participants targeted individual chatrooms on LiveJasmin.com, a webcam/porn site featuring live chat with girls, many of whom apparently do not speak fluent English. The raids consisted of flooding the chatrooms and making strange requests like "do a barrel roll" and "show me your keyboard."*
>
> *Soon enough, a YTMND user known as FlyingLaserJesus told one of the performers to place her shoe on her head, using the fractured English command of 'Put Shoe On Head', and soon enough, the phrase became the one line glory of the Live Jasmin Raids. -- **Know Your Meme (https://knowyourmeme.com/memes/put-shoe-on-head)***

I didn't know the backstory. I just saw the thread on 4chan.

Later, a popular anti-SJW YouTuber would use ShoeOnHead as her handle, and it is in this context that it is best known today.

Here are some other notable examples of raids:

On July 10, 2008, 4chan users caused "F— Google" and the swastika unicode character to rise to the top of Google's search results for a few hours before Google noticed and quickly changed how their top search results feature worked.

In October 2008, 4channers started a hoax about the death of Steve Jobs, CEO of Apple, causing a significant fall in the price of Apple's stock.

In 2009, 4chan users mass voted in—and may have even hacked—the Time 100, the list of the 100 most influential people of that year. The winner was moot himself, and the first letters of the names of the top winners spell out "mARBLECAKE ALSO THE GAME", a reference to two popular 4chan memes at the time.

In July 2010, 4channers mass voted in a poll of which country Justin Bieber would next perform at. They made North Korea the number one answer.

They did another mass vote in 2012 for a Taylor Swift concert and ended up sending her to a school for the deaf.

In August 2012, they mass voted in the poll for Mountain Dew's Dub the Dew event, which was a vote for what the new green apple flavor of Mountain Dew would be. They filled the top ten responses with things like "Diabeetus" and "Hitler did nothing wrong".

4channers created a fake promotional poster in 2014 that falsely stated that the new iPhone update, iOS 8, would allow their iPhone to be charged by placing it in a microwave and turning it on. A handful of people did this, and subsequently destroyed their phones. Multiple news outlets had to warn people that the microwave charging was just a hoax. -- **A Cultural History of The Internet** *(https://culturalhistoryoftheInternet.com/student-projects/fall-2020/4chan/)*

Raids and ops would later become an important tool when the Alt Right grew out of 4chan, being used as a tool in their arsenal to further their political beliefs, whether these beliefs were genuine or simply a means of trolling "libtards" for the lulz. This technique is still sometimes effective, but they can be put down very quickly by the extremely censorious modern Internet, which has access to much more effective means of moderation, such as AI algorithms. Recent campaigns such as the #BanTheADL hashtag on Twitter might be considered examples of "raids," but they differ slightly in character in that they are more organized and directed towards a specific political aim or promoting a specific message, rather than anarchic and with the primary aim of disruption. They might fall more into the category of "op" than "raid" since an "op" does not carry the same connotation of deliberate disruption, but more emphasizes the coordinated nature of the attack.

The Rules of the Internet

The Rules of the Internet is a meme created on 4chan in 2006. It is a good illustration of the culture on 4chan during this time.

1. Do not talk about /b/

2. Do NOT talk about /b/

3. We are Anonymous

4. Anonymous is legion

5. Anonymous never forgives

6. Anonymous can be a horrible, senseless, uncaring monster

7. Anonymous is still able to deliver

8. There are no real rules about posting

9. There are no real rules about moderation either - enjoy your ban

10. If you enjoy any rival sites - DON'T

11. All your carefully picked arguments can easily be ignored

12. Anything you say can and will be used against you

13. Anything you say can be turned into something else - fixed

14. Do not argue with trolls - it means that they win

15. The harder you try the harder you will fail

16. If you fail in epic proportions, it may just become a winning failure

17. Every win fails eventually

18. Everything that can be labeled can be hated

19. The more you hate it the stronger it gets

20. Nothing is to be taken seriously

21. Original content is original only for a few seconds before getting old

22. Copypasta is made to ruin every last bit of originality

23. Copypasta is made to ruin every last bit of originality

24. Every repost it always a repost of a repost

25. *Relation to the original topic decreases with every single post*

26. *Any topic can easily be turned into something totally unrelated*

27. *Always question a person's sexual preferences without any real reason*

28. *Always question a person's gender - just incase it's really a man*

29. *In the Internet all girls are men and all kids are undercover FBI agents*

30. *There are no girls on the Internet*

31. *TITS or GTFO - the choice is yours*

32. *You must have pictures to prove your statements*

33. *Lurk more - it's never enough*

34. *There is porn of it, no exceptions*

35. *If no porn is found at the moment, it will be made*

36. *There will always be even more fucked up shit than what you just saw*

37. *You can not divide by zero (just because the calculator says so)*

38. *No real limits of any kind apply here - not even the sky*

39. *CAPSLOCK IS CRUISE CONTROL FOR COOL*

40. *EVEN WITH CRUISE CONTROL YOU STILL HAVE TO STEER*

41. *Desu isn't funny. Seriously guys. It's worse than Chuck Norris jokes.*

42. Nothing is Sacred.

43. The more beautiful and pure a thing is - the more satisfying it is to corrupt it

44. Even one positive comment about Japanese things can make you a weaboo

45. When one sees a lion, one must get into the car.

46. There is always furry porn of it.

47. The pool is always closed.

-- **The Rules of the Internet** (https://knowyourmeme.com/memes/rules-of-the-internet)

Conspiracy Theories

Reflecting its "free speech absolutist" attitude, conspiracy theories have long been a staple of the Internet. However, the Internet completely transformed conspiracy theories.

A meme among anon was, "pics or it didn't happen." Although the Internet loved conspiracy theories, it loved flamewars (threads where people roast each other) and Internet arguments even more. And, of course, it was always suspicious of information that could simply be a troll. Thus, the claims of conspiracy theorists were subjected to harsh scrutiny. However, the conspiracy theorists also had the entirety of the information of the Internet (which at the time, was almost completely uncensored) at their fingerprints. Thus, conspiracy theories became a sort of an op of their own. They were highly collaborative processes, where anon would collect evidence such as citations from books, official documents such as FBI crime statistics, videos, images, and so forth, and then craft memes, extremely elaborate infographics, and perhaps entire wikis explaining and arguing for the theory. Critics of the theory would likewise create their own counter-memes in an attempt to debunk the theory.

Thus, conspiracy theories grew from mere speculations and rumors to what was essentially the birth of a new academic discipline. Prior to this, perhaps a handful of people, with extremely limited capacity to collaborate and extremely limited access to information, were able to study conspiracy theories to this level of rigor. Everyone else had to simply choose between taking the words of journalists, academics and government officials at face value, or else relying on a rumor they heard from their other Boomer friend.

This is one of the greatest unrecognized generational divides between pre-Internet and post-Internet generations. I noticed this during the Stop the Steal movement. While there were both young and old people represented, their choice of conspiracy theories was totally different. The conspiracy theories of the older generation amounted to little more than wild rumors and speculations, with little evidence offered to back them up. Nefarious actors such as communists from Venezuela somehow were able to manipulate American elections through dubious means, they claimed. One Boomer told me that the "real ballots" were all marked with some sort of secret watermark.

A good example of the difference between pre- and post-Internet conspiracy theories is Q-Anon, and how it was treated by the pre- and post- Internet generations. Q-Anon actually began on 4chan, where it was met with a mixed reception. Some anon believed that Q-Anon's cryptic posts really were from some anonymous leaker embedded in the Trump White House. This was not entirely implausible. By this point in time, there actually had been genuine leaks released on 4chan. In fact, it was not an uncommon occurrence. A leak posted on 4chan was what started GamerGate, mass shooters have leaked their plans on 4chan, and during the 2016 election 4chan would be a major disseminator of the Jon Podesta emails leaked by Wikileaks. As of this writing, the latest leak of classified documents on 4chan was April 2023, referred to by Wikipedia as the "2022–2023 Pentagon document leaks" (*https://en.wikipedia.org/wiki/2022%E2%80%932023_Pentagon_document_leaks*).

However, LARPing as (pretending to be) a leaker online was also common. An early example being Jon Titor, a poster from from 2000-2001 claiming to be a time traveler. So many anon responded to Q-Anon with the typical refrain of "pics or it didn't happen." As time went on and Q-Anon's predictions that Trump was playing "4D Chess" and was about to take down the Deep State and become the God Emperor failed to materialize, less and less anon took Q-Anon seriously. It even became a meme -- "*just two more weeks!*" -- referring to the fact that Q-Anon would make a major prediction that we just had to wait "two more weeks" and then a major event would occur (which never happened).

Meanwhile, Q-Anon made its way to platforms like Facebook with a much larger Boomer population, in part due to being heavily astroturfed and promoted by Left Wing journalists such as Jared Holt of Right Wing Watch. Once in the hands of the Boomers, it exploded in popularity. Soon Boomers were clad head to foot in Q-Anon t shirts and merch. Even after the events of J6, Boomers in Q-Anon communities continued to concoct ever more ambitious tales about Q-Anon. They attributed Q-Anon to various figures such as Michael Flynn, and claimed that Trump was still actually President running the country from the shadows, and was about to announce this -- presumably in just two more weeks. None of this was challenged by flamewars or infographic memes from their own community debunking their claims. Instead, every claim simply became amplified by the manic Boomer hivemind. Whatever might be said about 4chan conspiracy theories, the adversarial and trollish nature of the Wild West Internet ensured that these type of runaway Boomer conspiracy theories become relegated to self-parodying ironic versions of themselves by the time they reached such a critical mass, by which time they would be considered "Reddit" and "cringe" "normie memes" (or in this case "Boomer memes").

Nonetheless, the more sophisticated conspiracy theories of the post-Internet generations would have an enormous impact on Internet politics, opening a door for alternative explanations for political and historical developments that did not rely on the authority of the media and were not approved by the establishment. This created the seed which would blossom into a dissident political narrative that challenged all the presuppositions and assumptions made by the liberal thesis, with plenty of information organized by countless anon and put through the crucible of relentless scrutiny by others.

/new/

/new/ was the board for news on 4chan. It was created in 2010 along with the board /int/ - International. It was common for moot to add new subject matter boards from time to time. But this time, the creation of this obscure board, in one small corner of an anime imageboard on the Internet, would create the first crack in "the end" of history.

The culture of /new/, and its better-known successor, /pol/, was extremely unique. Part of this was due to the structure of 4chan itself, which allowed for total freedom of speech, total transparency, total anonymity, and equality in its treatment of posts. But the other important part was the content of the board itself. /new/ transformed into the de facto politics board of 4chan. However, the political content of /new/ could not be found anywhere else. That is because, in 2010, the Overton Window of mainstream political discussion IRL was extremely narrow.

On one hand, were the Republicans, led by neocons such as George W Bush. These neocon's highest values were essentially:

1. Capitalism and "small government" - *With an emphasis on tax cuts for corporations, "the free market" (ie few regulations or restrictions on the private sector), cutting "government spending" on programs such as welfare, and "free trade" (ie reducing trade restrictions and creating a more globalized market).*

2. Strong Military - *High military spending, and military interventionism abroad (acting as "Team America: World Police"). It was the Republicans who were responsible for the wars in Iraq and Afghanistan, which were by this time extremely unpopular.*

3. The Patriot Act - *The Patriot Act, which included more government surveillance of American citizens (ostensibly in order to prevent terrorism) often in violation of the 5th amendment. This was blamed on the Republicans as one aspect of the "War on Terror."*

4. Libertarian governance mixed with "Religious Right" rhetoric - *Most of the Republican base were socially conservative Christians. This "Religious Right" of the 1980s-2000s was a major force in culture, and sometimes politics. This "Religious Right" fought for tougher laws against abortion, opposed gay marriage, and tried to promote moral decency by, for example, adding content warning stickers to offensive material. However, there was also a large libertarian contingent against "legislating morality," arguing that it was not the concern of "Big Government" but a personal matter to be decided by each individual. By the late 2000s, the Religious Right had become unpopular, and the more libertarian attitude against "legislating morality" was growing.*

As a result of the unpopularity of the War on Terror and the Patriot Act, Obama was elected in 2008. Obama promised "change." Change such as ending the Iraq war, closing Guantanamo Bay (where suspected terrorists had suffered what were considered human rights abuses), and a vague notion that the excesses of the Patriot Act would be reversed. This put the opposite party, the Democrats, in the White House. At the time, the Democrats stood for:

1. Labor - *More government spending on social welfare programs. Strong unions. Higher minimum wage and greater worker's rights. Creating a universal healthcare plan for the country. More regulations on businesses, for example to protect the environment.*

2. Peace - *Ending the Iraq and Afghanistan wars, which some said were for "oil."*

3. "Human Rights" - *Such as closing Guantanamo Bay and fighting discrimination against Muslims. Some also assumed that this would also include a rolling back of the Patriot Act.*

4. Social Progressivism - *More tolerance for homosexuality (although even Obama did not advocate for gay marriage), and some affirmative action. This would, of course, become the cornerstone of the Democratic party after the Great Awokening, but at the time it was less extreme relative to what it would become.*

5. Tolerance - *Unlike the Left of today, the Left of the time was much more liberal. They were in favor of freedom of speech, for example, including "shock humor" which was often targeted against the "Religious Right." They even defended homosexuality on these grounds – ie "it doesn't affect you what someone does in private, so why should you care?" However, there were some instances in which they would become politically correct, such as if a white person called a black person the N word. There was even a much smaller "political correctness" movement in the 1990s (although it was ultimately unsuccessful).*

Since President Clinton, much of the Democratic Party platform existed in a much more moderate form. The Democratic Party was for labor, true, but it lacked the heavily socialist elements of the New Deal era, and the unions were somewhat of a holdover from the past. Clinton had taken a much more pro-business stance than previous, more ideological Democrats, with actions such as NAFTA. They were for peace, but not absolutely and in all circumstances like their hippie predecessors (Clinton would order airstrikes against Iraq in 1998). They were for Civil Rights, but in an earlier incarnation that emphasized a "colorblind" society.

The Republicans followed a similar path towards moderation. They were for "small government" but wanted to keep entitlements like Social Security alive. They were against "government spending," but not if it concerned the military or bailouts for large corporations and banks (and they in fact ended up spending just as much as the Democrats in the end). And of course, they were in total agreement on Civil Rights issues in emphasizing a "colorblind" society--though they were perfectly happy to strip away civil liberties in the name of protecting America from "terror."

In the end, Obama did not deliver on his promise of change. Instead, he delivered more of the same. Rather than ending the Patriot Act, the government's illegal surveillance of American citizens expanded. Rather than ending the bank bailouts, he continued them. Rather than closing Guantanamo Bay, it remained open. And rather than ending the wars in Afghanistan and Iraq, he expanded the war to new fronts such as Libya and Syria.

In the end, both parties in effect were:

- Unwilling or unable to prevent military adventurism abroad

- Unwilling or unable to protect civil rights from the incursions of the government through laws such as the Patriot Act

- Served businesses over the people (ie bailing out banks and corporations while allowing ordinary people to suffer)

- In favor of shipping jobs abroad to increase the GDP and benefit the rich while causing Americans to compete in a globalized labor market

- In favor of mass immigration that had various social and economic effects that benefitted immigrants and big business at the expense of the American people

It seemed that no matter who Americans voted for, the policies of the American government would not change. In addition, there was really no political alternative to the "uniparty" of the Democrats and Republicans. 3rd parties, such as the Reform Party of Ross Perot, or non-mainstream candidates such as Ron Paul and Patrick Buchanan, never seemed to be able to be elected. Ideas such as communism, fascism, democratic socialism, and nationalism were laughable fringe ideologies relegated to an older time before the End of History. (Although libertarianism was seen as a viable and popular alternative, as we shall see). However, on /new/ and later /pol/, this was not the case.

The combination of free speech absolutism, anonymity and the prevalence of fringe and conspiracy theories led to an explosion of political creativity and diversity online. The Overton Window was abolished. On /new/, users ran the gambit from anarchists, Egoists, "tankies" (orthodox Marxists), progressives and "classical liberals" to Christian theocrats, monarchists, anarcho-capitalists, and, of course, fascists. Politics went all the way back to first principles. Discussions were not about Republicans and Democrats, but instead fundamental questions such as "what is the nature of the state?" "Where does sovereignty come from?" "When is the use of force legitimate?" and so forth. Of course, they were drenched in irony, memes, and trolling, but this was the essence of the discussion.

In addition, alternate histories, told through the lens of fringe ideologies such as Communism, anarcho-capitalism, or fascism were presented. For example, one might make a thread about how North Korea was actually the "good guy" and Juche was created in response to American intervention into North Korean affairs, forcing it to create an entirely self-reliant system that did not rely on foreign trade. Unlike South Korea which had unsustainable demographics, in North Korea the birthrate was healthy. They had conservative moral values, unlike the degenerate South Koreans. The thread would be accompanied by historical photos, North Korean propaganda, excerpts from books about North Korea or quotes from North Korean political figures that advocated for this framing of history.

From this primordial soup of political discussion, the Alt Right would eventually be born. But why did it take the form it did? To a large extent, it is simply because this Nazi imagery was the most shocking and edgy. While 4chan was host to genuine political discussion, though cloaked in irony, the main focus of the site was still nihilistic trolling. Nazi imagery was the most likely to "troll" people, because it was the most likely to get a reaction. And so /new/ and later /pol/ would gain infamy as a "Nazi" board, but this was partially tongue-in-cheek. Users leaned into the reputation because they thought it was funny. 4chan users found pretending to be a Nazi so much fun that they added it to their repertoire of shock humor that they could use to troll and raid other parts of the Internet. They studied the Third Reich in order to troll more effectively. And so, while all sorts of political opinions could still be found on 4chan, and there was never any organized campaign to turn the site towards a particular ideology, those that were Nazi-inspired (one cannot call them totally conventionally Nazi, as they were clothed in anime and Pepe the Frog) quickly become the most influential of the various political ideologies on the site.

The original incarnation of the "Alt Right" heavily adopted Nazi imagery, but it was still essentially libertarian in ideology. Many early figures, such as Sam Hyde, were not really political activists, but simply trolls trying to "trigger" Leftists for the lulz. What they really believed in was political incorrectness. That, and later Trump, the incarnation of this principle, were the only uniting forces of the movement. The actual politics of the Alt Right were extremely varied. There were classical liberals, libertarians, and even liberals who voted for Obama but still stood for free speech absolutism. Of course, there were genuine neo-Nazis and white nationalists as well -- Alt Right figures would eventually march shoulder to shoulder with David Duke at Charlottesville -- but it was inaccurate to call it a genuine neo-Nazi or white nationalist movement until its latest days in 2017, after Trump had already ascended to the throne and right before the Alt Right would cease to exist.

But why is it the edgiest imagery? Why is it that it is so offensive? The communists committed terrible atrocities, and killed even more people than the Nazis, so why was the hammer and sickle not as shocking as the swastika? It was people beginning to ask themselves these questions that would transform the ironic Alt Right into the more genuine Dissident Right. The explanation is that because Nazism represents, in effect, a previous thesis from the early 20th century, which the liberal antithesis was itself created in response to. This is why it is the most taboo of taboos. This is why Hitler is the most evil of all evils. The reaction away from absolutist ideologies such as Nazi Germany is what set forth the status quo in which we are living in the final years. Therefore, it is the inevitable force of the historical dialectic that draws it out again. Of course, history does not repeat. But, as Mark Twain said, it does "rhyme." The Alt Right, while inspired by the forbidden and discarded ideas of fascism, is not identical to it. Just as Vaporwave, which would become the musical movement associated with the Alt Right, did not perfectly replicate the music of the 1980s which inspired it, but resurrected these ideas in order to transform them into something totally new and modern.

In 2011, one year after the creation of /new/, moot would delete the board, claiming that it had "turned into Stormfront" (Stormfront was the name of a neo-Nazi website).

As for /new/, anybody who used it knows exactly why it was removed. When I re-added

the board last year, I made a note that if it devolved into /stormfront/, I'd remove it.

It did -- ages ago. Now it's gone, as promised.

-- moot, January 17, 2011 (https://webcitation.org/6159jR9pC? url=http://content.4chan.org/tmp/r9knew.txt)

But a few years later it would return in it's better known form as /pol/ - politically incorrect. The birthplace of the Alt Right.

Ron Paul /b/

In the meantime, the Internet continued to have an essentially libertarian character. In many ways, libertarianism hit the peak of its popularity during this time, in the shape of Ron Paul, who ran for president in 2008 and 2012.

Libertarianism was seen as an alternative to the "uniparty" of Democrats and Republicans, and the vessel for the "change" that the country so desperately wanted but which Obama had failed to deliver. Ron Paul ran on a platform that promised to return America to a version of itself which conformed more closely to its roots and stated values. A non-interventionist foreign policy and end to the wars, an end to alphabet agencies such as the NSA and CIA that were a threat to the rights of Americans, and an extreme reduction of the scope of government to basically pre-FDR levels.

Although not an incredibly important part of political history in the long run, it's important to touch on briefly to illustrate the libertarian nature of 4chan. After his failed presidential bid, anon would create memes of Ron Paul with the caption "it's happening!" implying that Ron Paul's predictions of the disastrous consequences that would occur to America if his platform was not adopted were coming to pass. Ron Paul was often photoshopped to have glowing "lazer beam" eyes, perhaps the first time this had been done. As of 2023, over a decade later, photoshopping "lazer eyes" onto various politican to show how "based" they are is still a staple of political memes. Users on /b/ even began to use Ron Paul's name to greet one another -- "Ron Paul, /b/!" *(Author's note: this one may be a rumor. While I do not remember encountering it firsthand, I do remember Ron Paul's popularity on 4chan. I have not been able to find the meme on Know Your Meme or elsewhere, but I will still include it for posterity as a part of Internet mythology).*

The media attacked Ron Paul as a quack, just as it had to all figures who dared offer an alternative to the uniparty. The tactic worked excellently, Ron Paul failed to get the nomination, and the establishment of both parties were happy for it. And so "change" would once again be crushed by the system. Right up until 2016.

Epic Fail Guy and Anonymous

*In late 2006, stick-figure comics depicting a character who is bound to fail at everything he does started to appear on 4chan. The Character soon became known as "Epic Fail Guy." -- **Know Your Meme** (**https://knowyourmeme.com/memes/epic-fail-guy**)*

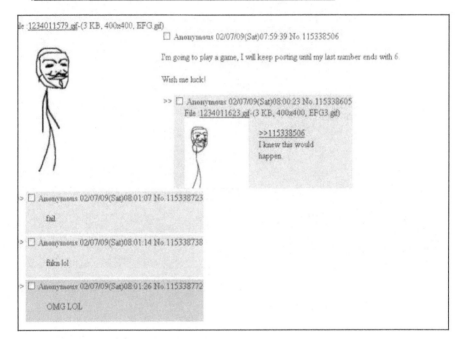

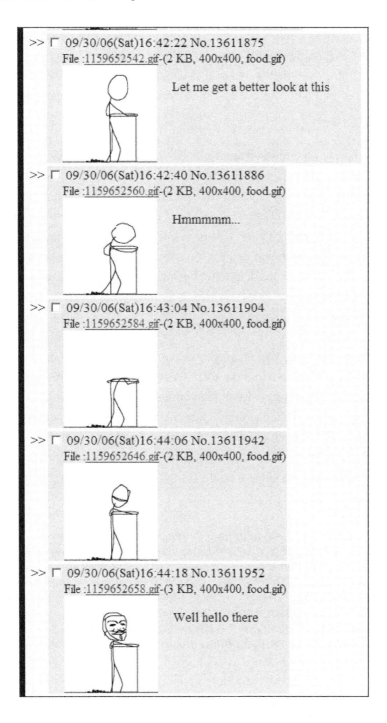

Epic Fail Guy was a series of comics posted by an anonymous drawfag at random times (people would screen shot the original threads and post the screen shots for anon that were not lucky enough to be around for the original thread). Epic Fail Guy was a stick figure comic about a guy who continually fails.

Although barely remembered anymore, he was at one point an extremely popular meme on 4chan, probably the most famous drawfag comic of all time until the creation of "rage comics" in the early 2010s. One comic, posted in 2006, featured Epic Fail Guy finding a Guy Fawkes mask (from the movie V for Vendetta) in a trash can and putting it on. He would continue to appear with the mask in subsequent comics. As a result of the popularity of this meme, the Guy Fawkes mask quickly became a symbol of 4chan as a whole. Depictions of 4chan in memes, for example, might feature an anonymous figure wearing a Guy Fawkes mask.

As with Pepe the Frog, Wojak, and other popular memes, the Guy Fawkes mask continued to evolve into the form we know today over the course of several years. The next important development in its history was "Chanology" in 2008. "Chanology" was the first time that 4chan went out into "meatspace" (the opposite of "cyberspace") and tried to troll people "IRL." Their target was The Church of Scientology, which reportedly was involved in the greatest sin one could commit against the Internet: censorship.

On January 16th, 2008 after the Church of Scientology issued a copyright violation claim against YouTube for hosting material from the Cruise video. The project was publicly launched via a video uploaded to YouTube on January 21st, 2008 entitled "Message to Scientology" on the channel Project Chanology. The video states that Anonymous views Scientology's DMCA action as Internet censorship, asserting the group's intent to "expel the church from the Internet." -- Know Your Meme (https://knowyourmeme.com/memes/events/project-chanology)

Many of the IRL trolls referred to their organization as "Anonymous" and appeared in public wearing the Guy Fawkes mask as a reference to 4chan. This was the origin of "Anonymous" as an activist group, and their association with the mask.

From then on, the newfound "Anonymous" would embark on many troll campaigns.

> **Operation Lioncash -** *Operation Lioncash is a graffiti practice initiated by the online group Anonymous in April of 2008, which involves drawing a lion face emoticon (">:3") over portraits on banknotes and releasing them back into circulation. According to its mission statement, the purpose of the global operation is to convert all regional currencies into Lioncash.*

> **Operation YouTube -** *Operation YouTube (also known as "YouTube Porn Day") was a series of adult video spamming raids launched by Anonymous which took place on YouTube in early June 2009.*

> **Operation Teaspoon -** *Operation Teaspoon was a campaign started in July of 2010 against the Oregon Tea Party for using the Anonymous slogan "We are Anonymous. We are Legion. We do not forgive. We do not forget. Expect us." Prior to its usage in bumper stickers, the slogan had been seen on protest signs and as the official description on the Tea Party Patriots website. Anonymous members retaliated by spamming the Oregon Tea Party Facebook with memetic catchphrases like "desu" and "derp". --* **Know Your Meme**
> **(https://knowyourmeme.com/memes/subcultures/anonymous)**

Eventually, parts of "Anonymous" would begin incorporating more and more activism in their activities, and use increasingly more sophisticated hacking techniques, hacking Sony and government entities such as the FBI.

> **Operation Payback -** *Operation Payback was a series of DDoS attacks organized by Anonymous that started on September 17th, 2010 against major entertainment industry websites such as the websites for the Recording Industry Association of America and the Motion Picture Association of America.*

Operation Sony - *After the Sony Corporation pursued legal action against the hackers George Hotz and Egorenkov, a contingent within Anonymous networks began attacking Sony-branded websites in a campaign named Operation Sony in April of 2011*

Operation BART - *Operation BART (#OpBART) is an Anonymous hacktivist campaign that was launched against San Francisco's Bay Area Rapid Transit (BART) websites following its disruption of cellphone services in select subway stations in August of 2011. According to the group's press release, the BART authorities disabled cellphone signals on its stations on August 11th, 2011 after receiving reports about a planned protest over fatal shootings of passengers by transit security officers.*

Operation Megaupload - *Operation Megaupload is a distributed denial-of-service (DDoS) campaign launched by online hacktivist group Anonymous in retaliation against the U.S. Justice Department's seizure and closure of file-hosting service Megaupload in January 2012. On the day of launch, 10 high-profile government and music industry websites were reportedly brought down, which was described as "one of the largest scale cyber attacks ever carried out" by an Anonymous-affiliated channel @Anonops. -- **Know Your Meme (https://knowyourmeme.com/memes/subcultures/anonymous)***

As Anonymous was not a membership organization with a formal structure and hierarchy, anyone could claim to be part of "Anonymous." As a result, there were many Anonymous offshoots, such as LulzSec, a smaller, more experienced group of hackers. Many of Anonymous's more advanced hacking operations were carried out by these groups (many of whom eventually faced serious federal charges).

LulzSec was the computer hacker group that was responsible for the 2011 Sony Pictures attack, among other high-profile attacks. LulzSec is a contraction of "lulz" for laughs and "security," which hackers like to compromise. During their peak activity in 2011, LulzSec broke into government and private computer networks, disclosing terabytes of confidential data, including usernames, passwords, and other personally-identifying information.

LulzSec claimed responsibility for taking down the CIA website. LulzSec's attacks are credited in the security community for raising awareness of the risks of insecure systems and the inherent security risk of reusing a password. It gained attention due to its high-profile targets and the sarcastic messages in the aftermath of its attacks.

*On June 26, 2011, LulzSec released a "50 days of lulz" statement, claiming the groups intended to end their attacks, that LulzSec consisted of seven hackers, and that they would shut down their website. Although the original LulzSec group appeared to disband, a potentially related group calling themselves LulzSec Reborn in 2012 attacked the military dating site militarysingles.com, followed several months later by public disclosure of 10,000 Twitter user account passwords. -- **Bugcrowd (https://www.bugcrowd.com/glossary/lulzsec-hacker-group/#:~:text= LulzSec%20was%20the%20computer%20hacker,which%20hackers %20like%20to%20compromise.)***

*One of the founders of LulzSec was computer security specialist Hector Monsegur, who used the online moniker Sabu. He later helped law enforcement track down other members of the organization as part of a plea deal. At least four associates of LulzSec were arrested in March 2012 as part of this investigation. Prior, British authorities had announced the arrests of two teenagers they alleged were LulzSec members, going by the pseudonyms T-flow and Topiary. -- **Wikipedia (https://en.wikipedia.org/wiki/LulzSec)***

"Anonymous" is no longer really a relevant group. Shortly after it entered the public consciousness in the early 2010s, a distinction began to grow between 4chan and Anonymous as two separate entities. As "Anonymous" became popular as a "hacktivist" group, 4channers began to stop using the Guy Fawkes mask to represent themselves and stopped referring to themselves collectively as "Anonymous" (but still continued to refer to themselves as "anon"). Eventually Anonymous would be seen as "cringe" and become associated with Leftist causes like Occupy Wall Street which the newly Right-leaning 4chan wished to distance itself from.

Still, Anonymous played an important part of the Internet's discovery of its own power to influence real-world events and pioneered the combination of trolling, hacking, and activism that would later be used by the Alt Right and Dissident Right. As of 2023, the Guy Fawkes mask is still a part of the popular lexicon. Its contemporary meaning is as a symbol for all hackers in general.

Sarah Palin email hack

During the 2008 election, Vice Presidential candidate Sarah Palin's personal Yahoo email account was hacked, and posted on 4chan's /b/ board. Anon then raided the email address and began posting her personal information on the site.

This is notable as one of the first times that 4chan "hacktivism" would play a part in a presidential election. A bit later, after the hacker was caught, moot was also summoned to appear in court to testify about the incident. This led to a humorous moment when moot had to explain 4chan cultures, memes, and lingo to the normies of the court.

Q. And is there any significance to "new fags"?

A. That is the term used to describe new users to the site.

Q. What about "b tard"?

A. It's a term that users of the /b/- Random board use for themselves.

...

Q. "Rickroll"?

A. Rickroll is a mean or Internet kind of trend that started on 4chan where users -- it basically a bait and switch. Users link you to a video of Rick Astley performing Never Gonna Give You Up. – **moot's testimony in United States of America vs David C. Kernell, Aug 10 2010 (https://web.archive.org/web/20100820204109/http://i.cdn.turner.com/ dr/teg/tsg/release/sites/default/files/assets/poole-testimony.pdf) (https://www.businessinsider.com/4chan-founder-moots-weird-testimony-in-sarah-palin-email-hacking-trial-2010-8)**

Occupy Wall Street

It's interesting to note that the dissident movement that would eventually spawn Trump started not with him but with Obama. The dissident movement started as a desire for "change" that began after 9-11 and the financial crisis of 2008, and then changed shape and evolved, first manifesting itself as Obama and Occupy Wall Street, then as Libertarianism and Ron Paul, then as the Alt Right and Donald Trump, and finally as the Dissident Right of today. In the future, who knows what shape it will take? Likely, due to the dialectical process, it will still be Right Wing. But, if it had been successful in reforming the system at an earlier stage, such as through Occupy Wall Street, perhaps it might have taken a very different form.

Occupy Wall Street was a series of protests in New York City which lasted from September 17 to November 15, 2011. Copycat movements also arose in other American cities. The protesters occupied Zuccotti Park, carrying signs such as *"We are the 99%!"* Although its specific goals were a bit vague, it generally was a reaction to anxiety caused by the 2008 financial crisis, where the financial industry was bailed out by the government, while ordinary people were told to "pick themselves up by their bootstraps" and not expect "handouts." There was a growing sentiment that the government was run not for the benefit of Americans (the 99%), but rather for a small number of wealthy and influential people at the top (the 1%). (Note that this sentiment would eventually transform into the populism of Trump, rephrased in less explicitly economic terms, as the "elites" and the "establishment" versus the "American people")

The initial protest was started by AdBusters (a Canadian anti-consumerist organization) and attended by a variety of different groups and individuals. Many online communities, such as Reddit, encouraged their users to attend. This included Anonymous, who showed up to the protests in their characteristic Guy Fawkes masks. The protests, while involving organized groups such as AdBusters, also involved many independent actors, with no clear structure or hierarchy. In many ways, it mirrored the anarchic and decentralized hacktivism of Anonymous. Many of the participants organized and communicated online using Twitter, Reddit, 4chan and various other platforms.

It also featured independent journalists such as Tim Pool. These journalists were able to cover the protests on their private YouTube channels or Twitter accounts, or simply post their coverage on 4chan or Reddit if they desired. It's important to note this development. It represents the beginning of the fracturing of the news and the end of the monoculture. In the future, consumers no longer had to simply follow the mass media news "transmitters," but could instead turn to these independent news outlets or to social media. And they could follow an independent organization that shared their specific politics. Socialist and progressive people could follow *The Young Turks*, while conspiracy enthusiasts could follow Alex Jones, and the far-Right could see what other anon were posting about the protests on /pol/. This would have a major effect on the 2016 election.

Occupy Wall Street foreshadowed what would become major themes of the rise of Trump in 2016: dissatisfaction with the American establishment, decentralized Internet activism, and the explosive growth of social justice politics on the Left. It was the latter of these that is said to have ended Occupy Wall Street. Those who I have talked to who were a part of the protests in NYC, described it to me this way. The "leaders" of the Occupy

Wall Street were "too white and too male" and factions in the movement began to form calling for new leadership. This led to fracturing in the movement, and its eventual weakening and lack of solidarity made it easier for police to begin removing people from the park.

Occupy Wall Street would be the last time that economic issues were the main focal point of the Left. In the years to come, it would be entirely dominated by the explosive growth of social justice progressive "identity politics" or "wokeism."

Encylopedia Dramatica Becomes Oh Internet: the First Domino That Would Lead to Trump, J6, and the End of the End

On April 14, 2011 an event would occur on the Internet that forever changed world history. *Encyclopedia Dramatica* was deleted. This may sound like a joke, but it is not. The ripple effects of this action would eventually lead to the creation of the Alt Right, the proliferation of dissident ideas on the Internet, the Great Meme War, and then the election of Donald Trump.

Encyclopedia Dramatica, essentially, a 4chan version of Wikipedia. It used the same wiki software as Wikipedia, but with the shock humor of 4chan, including its staples of pornography, gore, obscenity and extreme racism. In addition to articles on various subjects, such as you might find on Wikipedia, *Encyclopedia Dramatica* (sometimes abbreviated as ED) also served as an early version of "Know Your Meme," chronicling the history of various memes, as well as events in Internet history, raids, and e-drama (with many e-celebs gaining their own ED page). Newfags who were not yet acquainted with 4chan culture often went to ED to learn the lore.

Aboriginals are the niggers of Australia. They are the most primitive animals on the planet and have an average iq of 50. These subhuman relics of human evolution are the greatest living proof of the inequality of the races.

They are typically called coons, noongahs, boongs, abos or black cunts by every Australian. The proper name for a young aboriginal is Lake Angel. – **The Encyclopedia Dramatica article on Aboriginals. (https://encyclopediadramatica.online/Aboriginal) I tried to find a better example of an ED article, but as of September 2023, the site is in a broken and mostly unusable state. This article is known for being removed from the Google search engine, an early example of the Internet censorship that would become commonplace during the Censorship Era**

Then, one day, *Ecyclopedia Dramatica* was gone, and users were redirected to a page called Oh Internet, a safe and advertiser-friendly page.

"OhInternet covers anything related to Internet culture from people to memes to websites and more. Our aim is to be a complete guide to the Internet's past, present and future and we want you to participate.

-- OhInternet's description of itself, April 14 2011. It seems that they basically wanted to create "KnowYourMeme," which serves a similar purpose to ED, but presents history in a straightforward manner without intentionally offensive content and shock humor

*OhInternet (also known as OhI, OhShitternet, Know Your Meme 2: Electric Boogaloo, or old ED's purported killer) was the fetid afterbirth spilling from the diseased uterus of Encyclopedia Dramatica's heartbreaking temporary downfall of April 2011. Created by morbidly obese traitor-hipster Sherrod Ellen DeGrippo and her sysop sheep, OhI was basically a carbon copy of Know Your Meme, except instead of cataloging memes with a pseudo-scientific flair, it depressingly and relentlessly tested the reader's tolerance for tepid, pretentious, and smarmy articles about HILARIOUS Internet CULTURE. It was among the Internet's most naked and obvious attempts to gain Jew gold at the expense of content, though this was vehemently denied by the grossly corpulent and badly-aging liar who orchestrated this unforgiveable, unabashed treachery. Going from an awesome wiki about drama to an almost offensively bland catalog of memes and milquetoast "columns," OhI was universally panned by the Internet during its thankfully brief existence. -- **Encyclopedia Dramatica's description of OhInternet (https://encyclopediadramatica.online/OhInternet)**

Later that year, during a panel discussion, moot would criticize the decision to unilaterally destroy an Internet community without caring about the opinions of the members of that community. Realizing that he had done the same thing himself to /new/ earlier that year, moot decided to revive the board on October 23, 2011, with a new name: /pol/ - politically incorrect.

As a result of this decision, the proto-Alt Right, which might have been snuffed out in 2011, instead was allowed to ferment for 4 more years. If the Alt Right social phenomenon, and the greatest of all ops: The Great Meme War, had anything to do with the rise of Trump – as many say it did – then this small decision would set off a chain of events that would change the trajectory of the world forever and restart history.

As it turned out, 2011 was a very important year in the chain of events that would lead to the rise of the Dissident Right and the Trump Era of politics. But not as important as what would come after it in the year 2014.

Chapter 2 - 2014: The Greate Awokening and Its Consequences, GamerGate, Anti-SJWs, Million Dollar Extreme, /pol/

2014: The Current Year Begins

There are a number of dates one could choose for the Trump Era. Although Trump left office in 2021, he has still been a major focal point of throughout the Biden presidency, and may be in office again until 2028. Most would begin in 2015, when Trump announced his candidacy. But I would place the true start of the Trump Revolution was in 2014, when the Dissident Right really began to take form. This is the year when the Internet went from libertarian, nihilistic, and really apathetic to politics, to a true political force. Anyone familiar with the Internet will recognize this as the year when one of the most infamous events in Internet history took place: GamerGate.

"It's about ethics in video game journalism!"

-- A superchatter watching a city block in Minneapolis being burned to the ground during the 2020 BLM riots on The Killstream with Ethan Ralph livestream

There is a meme on the Internet that we are living in a "post-GamerGate world," ascribing all of "Clown World," including Trump, the 2020 BLM riots, the January 6 capitol riot, etc. to the consequences of GamerGate.

Someone could probably write an entire book about this event alone. But not me. The truth is, I was actually not very interested in GamerGate at the time, having already been somewhat redpilled by /pol/ and Million Dollar Extreme prior to the event. So I was not really surprised that events unfolded as they did, already possessing a jaded view of the media and politics. Still, due to its immense importance, I will give an extremely brief rundown of the events of

GamerGate and 2014. But first, we need to go back even further, all the way to the days just after Occupy Wall Street, in 2011. During this time, an even more important phenomenon than GamerGate occurred: The Great Awokening.

The Great Awokening (circa 2011)

*In the past five years, white liberals have moved so far to the left on questions of race and racism that they are now, on these issues, to the left of even the typical black voter. -- **vox.com, April 1 2019 ,"The Great Awokening", (https://www.vox.com/2019/3/22/18259865/great-awokening-white-liberals-race-polling-trump-2020)***

Our results document a marked increase in the prevalence of prejudice-denoting words in news media discourse within the 2010-2019 time frame. The trend precedes the emergence of Donald Trump in the political landscape for most of the terms analyzed but appears to accelerate after 2015. The abrupt and dramatic changes in word frequencies suggest the existence of powerful underlying social dynamics at play.

*It is noteworthy that prejudice-denoting words are markedly increasing in prevalence alongside long-term decreases in overt expression of prejudice yet recent increases in the perceived prevalence of such prejudice among the general public. It is our hope that the detailed characterization of the phenomena presented here can pave the way for future studies looking in-depth at potential causal factors for the trends described herein as well as the impact of news media rhetoric on public consciousness and the social implications of growing perceptions of prejudice severity among the general population.– **David Rozado, Jul 19, 2021 "Prevalence of Prejudice-Denoting Words in News Media Discourse" (https://davidrozado.substack.com/p/ppdwnmd)***

The Great Awokening was a political shift in the Left Wing in the early 2010s. During the shift, the Left Wing went from a party centered around economic issues and liberalism to the Left that we know today, dominated by "social justice," often prescribed to the public by militant ideologues ("social justice warriors") through illiberal means. It is equivalent to what people call "wokeism" today.

It is unknown exactly how and why the Great Awokening started. These social justice ideas had been taught in some far-Left circles in academia for decades, sometimes reaching back all the way to the 1960s or earlier. They also were popular among a small minority of young people in some online communities, such as Tumblr, whose ideas of "fat acceptance," "white privilege," "multiple genders" etc. were seen as a fringe Left Wing counterpart to the fringe Right Wing ideas circulating on 4chan's /pol/. They were also popular on Left Wing independent news publications such as *Buzzfeed* and *Jezebel* (which extended into the realm of gaming journalism, a detail that is about to become very important). Some say that the rise of these independent journalists around the same time as Occupy Wall Street caused these issues to enter the public consciousness, and were then picked up by larger publications.

Another popular theory, which has not been definitively proven, is that the Great Awokening was a direct answer to Occupy Wall Street by the establishment. According to this theory, "the powers that be" used their control over mass media to intentionally stoke racial conflict in order to divide the 99% over social and cultural issues, so that they could not unite against the 1% over economic concerns. In a way, this is the opposite of the former theory, claiming a top-down origin due to mass media rather than a bottom-up origin due to the disruptive force of the Internet.

This theory is supported by the convenient timing, and the supposed role of identity politics in helping to disintegrate Occupy Wall Street (as has been attested to by people involved in the movement). However, it could be that the beginnings of "woke" politics were simply already present organically by the time of Occupy Wall Street to a sufficient degree as to cause conflict along identity lines within the movement to occur. It also relies on the assumption that the 1% perceived Occupy Wall Street as a threat, despite it having virtually no effect on public policy in any way. It also assumes that America's racial and identity divisions are somehow imposed on Americans inorganically by the establishment rather than being innate, something that is

not borne out in the long history of organic racial conflict that did not need to be manufactured in this way.

Whatever the explanation, this political realignment occurred first in the media. Starting around the year 2011, the media began to be filled with social justice narratives, with a pronounced increase of articles dedicated to racism, sexism, white supremacy, anti-Semitism, homophobia and even transphobia (even though transgenderism was a non-mainstream topic in 2011, four years before Obergefell).

*Figure 4 illustrates the increasing prevalence of words denoting different types of prejudice in two prestigious newspapers in the United States: The New York Times (in blue) and The Washington Post (in red). A clear trend of increasing prevalence of prejudice related terms is apparent with words such as racist or sexist increasing in usage between 2010 and 2019 by 638% and 403% in The New York Times or 514% and 141% respectively in The Washington Post. The yearly usage of prejudice related words is highly correlated between both outlets as shown by the Pearson correlation coefficient, r, in the upper left corner of each plot. – **David Rozado, Jul 19, 2021, "Prevalence of Prejudice-Denoting Words in News Media Discourse" (https://davidrozado.substack.com/p/ppdwnmd)**

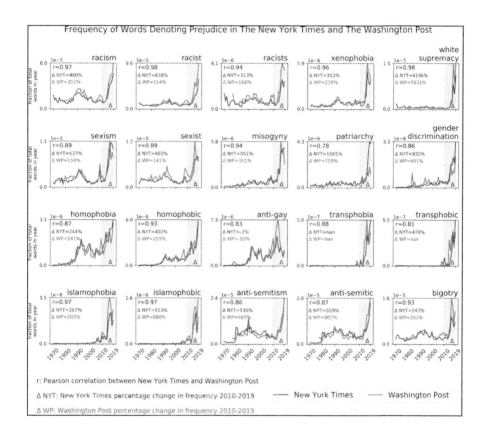

Frequency of Words Denoting Prejudice in The New York Times and The Washington Post

r: Pearson correlation between New York Times and Washington Post

Δ NYT: New York Times percentage change in frequency 2010-2019

Δ WP: Washington Post percentage change in frequency 2010-2019

This text is not meant to serve as a rigorous study of the Great Awokening. However it is important to note the basic timeline, as in many ways the far-Right is a reaction to this phenomenon, rather than the other way around. As David Rozado (one of the first to draw attention to this phenomenon) concludes, this uptick in coverage of identity and culture based issues did not coincide with any uptick in racist attitudes. Race relations were fairly stable in the 2000s, with a "colorblind" consensus in both the mainstream Right and Left Wing. America had just finished electing its first black president to his second term in the White House. However, the Great Awokening changed the media's coverage of what few racially charged events did occur.

> *"If there had been no Twitter or Facebook," Columbia University's John McWhorter, an early and somewhat skeptical observer of the Awokening, tells me, "Trayvon [Martin] and Mike Brown would have had about as much impact on white thought as, say, Amadou Diallo did." -- vox.com, April 1 2019, "The Great Awokening", (https://www.vox.com/2019/3/22/18259865/great-awokening-white-liberals-race-polling-trump-2020)*

The Great Awokening represented a shift from the more liberal consensus of "colorblindness" in which Americans were encouraged to judge people as individuals and pretend not to notice race in any way, to "anti-racism" in which white Americans were encouraged to "check their privilege" and explicitly favor non-whites over whites, in order to make up for past discrimination against non-whites. This has also been called "equality of opportunity" (colorblindness) versus "equality of outcome" (anti-racism). Adherents of the new ideology claimed that race had no basis in genetics but was a "social construct," and that any differences in the material conditions of whites and non-whites must therefore be caused by racism, even if this racism was not explicit, but hidden somewhere beneath the surface. "Colorblindness," they said, was simply an effort by white people not to confront their "privilege" and combat this hidden racism.

The Great Awokening also resulted in the beginnings of "political correctness" and "cancel culture."

> Cancel culture is a phrase contemporary to the late 2010s and early 2020s used to refer to a cultural phenomenon in which an individual deemed to have acted or spoken in an unacceptable manner is ostracized, boycotted, shunned, fired or assaulted, often aided by social media. — **Wikipedia (https://en.wikipedia.org/wiki/Cancel_culture)**

This is when the shift from "free speech" being Left-coded to being Right-coded occurred. It was this that would set the stage for the conflict between the Great Awokening and the 4chan-influenced, politically incorrect culture of the Internet, which would result in GamerGate.

GamerGate: The New Year 0

"Gamers" — as the video game enthusiasts called themselves, especially in online communities — were already beginning to chafe against the Great Awokening. This was because of what gamers saw as the unnecessary injection of Left Wing "woke" politics into video games. Gaming journalism, which had grown into a large industry, was much more female and Left Wing than the gaming audience, which was predominantly white and predominantly male. On top of this, many gaming journalists were seen as not hardcore video game enthusiasts but rather journalists first and foremost, with video games simply being a lucrative beat.

Video games had begun to be attacked and critiqued by Leftists, especially feminists. Anita Sarkeesian's *Feminist Frequency* became popular with Leftist women.

*Since mobile, indie and retro inspired games are built on a legacy of
inequality in the medium the new wave of 80s and 90s nostalgia has
brought with it a resurrection of the worst of the old-school damsel in
distress stereotypes. Indeed, many of these new titles essentially function
as love letters to the trope as a way of paying homage to classic games of
years gone by. -- **Anita Sarkeesian, Feminist Frequency, Aug 1, 2013,
"Damsel in Distress: Part 3"
(https://en.wikiquote.org/wiki/Anita_Sarkeesian)***

Like many video games journalists, Anita Sarkeesian was not a video game
enthusiast, but saw video games as a new, 21st century avenue for her
journalistic and social justice aspirations:

*For me, the big picture has always been culture change, and pop culture
was just a vehicle and a medium through which cultural change can
happen or it can be influenced by; so it's not actually about video games.
But it's about video games, right? -- **Anita Sarkeesian, Fighting for a
Cause, June 24, 2016, "VidCon 2016 @34:06"
(https://en.wikiquote.org/wiki/Anita_Sarkeesian)***

Not only were gaming journalists seen as "not real gamers" who were hostile
to video games and intent on "shoving their politics down people's throats,"
but they were often directly hostile towards gamers themselves. Some of the
best example of this can be found in the reactions of gaming journalists to
"GamerGate" which exacerbated this hostility and made it more explicit. One
example is the infamous "The End of Gamers" blogpost, written by Dan
Golding on his Tumblr.

*The last few weeks in video game culture have seen a level of
combativeness more marked and bitter than any beforehand.*

First, a developer—a woman who makes games who has had so much piled on to her that I don't want to perpetuate things by naming her—was the target of a harassment campaign that attacked her personal life and friendships. Campaigns of personal harassment aimed at game developers are nothing new. They are dismayingly common among those who happen to be women, or not white straight men, and doubly so if they also happen to make the sort of game that in any way challenges the status quo, even if that challenge is only made through their very existence. The viciousness and ferocity with which this campaign occurred, however, was shocking, and certainly out of the ordinary. This was something more than routine misogyny (and in games, it often is routine, shockingly). It was an ugly spectacle that should haunt and shame those involved for the rest of their lives.

...

And lest you think that I'm exaggerating about the irrelevance of the traditionally male dominated gamer identity, recent news confirms this, with adult women outnumbering teenage boys in game-playing demographics in the USA. Similar numbers also often come out of Australian surveys. The predictable 'what kind of games do they really play, though—are they really gamers?' response says all you need to know about this ongoing demographic shift. This insinuated criteria for 'real' video games is wholly contingent on identity (i.e. a real gamer shouldn't play Candy Crush, for instance).

On the evidence of the last few weeks, what we are seeing is the end of gamers, and the viciousness that accompanies the death of an identity. Due to fundamental shifts in the video game audience, and a move towards progressive attitudes within more traditional areas of video game culture, the gamer identity has been broken. It has nowhere to call home, and so it reaches out inarticulately at invented problems, such as bias and corruption, which are partly just ways of expressing confusion as to why things the traditional gamer does not understand are successful (that such confusion results in abject heartlessness is an indictment on the character of the male-focused gamer culture to begin with).

...

The last few weeks therefore represent the moment that gamers realised their own irrelevance. This is a cold wind that has been a long time coming, and which has framed these increasingly malicious incidents along the way. Video games have now achieved a purchase on popular culture that is only possible without gamers.

...

On some level, the grim individuals who are self-centred and myopic enough to be upset at the prospect of having their medium taken away from them are absolutely right. They have astutely, and correctly identified what is going on here. Their toys are being taken away, and their treehouses are being boarded up. Video games now live in the world and there is no going back.

I am convinced that this marks the end. We are finished here. From now on, there are no more gamers—only players. -- **Dan Golding, "The End of Gamers" (https://www.tumblr.com/dangolding/95985875943/the-end-of-gamers)**

Kotaku, a major video game publication at the time, echoed these sentiments in the wake of GamerGate:

I've been working at Kotaku for nearly eight years now, and while I've seen some online kerfuffles over various issues in that time, I've never seen anything like the past two weeks.

There has been so much hate. So many angry words, so many accusations, over...what? video games? Women in video games? People who write about video games?

It would be absurd if it hadn't forced people out of their homes for fear of their personal safety.

...

"These obtuse shitslingers, these wailing hyper-consumers, these childish Internet-arguers — they are not my audience. They don't have to be yours. There is no 'side' to be on, there is no 'debate' to be had."

– Luke Plunkett, "We Might Be Witnessing The 'Death of An Identity'", Kotaku, August 28, 2014 (https://kotaku.com/we-might-be-witnessing-the-death-of-an-identity-1628203079)

Of course these sentiments did not arise solely as a reaction to GamerGate. Quite the opposite, GamerGate was a backlash by gamers against the contempt that these Left Wing journalists had for their own audience. In many ways, GamerGate was the entire Trump 2016 Campaign in miniature. An uprising by predominantly white male conservatives against an establishment and mainstream media that reviled them. Thus the meme that as of 2023, we are living in the 9th year AG (after GamerGate).

So what was GamerGate and how did it occur? Well, of course, it started on 4chan. 4chan culture and gamer culture were already tied closely together. Since the dawn of the Internet, there was a lot of crossover between fans of video games, fans of anime, and Internet enthusiasts. /v/ - Video Games was one of the largest and most popular boards on 4chan.

The controversy began with indie developer Zoe Quinn, and a text-based game created by her, *Depression Quest*. This game was in many ways the epitome of everything that the Left Wing movement, led by gaming journalists, wanted games to be. It was female, focused on narrative and themes rather than gameplay (thus allowing it to be a vessel for Left Wing propaganda), and lacked technical finesse (typical of the Leftist preference for art that is conceptual rather than demonstrating technical skill). Of course this game received rave reviews from mainstream video game journalists, while being loathed by the "gamer" community on 4chan (much as conservatives often trash other Left Wing art while critics praise it, a la Rotten Tomatoes movies where the critic score is 99% and audience score is 2%).

Meanwhile, a post by Zoe Quinn's ex-boyfriend, Eron Gjoni, was posted on 4chan, "exposing" Zoe Quinn.

*On August 16th, 2014, game developer Zoe Quinn's ex-boyfriend Eron
Gjoni published an online expose detailing their relationship called the
Zoe Post. In the expose Gjoni claims Quinn cheated on him with several
men in the gaming industry, including Kotaku journalist Nathan Grayson.
These claims were subsequently refuted by Kotaku editor-in-chief Steve
Totilo in a post on the website. In this post he claims that the only time
Nathan mentioned Quinn was in a post about a gaming competition
known as GameJam. The day following the publication of the Zoe Post,
YouTuber MundaneMatt uploaded a video critiquing Quinn's game
Depression Quest and commenting on the alleged affairs with men
working in the video game industry. The video was subsequently removed
due to a copyright claim allegedly by Quinn for using a still image from the
game. On August 18th, YouTuber Internet Aristocrat uploaded the first in a
series of videos titled Quinnspiracy Theory, in which he discusses the
issue of cronyism in gaming media and the indie game development
community.*

...

*As concerns over the alleged integrity of gaming journalists increased, it
was discovered that several were actively contributing money to Quinn's
Patreon account, including Polygon editor Ben Kuchera who had been
donating to Quinn for several weeks prior to writing an article about her
game. Kotaku writer Patricia Hernandez subsequently came under
scrutiny as well when gamers began investigating her alleged romantic
relationships with other video game developers. Similarly, many criticized
sound designer Robin Arnott for having an alleged affair with Quinn while
appearing as a judge in the Indiecade game competition, which gave
Quinn an award for Depression Quest –* **Know Your Meme
(https://knowyourmeme.com/memes/events/gamergate)**

Note, again, the role of the medium of 4chan in shaping events, its free
speech absolutist policy on /b/ and anonymity making it the perfect platform
for leaking information.

While the initial point of contention between game journalists and gamers
was "cronyism" — or, as it was commonly phrased "ethics in video game
journalism" — it ignited the other political rifts between the two groups,
escalating as it began to touch on more fundamental political divisions. The
first of these being censorship. As we have seen throughout this text, the

highest virtue of the Wild West Internet was freedom of speech and the greatest sin was censorship. It is amazing to think about now, but censorship was so uncommon on the Internet and yet so feared, that even the appearance of the slightest act that could be perceived as censorship was seen as a capital offense. Thus, the flagging of the initial MundaneMatt video for copyright infringement was treated as a heinous act of Zoe Quinn "suppressing the free speech" of her critics. It was the censorious reaction of the gaming media to these initial complaints, and their wanton contempt for gamers, which became the real focal point of the conflict.

It also led to the birth of an army of anti-SJW YouTubers, which would become mobilized in force throughout 2014-2016, becoming a central part of the Alt Right. Future Alt Right and Alt Lite personalities such as Milo Yiannopoulos, The Internet Aristocrat/Mr. Metokur, Ethan Ralph, Sargon of Akkad (AKA Carl Benjamin), and others gained massive Internet followings during GamerGate, which they would continue to harness throughout the rise of the Alt Right and election of Trump in 2016, before finally being banned, becoming embroiled in endless e-drama with one another, or being forced to moderate or reverse their views during the Censorship Era of 2017-2022.

GamerGate in a way pulled back the curtain to the inner-workings of politics for the first time for a young audience. They saw a coordinated attempt to suppress their voices and slander them by the entire media, and the contempt that the woke had for straight white males. It also exposed the inter-connectivity and cronyism between individuals in an industry and their ability to conspire towards common political ends or for personal gain. And they saw any criticism of this system met with allegations of misogyny and bigotry, an attempt to suppress their criticisms rather than address them at face value.

After the Zoe Post, many commentators online, including social justice bloggers, began to condemn the gaming industry, and the culture surrounding it, for being filled with sexism and misogyny. Many news sites began to report on these allegations, many of which saw this alleged harassment as proof of the sexism rooted within gaming culture. Among those who were targeted by this harassment included video game developer Brianna Wu, and actress/livestreamer Felicia Day.

On October 29th, 2014, video game critic Anita Sarkessian appeared on Stephen Colbert's late-night news show The Colbert Report to discuss sexism in the gaming industry. The clip of Sarkessian and Colbert's discussion was later uploaded to Comedy Central's YouTube channel (shown below), and was reported on by various sites such as The Verge and The Washington Post.

...

After several articles critical of the "gamer" identity were being posted on gaming news websites, people began speculating that journalists had worked together to promote a narrative against gamers that disagreed with them. On September 17th, Breitbart staff writer Milo Yiannopoulos posted a tweet hinting he had obtained information about a "co-ordinated approach" used by journalists who wrote the articles.

Later that day, Breitbart published and article titled "Exposed: The Secret Mailing List of the Gaming Journalism Elite," revealing a private Google group mailing list titled "GameJournoPros," purportedly used by gaming journalists cooperating to work against GamerGate. The article contained several screenshots taken from the mailing list, which discussed ways to approach the topic of Zoe Quinn and the GamerGate controversy.

-- Know Your Meme
(https://knowyourmeme.com/memes/events/gamergate)

Talk of GamerGate eventually started to become censored outright. First, on Reddit, and later, even on 4chan. On Reddit, Julian Assange even spoke out against censorship of GamerGate:

On September 15th, Wikileaks founder Julian Assange participated in an "ask me anything" thread on the /r/IamA Subreddit to answer about his new book When Google Met WikiLeaks.

After Redditor ShaskaOtselot asked for his opinion censorship of GamerGate discussions on Reddit, Assange replied that it was "pathetic." After another Redditor pointed out that ShaskaOtselot had been shadowbanned, Assange edited the post to point out that a user had been banned for asking him a question about censorship. On the same day, Julian Assange tweeted about this event using the hashtag #gamergate. -- **Know Your Meme (https://knowyourmeme.com/memes/events/gamergate)**

On 4chan, GamerGate threads flooded the boards of /v/, /b/, /pol/, and others. /v/ had practically been transformed into a GamerGate board. Eventually, moot would ban GamerGate, something that came as a surprise to many users and was almost unprecedented.

> *The decision to remove "GamerGate" threads has been poorly communicated, and that's my fault. Said threads are being deleted primarily because they violate our blanket "no personal information / raids / calls to invasion" rule. Spamming the reports system and creating multiple topics were also a factor, especially given /v/ is one of 4chan's fastest moving boards and has historically struggled with keeping topics limited to actual video games.*
>
> *Regarding a perceived lack of free speech/censorship -- many seem to misinterpret my advocating for anonymous communication and highlighting that it allows people to share things they otherwise wouldn't be comfortable with on other platforms as "you can say and do anything on 4chan," which simply isn't the case. We've had rules and moderators since the site was founded 11 years ago, and I've only reinforced this statement over the years, a la: https://archive.moe/q/thread/580080/#580135*
>
> *To those who actually want to use /v/ to discuss vidya and not a movement that has outgrown 4chan (a la Project Chanology) -- apologies for the inconvenience.*

-- moot, Sep 19, 2014

Censorship of GamerGate on 4chan was considered an unforgivable
grievance for many oldfags. They migrated to 8chan, a spin-off of 4chan
(with the difference being that instead of a small list of fixed boards, users
could create their own boards). 8chan started to gain a reputation as the more
hardcore version of 4chan, while 4chan, mockingly referred to as "halfchan"
by 8chan users, was for normies. moot began to be seen as a "cuck."

To be totally fair, given the nature of the Internet at the time, it is not
inconceivable that some crazed anon could have represented a credible threat
and done something crazy to Anita Sarkeesian or Zoe Quinn.

> On October 10th, an anonymous user on 8chan posted Wu's address,
> phone number and email to the /gg/ (GamerGate) board. Several users
> responded denouncing the post and raising suspicions that it was part of
> a false flag attack. That evening, Wu tweeted that she was contacting the
> police after receiving threats from a Twitter account named "Death to
> Brianna"
>
> ...
>
> On October 14th, 2014, video game critic Anita Sarkeesian tweeted that
> she canceled her talk at Utah State University when her requests were
> denied for pat downs or metal detectors after receiving death threats
> – **Know Your Meme
> (https://knowyourmeme.com/memes/events/gamergate) Note: Briana
> Wu was another female video game developer targeted by
> GamerGate**

It's not impossible to believe that the antagonists of GamerGate received
"death threats." But what, in the end, does that mean? Should someone
assume that that is a real threat that someone intends to act on, or simply an
idle threat that is designed to intimidate? Most likely the latter. On the other
hand, 8chan users have also posted their manifesto online before going on
mass shootings. So, if I was on the receiving end I would probably play it
safe.

While they were certainly trolled, "harassed" and "raided" by anon, I also share the view with most anon that it was played up for effect to feed into their narrative about being poor innocent victims of misogynist bullies. They seemed to revel in the fact that they were being attacked and made it the focal point of why people should empathize with them during interviews on *The Colbert Report* and in the gaming journals.

In addition to questions about the inner-workings of journalism, the controversy also raised questions about the true nature of women and feminism. Were negative stereotypes about female hypergamy really so incorrect? Were female professionals able to compete on their own merits, or only through manipulating men in power through relationships, sex, and playing the victim?

Eventually, the campaign would run out of steam and gamers would move on. But not before hundreds of thousands of young white males became redpilled for the first time as the result of the fallout from GamerGate.

Vivian James

GamerGate, like the early Alt Right, was still an essentially libertarian movement. It was not interested in challenging the basic assumptions of social justice or even feminism (such as the assumption that "men" and "women" should have similar roles in society). It was more concerned with holding the Left to their own standards of tolerance, liberalism, and not judging others based on immutable characteristics such as race or gender.

Like many Boomer conservatives today, they met accusations of "sexism" and "misogyny" by pleading with their accusers and insisting that they had simply made a mistake, and that they could prove these accusations false. This led to the creation of "Vivian James."

Vivian James was a female anime character created by /v/ which was supposed to represent their idea of a "female gamer" that they would have no trouble accepting as one of their own. A female gamer that was unconcerned with social justice issues, and simply wanted to play video games.

> *Vivian James is a fictional character conceived through a collaboration between 4chan's /v/ (video games) board and the indie game developer group The Fine Young Capitalists. The character can be viewed as an anthropomorphized avatar of the /v/ board community created in response to Zoe Quinn's purported attack on the second-wave feminist organization The Fine Young Capitalists (TFYC) while they were trying to fund a Game Jam to assist women's projects in gaming development.*
>
> *...*
>
> *By reaching at least $2000 in donations, 4chan gained the right to have a character of their design be placed in the video game that would result from TFYC's Game Jam. When /v/ noticed that they had reached the character design reward, multiple threads where created to brainstorm for ideas. This eventually led to the idea and design for what later would become Vivian James – **Know Your Meme (https://knowyourmeme.com/memes/vivian-james)***

Vivian James was depicted as a lazy, cynical redhead in a green and purple hoodie (green and purple were the official colors of /v/), with a four leaf clover hairpin in her hair (the four leaf clover is the logo of 4chan), and a scowl on her face.

She was often depicted in memes with the caption *"Can we just play some video games?" (https://knowyourmeme.com/photos/962902-vivian-james)* or *"Shut up and play video games" (https://knowyourmeme.com/photos/968813-vivian-james)* indicating her love of video games and indifference towards politics. Other memes depict her as scrolling /v/ or participating in the boards culture, indicating her authenticity and acceptance by the community — *"fuck, another me thread? Neo-/v/ sucks!" (https://knowyourmeme.com/photos/866890-vivian-james)* Another meme bears the caption *"I represent over 70k donated by so called*

'misogynists' to a campaign to encourage women in game development that was blacklisted by so called 'feminists'"
(https://knowyourmeme.com/photos/859342-vivian-james)

Of course, the charitable gesture of Vivian James was in no way reciprocated by the Left, and they had no interest in compromising. They ignored the gamers and continued to accuse them of sexism and misogyny.

> *Following the creation of Vivian James and the cooperation between 4chan and TFYC, The Fine Young Capitalists received negative feedback on both Twitter and Tumblr from certain feminist groups and supporters, claiming TFYC to be hypocrites, for dealing with 4chan in a friendly manner and accepting money and help from them. –* **Know Your Meme(https://knowyourmeme.com/memes/vivian-james)**

Vivian James serves as a stark reminder of how trying to offer an olive branch to the Left, rather than submitting passively to their entire worldview, usually works out.

SJWs and Anti-SJWs

GamerGate eventually spawned the "anti-SJW" era of YouTube, one that
lasted throughout the 2016 election and until the Wild West Era ended and
the Censorship Era began. Most of the channels involved, such as Sargon of
Akkad, grew directly out of making GamerGate content. These channels
moved from covering GamerGate drama to making more explicitly political
content that began to criticize "SJW" hypocrisy concerning feminism, white
privilege and other social justice issues. However, until perhaps the rise of
"Kekistan" (covered in chapter 3), they did not employ the same fascist-
inspired imagery or extreme Right Wing views of the Alt Right, usually
taking a classical liberal, "free speech" stance. Sargon of Akkad is a good
example of this kind of content, calling himself a "classical liberal" to this
day.

What is an "SJW"? SJWs, short for "social justice warriors," were people
who we might use the word "woke" to describe now. They were often
depicted as blue haired, fat, easily "triggered" feminists who probably
browsed Tumblr and watched Anita Sarkeesian. The word "social justice
warrior" was actually meant to be sarcastic initially, in a similar way to the
term "keyboard warrior," to imply that these people did not actually
participate in real activism but simply made impotent posts online
complaining about social justice issues. While doing nothing of substance in
the real world, they viewed *themselves* as "warriors" saving the world from
bigotry and oppression. However, over time, this aspect of the term was lost,
especially when the Alt Right truly became popular and caring about "social
justice" in the first place finally became "cringe."

Typical anti-SJW content were longform video essays critiquing social
justice warriors, usually from the stance that they contradicted purportedly
liberal beliefs. A typical anti-SJW argument would be similar to "affirmative

action is bad because it judges people by their skin color, not the content of their character."

However, other content would be better described as proto-Alt Right or Alt Right content. This content truly questioned the basic assumptions of liberalism, rather than criticizing hypocrisy or contradiction. This included the channels The Alternative Hypothesis (also known as AltHype for short) and Sean Last, who argued for "human biodiversity"(HBD) or "race realism." This was the belief that there are in fact genetic differences between the races, and this is what was ultimately responsible for racial inequalities, not racism. Rather than being hypocritical, affirmative action was intentionally anti-white, based on the racial grievances non-whites had against white people. That is why, they argued, Leftists did not care about the contradiction between affirmative action and "colorblindness," because they did not actually care about "colorblindness" in the first place. They simply supported whatever policy most benefited their non-whites, even if it was unfair or came at the expense of white people.

Other anti-SJW content included the popular "SJW feminist triggered compilation" style of YouTube videos which mocked SJWs. The cool, unbothered, and logical anti-SJW might "trigger" SJWs through over-the-top politically incorrect statements, or through Ben Shapiro-style rhetorical one-liners. The SJW, usually fat and grotesque with bright dyed hair and of ambiguous gender, would then be shown freaking out, crying and screaming hysterically in response.

Million Dollar Extreme

Around the same time, *Million Dollar Extreme* was growing in popularity on the Internet. *Million Dollar Extreme* was an underground, Rhode Island-based film and comedy troupe consisting of Sam Hyde, Nick Rochefort and Charls Carroll. Founded in 2007, they played a similar role to artists of the

1960s counter-culture such as Lenny Bruce, George Carlin and Monty Python. The most well-known member was founder Sam Hyde. Hyde was successfully able to combine surrealist comedy like Adult Swim's *Time and Eric* with the underground Internet's characteristic style of humor such as memes, trolling, meta-irony, political incorrectness and inspiration from video games and anime.

Sam Hyde was best known for his short "vertical videos" where he would shoot intentionally crappy comedy sketches featuring him recording himself, often in front of the mirror in his mom's house. These vertical videos featured bizarre impressions and characters, such as "Bowl Cut Tyler" and "Gamer Dude," dripping with irony.

> *Just went to a steampunk convention. Flew there in a steam-powered gyrocopter with my musket and my corncob pipe and my monocle and an ascot and a newsie cap and Doc Martens and suspenders. And my character's name is Humperdinck. That's my character Humperdinck. And I'm 32 years old, so I guess he's level 32. And I have a kid with my wife. And my wife...I could have gotten – if you're going to use a rating scale to rate women, which is disgusting. And if you do that you're a disgusting person – but my wife is a 6-point...you know my wife's a five. I could have gotten a 6.5 but I'm a disgusting pig. I'm a slob. I smell. I have bad hygiene. She has the worst hygiene. Which is why I'm comfortable with her. Because I'll take that choice. I will make that compromise. That's my, you know, that's what I'll do. I'll forego a 6.5 in favor of a sloppy five.– **Sam Hyde as "Gamer Dude" (https://youtu.be/z7qTPUj7wVc?si=LtqRpZj9nRtSa3Yj))***

Sam Hyde was especially known for incorporating Internet-inspired "meta-irony" in his humor. Most of his "characters" such as Gamer Dude was ironic, and meant to mock the people he was imitating. But Hyde would also imitate characters reminiscent of a typical 4chan user with far-right beliefs. Although done in the same "ironic" style, Hyde would drop subtle hints that in fact the character's beliefs were not entirely ironic, making it difficult to surmise which part of the character was a joke and which parts reflected Hyde's true beliefs.

He also filmed IRL trolling campaigns, such as his famous "Paradigm Shift 2070" in 2013 in which he managed to be invited to a TEDx talk at Drexel University as a guest speaker, claiming to be a video journalist and documentary filmmaker from Brooklyn.

> *"Sam Hyde is a video journalist and documentary filmmaker from Brooklyn, New York. His work spans every continent and has been featured on television and in print (Discover, NatGeo, Vice, and others). He recently returned from Mogadishu, the most dangerous city on earth, where he shadowed the heroic al-Mahamudwomen on their quest to clean up the streets and restore humanity to their war-torn country. In 2014 he will be investigating the methamphetamine trade in Mongolia."*
>
> *– **TEDx introduces Sam Hyde** (https://www.YouTube.com/watch?v=4jRoatZizQ0) (https://gothgordongekko.medium.com/sam-hydes-2070-paradigm-shift-f55872e5f77d)*

Hyde appeared on stage in a suit of armor resembling that of a gladiator and gave a rambling, incoherent speech full of meaningless buzzwords, much of it making ridiculous predictions about what the future of 2070 would hold, including *"state-enforced homosexuality,"* and a *"trash economy"* where people would *"use cubes of trash as money"*.

> *I was at a college, a second tier, not an ivy league school, a second choice school, and I was in a class. And there was a student in that class, okay? And the, the teacher, he was spouting some horrible nonsense, about how, it was something about how women's rights are not legitimate, something that everybody knew was false, but if anybody had spoken up, he would've taken extreme joy in failing them. Okay? Nobody spoke up. One person raised his voice. Once person started talking. The teacher couldn't believe it, the classroom couldn't believe it either. But in the end, he had logic on his side. And at the end of the day, he proved his point. That student was Albert Einstein. And that same sense of childlike play and innocence that we know from Albert Einstein, I can sense it in this room today.– **Sam Hyde, Paradigm Shift 2070** (https://www.YouTube.com/watch?v=4jRoatZizQ0) (https://gothgordongekko.medium.com/sam-hydes-2070-paradigm-shift-f55872e5f77d)*

This event would receive coverage from *Insider* magazine and other outlets, as well as achieving much attention from Reddit. Even Joe Rogan covered the video (Sam Hyde would later spam Joe Rogan for years trying to get on the show).

Million Dollar Extreme also produced more traditional sketch comedy videos, such as *Ideas Guy* and *Moms* which they posted to their YouTube channel. These videos featured surreal humor and over-the-top editing reminiscent of Adult Swim's *Tim and Eric*, as well as jarring, manic, intricate graphics created by Hyde, who had previously worked professionally in motion graphics.

Some of Sam Hyde or Million Dollar Extreme's other projects included:

- *KickstarterTV* - a multi-episode series where Sam Hyde would mock other creator's Kickstarter projects

- *Samurai Swordplay in a Digital Age* - an "IRL troll" much like *Paradigm Shift* where Sam Hyde was able to become a speaker at an anime convention, posing as "Master Kenchiro Ichiimada" and delivering a speech mocking anime and Japanese culture

- Standup comedy where Sam Hyde would troll the mostly liberal audience with increasingly misogynistic, homophobic and anti-Semitic humor

- In 2014, Sam Hyde created a Kickstarter campaign to crowdfund a "pony dating simulator for Bronies" based on the cartoon *My Little Pony: Friendship is Magic*

Sam Hyde's videos, especially his vertical videos, circulated on 4chan and gained a cult following among anon. They were staples at the time of the website SynchTube, a site popular with 4channers which allowed users to hang out and watch YouTube videos together. It was clear from his humor, familiarity with chan culture, and /pol/-inspired politics that he himself was anon, and 4chan considered him one of their own.

Sam Hyde also became the subject of another troll campaign, this time not of his own devising. During a school shooting or other tragedy, trolls would call into major news stations claiming the killer had been identified as "Sam Hyde." The media would then report this information without confirming it, unaware of the joke or who Sam Hyde was. Anon would then clip the news report and post it on 4chan or Twitter, often with the tagline "he can't keep getting away with it!"

This joke hit its height on February 25 2022, when congressman Adam Kinzinger was duped into tweeting a photo of Sam Hyde's face photoshopped onto the body of a fighter pilot, which claimed to be the "Ghost of Kyiv"

> *The #ghostofkyiv has a name, and he has absolutely OWNED the Russian Airforce. Godspeed and more kills, Samuyil!*
>
> *– Congressman Adam Kinzinger , US House of Representatives for Illinois's 16th district, tweeting a picture of Sam Hyde*
> *(https://twitter.com/BushidoToken/status/1521190811408510979)*

In 2016, *Million Dollar Extreme* would get picked up by Adult Swim, where they created *"Million Dollar Extreme: World Peace."* It ran for one season, where it received successful ratings. However, Sam Hyde would become a victim of "cancel culture" due to his high profile support for Donald Trump and financial donation to the Alt Right publication *The Daily Stormer*. Charls and Sam would have a falling out over the cancellation of the show, Charls blaming its cancellation on Sam's online antics, and *Million Dollar Extreme* broke up. They would not be brought back together until 2023.

/pol/

/pol/ by now had evolved into something basically resembling the Alt Right, with a true far-Right ideology. However, it was still very much fused with the "shock humor" of 4chan, and was not a serious political movement, but rather steeped in irony and "troll" culture, making it difficult to determine if its users actually believed what they were posting or if it was simply "for the lulz." /pol/ was still a small subculture relegated to 4chan. Although there was much crossover given their common enemy of SJWs, the anti-SJW movement was far bigger, and centered around YouTube and other sites like Reddit, rather than 4chan.

It's hard to say whether the Alt Right truly existed at this point, or whether it was still the proto-Alt Right, continuing to gestate on /pol/. The Alt Right never truly became the Alt Right until it was galvanized by Trump. /pol/ was solely an anarchic, Internet phenomenon. Nobody really thought that it would ever be a serious political movement. Who would they even try to elect? Who would even accept their support? And /pol/ did not even truly have a clear political philosophy. It was still a mishmash of trolls, libertarians, and various other ideologies. The only thing they all had in common was being politically incorrect. Then, out of nowhere, arose Trump: the politically incorrect candidate. "The chaos candidate" as he was called in the press. Much like the chaos that /pol/ wished to unleash on the world.

Even the support for Trump was half-earnest and half-joke. /pol/ did not support him primarily for his politics, but because it would be funny. Mostly, they just wanted to watch the world burn. However, /pol/ culture, or the proto-Alt Right, or the Dissident Right, however you want to think of it, was growing precipitously on the Internet, driven by the larger anti-SJW movement.

A smaller minority were more earnest in their politics. Eventually, the proto-Alt Right, like other movements that began online, started to slowly make their way IRL. Dissident Right podcasts such as *The Daily Shoah* (a part of the podcast network TRS) began to appear. Anon began to acquaint themselves with far-Right literature such as Julius Evola, or Richard Spencer's publication *The Radix Journal*. Some anon even began to form or join white nationalist organizations such as "Identity Europa." White nationalist propaganda such as the satirical show *Murdoch Murdoch* (which was a sort of Alt Right version of *South Park*) and *White Rabbit Radio* (a series of cartoons such as "anti-Racist Hitler" which explained white demographic replacement using a "woke" version of Hitler who tried to perform a second holocaust by telling Jews to "check their privilege" and replacing them with gentile immigrants) began to circulate alongside *Million Dollar Extreme* and Sargon of Akkad. Bits of a genuinely far-Right ideology were beginning to form.

However, in the main, the movement was still dominated by edgy libertarians. *The Daily Shoah,* a racist and anti-Semitic podcast hosted by Mike Enoch, and *The Daily Stormer,* a far-Right online publication created by Andrew Anglin, both included over-the-top, explicit, intentionally shocking Nazi imagery, but were originally satirical (much in the same vein as *Encylopedia Dramatica*). It was not until the end of the Alt Right around 2017 that both had become genuinely political, with *TRS* going so far as to start its own political party, "The National Justice Party," in 2020.

The majority of anon, even those who lurked /pol/, were only dimly aware of these genuinely fascist and white nationalist developments. I personally did not know of the existence of *The Daily Shoah* until well after Trump became president in 2017, nor was I aware of Identity Europa until 2019, well after Charlottesville. It would not be until 2017, after Trump miraculously was elected, that the Alt Right was ever a serious political movement. Whatever fascist imagery they may have employed, and however much of the "irony" might have actually been "meta-irony," the movement would still primarily be focused around two pillars: rejection of political correctness and "burn it all down" anti-establishment sentiment, both embodied in the person of

Donald Trump. The fact that there were actual white nationalists like Richard Spencer (one person who anyone in the Alt Right would have recognized due to his high profile mainstream media interviews) amongst the Pepe the Frog-avatared edgy teenagers really just made things funnier. The Alt Right was also a "big tent movement." True, it may have included Richard Spencer, but it also included just as many classical liberals, or edgy trolls like Sam Hyde. People might accept one or two far-right beliefs from /pol/, like anti-feminism, but reject others, like anti-Semitism. There was a large spectrum of vaguely Right Wing, vaguely anti-establishment beliefs that any one person's true beliefs, under the trolling, might fall under.

Until Trump's inauguration, it was all just for the lulz.

Chapter 3 - 2015 & 2016: The Alt Right, Trump, The Great Meme War

If an entire book could be written about GamerGate, an entire library could be written about the Trump Presidential Campaign in 2016. As with GamerGate, I will not be giving a play by play of the entire campaign. I will be forced to leave out many memorable and important moments.

Also, a slight warning for my normie audience, you might call it a trigger warning. This is a chapter in which some of the most offensive, racist, anti-Semitic and explicitly Nazi content will appear. I try to explain at length the historical context in which it occurred, and the importance the use of this shock humor.

While my beliefs had already been influenced by /pol/ by this time, I would only consider myself to be something like half-redpilled. I entertained the ideas I read about on 4chan and found them fascinating, but I was unsure whether to believe them or not and I certainly did not hold them with conviction. I never accepted wholly white nationalist or neo-Nazi beliefs, but I did believe that the Alt Right held within it some valid critiques of liberalism.

Some people would recognize these valid critiques (the kernel of truth from within the chaotic explosion of the Alt Right) and develop them, thus influencing the Dissident Right of today. Others simply moved away and abandoned the movement after it stopped being about lulz and trolling SJWs and matured into a real political movement, dropping the shocking Nazi imagery and shock humor but retaining far-right anti-establishment ideas.

I don't mean to brag, but I predicted all of this in 2016. I remember being invited into my Leftist friend's groupchats in 2016. All of them, of course, predicted that Trump was going to be the next Hitler. Not being aware of my real views and assuming I was on their side (given my socially liberal libertarian lifestyle at the time: drugs, parties, etc.) they invited me to these groupchats where they would feed off of each other's paranoia and grow increasingly hysterical. My response was simply this: "the Alt Lite is more important than the Alt Right."

"The Alt Lite" referred to a faction within the Alt Right that was more moderate, classically liberal, and much more akin to the larger anti-SJW trend than the /pol/-dominated Alt Right, which by this time involved genuine white nationalists such as Mike Enoch, Richard Spencer and Andrew Anglin among the trolls. My logic was simply as follows.

Prediction 1: Trump would not become Hitler

1. America was already almost 50% non-white.

2. Therefore, even if you wanted to turn America into a white ethnostate, its demographics simply made it logistically impossible to do so. People might be willing to post a racist Pepe the Frog meme, but the majority of them would not be willing to comply with oppressing their own friends and relatives.

3. Therefore, it was impossible for white nationalism to ever become a reality in America in 2016.

Prediction 2: The Alt Lite would become mainstream, but the Alt Right would not

1. Unless the Internet was totally censored and shut down, Chinese style, the Streisand effect meant that Alt Right ideas would continue to spread and become mainstream (I never thought that that could happen to the Internet, but it began to happen just one year later).

2. However, as these ideas spread, they would become diluted and less extreme. Because of American demographics (see P1-1) they would also have to become palatable to non-whites and whites with non-white friends and relatives. This point was supported by the fact that much of /pol/ itself was non-white. In pictures I had seen of IRL /pol/ meetups, the demographics were similar to the demographics of America, with as many hispanics and Asians and there were whites. There was even a black person or two and maybe even a Jew.

Prediction 3: Trump would be assimilated

1. Most politicians say whatever will get them elected, then conform to the uniparty after they get elected. So Trump might not even genuinely believe what he says.

2. Even if Trump succeeds in getting elected, and even if he genuinely believes in his campaign promises, he has no base of power to set them into motion. Trump came out of nowhere. He had no movement behind him, not even a faction within the Republican party, and the establishment Republicans hated him and were dominated by never-Trump neocons right up until he became President.

3. Therefore, the Trump administration would not live up to the hype. Its actual policy decisions would basically be the same as a normal Republican administration, albeit it with extremely unorthodox rhetoric.

Although I got some of the details wrong, my predictions have held up better than anyone else who I personally know. The same cannot be said for the hysterical Leftists in the groupchat. The only people who made more accurate predictions than me are people I do not know personally: professional influencers who do politics for a living.

Because of prediction 3, I actually never ended up voting for Trump until 2020. I came close to doing so, and I did secretly love Trump and hoped that he would win, but something a few days before Election Day changed my mind. At my office, there were TVs all over the place tuned to the news, mostly business channels but also CNN, MSNBC and Fox. This made it possible for me to follow politics literally all day, every day, while browsing

4chan on my phone (I had a cushy desk job). A few days before the election, Fox News ran a segment where they predicted who Trump might assign to his cabinet if he were to win. Every name was somebody I hated, like Mitt Romney, Michael Bolton, or Paul Ryan. *"Wait a minute? Am I just being tricked into voting for a Republican?"* I thought. Thus, I never voted in the 2016 election and instead stayed home. My first vote for a Republican was during the 2018 election, by which time I had been convinced that Trump was the real deal.

As a result, I never got to fully participate in the victory of 2016.

Trump Comes Down the Escalator

"Trump formally announced his candidacy on June 16, 2015, with a campaign rally and a 46 minute speech at Trump Tower in New York City. In the moments before his announcement, he came down the golden escalator at Trump Tower, which has since become a metonym for Trump's announcement."

...

Trump declared that he would self-fund his presidential campaign, and would refuse any money from donors and lobbyists.

...

Following the announcement, most of the media's attention focused on Trump's comment on illegal immigration: "When Mexico sends its people, they're not sending their best ... They're sending people that have lots of problems, and they're bringing those problems with [them]. They're bringing drugs. They're bringing crime. They're rapists. And some, I assume, are good people." **-- Wikipedia's entry on the Trump 2016 Campaign announcement (https://en.wikipedia.org/wiki/Donald_Trump_2016_presidential_campaign)**

From the very first announcement speech, Trump became the human embodiment of the Alt Right's two major focal points: anti-establishment sentiment and, most importantly, political incorrectness.

The anti-establishment sentiment, which had been growing for quite some time since at least the 2008 financial crisis (and really since 9-11) was a feature of both sides. Similarly to Trump, Bernie Sanders ran on a populist, anti-establishment message with a self-funded campaign that had extremely popular grassroots support. In fact, at the time I missed most of the Republican primary due to following Bernie Sanders, whose campaign I donated to and for whom I voted for during the primary. It was only after Bernie Sanders's loss to Hillary Clinton that I began shifting my attention to Donald Trump.

But it was impossible to miss the other focal point of Trump's campaign, political incorrectness. His comments about illegal Mexican immigration would usually spell the end of a typical presidential candidate's campaign. The media of course called his comments racist against Mexicans. But some defended them, saying that Trump was not referring to all Mexicans, or even to all immigrants, but exclusively to illegal immigrants. Note the use of typical anti-SJW rhetoric, which does not challenge concepts such as racism on a fundamental level, but rather defends itself against allegations of racism in a particular case. Trump himself offered no apology, as would be expected in normal circumstances. Instead, Trump stood by it, commenting *"somebody's doing the raping."* Immigration (and, in reality, white demographic replacement, though not explicit) would become the cornerstone of Trump's campaign with his promise to build a "great, great" wall across the entire border with Mexico, and claiming that Mexico would pay for it.

This was only the beginning of Trump's politically incorrect comments. Every single day, there would be a new headline bearing a new Trump controversy. One memorable moment included mocking former Republican presidential candidate and bloodthirsty warmongering neocon John McCain.

> *At a July 18, 2015, event Trump described McCain as a "loser" and added, "He's not a war hero. He was a war hero because he was captured. I like people who weren't captured." – **Wikipedia (https://en.wikipedia.org/wiki/Donald_Trump_2016_presidential_cam paign#Conservative_movement)***

In December of 2015, he proposed an "Islamophobic" ban on Muslims entering the country:

> *On December 7, 2015, in response to the 2015 San Bernardino terrorist attack, Trump further called for a temporary ban on any Muslims entering the country. He issued a written statement saying, "Donald J. Trump is calling for a total and complete shutdown of Muslims entering the United States until our country's representatives can figure out what the hell is going on" -- **Wikipedia (https://en.wikipedia.org/wiki/Donald_Trump_2016_presidential_cam paign#Temporary_Muslim_ban_proposal)***

In a typical campaign, any one of these statements would have been suicide. Instead, with each new headline and controversy, Trump only became more and more popular. Attacking Trump in the media, a tactic that had sunk so many other anti-establishment campaigns, such as Ron Paul, was completely backfiring. The establishment had no idea how to counter this. For the first time, the spell had been broken.

The Alt Right unleashed

Trump's epic trolling instantly drew the attention of 4chan (all of 4chan, not simply /pol/, although /pol/ was starting to eclipse /b/ in terms of cultural output by this time) who decided to throw their support behind Trump and try to get him elected for the lulz.

In addition to support for Trump being an epic troll, 4chan's power only seemed to be growing, and it was easer to test this power. After the Anonymous hacktivism of the late 2000s and early 2010s, anon gained a sense of invincibility, always trying to push the limits of how far its decentralized "ops" could go in shaping events IRL.

But Trump's support was not merely limited to 4chan. Trump was also extremely popular on YouTube, Twitter and even parts of Reddit (which was seen as a center-left site, especially in contrast to 4chan).

Trump also united the many different anti-SJW ideologies (including many libertarians, anti-woke classical liberals, and conventional Republicans), white nationalists such as Richard Spencer, and /pol/ with its army of online trolls. It gave them a central mission: elect Donald Trump to the White House. It was this moment of unity and clarity of purpose that marked the definitive beginning of the Alt Right.

Etymology of the Alt Right

The name "Alt Right" was popularized by Richard Spencer, and many erroneously paint him as some sort of de facto leader. This is not really accurate. First of all, the movement was entirely decentralized, and while there were some well known figures like Richard Spencer, none of them rose to the level anyone could call a "leader." In contrast, Nick Fuentes is the undisputed leader of the America First movement, one of, if not the, major faction in the Dissident Right of today. Neither Richard Spencer nor any other individual ever rose to this level of prominence in the Alt Right movement.

Richard Spencer also popularized the term to describe a phenomenon that was by that time well underway, not one that he was responsible for creating. It was, however, a fitting term, reflecting the "big tent" nature of the movement. The Alt Right was not really about white nationalism, although this was one ideology under this tent. It really was a term that encompassed anyone who was Right Wing, but did not fit in with the conventional Republican party. Some of the ways in which they differed from the Republican party of the time included:

- Support for Trump

- Political incorrectness

- Distrust of both the Republican and Democratic parties

- Lack of respect for traditions, rules, and decorum in general (a "burn it all down" attitude). This was in stark contrast to mainstream Republicans, who sold themselves as the "adults in the room" and acted like the "bigger man," by following norms to the letter, even when this meant political defeat

- Opposition to foreign wars such as the war in Iraq and Afghanistan

- Economic populism rather than emphasizing the "free market"

- Nationalism and a protectionist foreign economic policy as opposed to "free trade" and globalism

- Opposition to immigration instead of support for a pathway to citizenship

- Criticism of the central tenants of liberalism (ie race realism over "colorblindness," historical revisionism vs explicit condemnation of fascism, questioning of feminism and homosexuality -- although this applies more to the Alt Right than to Trump himself)

- Atheism or agnosticism as opposed to Christianity (although this last point is complicated)

A note on the last bullet point, which is a bit of a paradox. The Republican party was at the time associated with social conservatism and the "Religious Right." This was certainly true of the base. And the establishment leaders, such as George W Bush would invoke the name of God and make concessions with the base over issues such as abortion. However, while Christian in rhetoric, the establishment considered these religious concerns a personal matter, and not the role of "big government" to legislate from the top down. As such, they were often seen as being "liberals from five years ago," adopting opposition to the latest liberal cause such as transexuality, while conceding on social causes from five years ago such as gay marriage.

In contrast, the Alt Right was the exact opposite. The part of the Alt Right that leaned more towards the far-right or fascism considered things like homosexuality, drugs, and even tattoos "degeneracy" and advocated for their abolition. However, they themselves were often the biggest degenerates of all. This is because the Alt Right was mostly agnostic towards religion. Many of its prominent figures were atheists like Richard Spencer. Nietzsche was popular among this contingency. There were many Christians in the movement, but there were just as many pagans who considered "christcuckery" to be "Jewish subversion" of the "ancient gods" of the white race, such as Thor and Odin.

This contradiction would eventually be resolved during the Optics Wars, when Christian Nationalism and social conservatism became a central part of the movement. But in the Alt Right, this Christian element was noticeably absent. While the Alt Right criticized earlier libertarian arguments for social liberalism (ie "the government shouldn't legislate morality") in favor of a more explicitly authoritarian government, this "social conservatism" was not a product of Christianity.

Trump was most certainly no social conservative, and even accepted LGBT openly during the 2016 campaign. Many even thought that the Trump campaign meant the universal acceptance of "gay rights" by both major parties, a claim that would later be made by Rick Grenell, an openly gay member of the Trump administration.

Mr. Bond and Moonman

"Sicker than your average coon slayer / Skin as white as snow and I dress like a player / I'm Moon Man / representing White Power / I'm the man of the hour / Yake a trip to the showers"

-- Moonman, Notorious KKK Pt.2

Why would anyone be proud to be black? / Your whole fucking race is addicted to crack / I'm Moon Man, representing "White Power" / I stack bodies higher than Trump Tower / Control the memes, control the planet / Fascism is back and the left can't stand it / Death camps for the blacks, sit back and relax / Right wing death squads prepare to attack

-- Moonman, Right Wing Death Squads

I bring the 1940s the fuck back / I'm a Nazi you can't stop that / Rolling on commies take the block back / Democrats running to the cuck shack / Bring those 40s the fuck back / I'm a Nazi you can't stop that / Rolling on commies / Take the block back / Homos running like a rocket

Now why'd you like a racist party with anti-Semites in it / They already lost the game / Why you still trying to win it? / What did they ever do to you / Why do you hate those Jews?

-- Mr. Bond, Fashout

Let the Frankfurt School corrupt these Whites / Make a happy merchant's paradise

Push the six gorillion guilt on Whites / It's a happy merchant's paradise

Our feminism breaks their family ties / Make a happy merchant's paradise

Have our media promote race-mixing Whites / It's a happy merchant's paradise

-- Mr. Bond, All White Paradise

I do not endorse the above lyrics. I also don't endorse the *Encyclopedia Dramatica* excerpts from earlier, or for that matter, any of the excerpts in this text. I especially disavow violence, that should go without saying. The above lyrics are included to illustrate the extreme shock humor of the Alt Right.

Moonman and Mr. Bond were two Alt Right content creators who would upload parody raps such as the one above. Moonman used a computer-generated voice and the McDonald's character "Mac Tonight" as his avatar (a character who, like Pepe the Frog, had started out as a non-racist meme on the website YTMND but then became appropriated by the Alt Right).

Moonman took the typical Alt Right approach of simply being as shocking and racist as possible by saying racial slurs over and over again and describing going around killing black people, Jews, and homosexuals.

Mr. Bond seemed to have been a legitimate Nazi. Most of his songs revolve around praising Adolf Hitler and advancing the cause of Nazism. Tragically, his song "Power Level" would be used in the livestream of the Halle Synagogue shooter in 2019.

I was not really into this stuff, although I did come across it from time to time. At the time, the Internet was full of extremely offensive content, so I didn't think much of it. I can't find many of the other Moonman and Mr. Bond songs that I remember from almost a decade ago because I do not know their names, but here are some of the titles that appear in an Odysee search for Mr. Bond: "Pop Some Fags," "Fascist," "Kill All Faggots,"

"Concentration Camp" and Moonman: "Ni**erland," "Go Kkkrazy," "The Klansman," "49 Faggots and 1 Doon Coon," "Notorious KKK."

This is how extreme the most extreme parts of the Alt Right became. This material was openly available on YouTube, Spotify, Apple music and Twitter during 2016. To their credit, Leftists were not entirely unjustified in their fears of fascism in some ways, since there were genuine fascists in the movement. Indeed, in the coming years, there would be mass shootings inspired by the Alt Right, their manifestos rife with /pol/ memes.

However, although it should be easy for anyone to disavow these songs, even in this extreme case there is another side to the story.

> *Mr. Bond was arrested at his home in Paternion, Carinthia, Austria and has been held in detention at Josefstadt Prison since his arrest on January 20, 2021, for "producing and broadcasting Nazi ideas and incitement to hatred". In 2022, he was found guilty and sentenced to 10 years in prison. Hassler's younger brother, the manager of his anti-Semitic website, was sentenced to four years in prison.* **-- Wikipedia (https://en.wikipedia.org/wiki/Mr._Bond_(musician))**

Even if you condemn the content of Mr. Bond or Moonman's speech, is it still appropriate to go so far as to arrest them for it?

I spent a lot of this text defending the Alt Right and adding context to the movement, but it's important to remember why the Alt Right ultimately failed and where it went too far. In one sense, it was the concept of "free speech absolutism" taken to its furthest extreme. Is it really too far to create a parody rap song with violently genocidal racist lyrics? The speech itself, taken in isolation, isn't hurting anybody. On the other hand, it may in fact have played some part in inspiring real world violence. So does that mean that "free speech absolutism" is invalidated as a serious principle? Should people like Mr. Bond, who did not commit any violent act themselves, but inspired others to do so, really be arrested simply on the basis of their speech?

On the other hand, the Alt Right would later give birth to more valid critiques of far-left social justice politics by the Dissident Right, which does not advocate for race-based violence against minorities. Even political activists such as Chris Rufo, LibsOfTikTok, Jordan Peterson and Matt Walsh can be said to be partially influenced by the Alt Right. If it were not for a policy of free speech, the reforms that Right Wingers believe are necessary for society could never be openly discussed. So is the cost of allowing "hate speech" to proliferate worth it, in order to receive the benefits of free speech and the necessary societal reforms it provides? And if we allow far-left speech, such as Communism (itself responsible for tens of millions of lives) to go uncensored in society on the basis of free speech, must we also allow far-right speech such as fascism? If we allow far-left speech, but not far-right speech, then is it not simply inevitable, given enough time, that society will ultimately drift further and further to the radical Left, making any opposition to the Left's agenda impotent?

In the end, the true value of the Alt Right is to provoke a conversation about these deeper intellectual topics. That is why I have taken pains to contextualize it throughout this text, rather than simply dismissing it due to some of its worst personalities. However, in my opinion, the ultimate failure of the Alt Right is that it was rooted in extreme nihilism. Yelling racial slurs at people in order to "troll" them is not the basis for a legitimate political movement. Neither is trying to one-up each other to see who can be more offensive to impress people on the Internet. What you get with that, eventually, is Mr. Bond and the synagogue shooter.

However, if we consider it in context, it was a necessary step at the time. Just as Trump was able to defeat the media slander that had buried respectable-presenting candidates, such as Ron Paul, by doubling down and leaning into the controversy, so too was the Alt Right's extreme offensiveness necessary to defeat political correctness and allow the beliefs of the social justice Left to be critiqued in the first place. This would have been impossible if one wanted to uphold his respectability in the face of an unreasonable, radical Leftist opponent, a strategy that had failed conservatives for decades.

The Alt Right was a destructive force that could only burn but could not build. It was missing a positive vision for society, such as the one that God can provide. It had critique and mockery, but it did not have virtues of its own. In that sense, it really was born out of hate. Still, for the moment, burning had some utility in and of itself.

Can't Stump the Trump

Not all Alt Right memes went to the extreme level of Mr. Bond and Moonman. Just as typical, were videos that were much more tame like "Can't Stump the Trump".

> *On July 28th, 2015, the conservative news site The Ralph Retort published an article titled "Can't Stump the Trump," which lauded Trump's ability to deflect criticism. On August 9th, YouTuber ZarosTemplar uploaded a montage parody titled "Can't Stump the Trump," featuring footage of Trump from the first 2016 Republican presidential debate*
>
> **-- Know Your Meme (https://knowyourmeme.com/memes/cant-stump-the-trump)**

Note the mention of *The Ralph Retort*. This was a publication created by Ethan Ralph, one of the main protagonists of GamerGate a year earlier. Later, he was also creator and host of the livestream show *The Killstream*, one of the few places where one could watch unedited footage of the BLM riots or openly question Covid during 2020, during the height of the Censorship Era. After the Capitol riot on January 6th 2021, which he broadcast live on *The Killstream*, he would be removed from all livestreaming platforms, and forced to move his show onto Nick Fuentes's platform Cozy.tv, until moving to Rumble after a falling out with Fuentes in the summer of 2023. This is one example of the through-line from GamerGate, through Trump and the Alt

Right, all the way to the Dissident Right of today. But back to "Can't Stump the Trump."

"Can't Stump the Trump" was a series of videos created by Comrade Stump. It was a montage of clips from Trump's press conferences or presidential debates, edited in the style of other montage video memes of the day. It is a perfect example of the Great Meme War, Trump memes, as well as what Internet culture generally looked like during its height of sophistication and popularity.

Video begins with Trump at a podium during the primary debates.

Narrator (taken from a National Geographic-style nature documentary): *It's a nimble navigator. And some can be highly venomous. Just like the tarantula it's killing, the centipede has two curved hollow fangs which inject paralyzing venom. This centipede is a predator.*

Camera zooms in on a still photo of Trump as a dubstep buildup plays.

Trump: *I think you heard me, you're having a hard time tonight.*

Dubstep drop. Cut to Trump at a press conference, heckling a journalist from Univision

Trump: *Go back to Univision!*

Dubstep breakdown continues to play as money falls from the sky over Trump's podium.

Trump: *Go ahead!*

An image of a sniper rifle from a first person shooter appears over the journalist's head. The camera zooms through the crosshairs of the rifle.

The text +100 appears over the scope in red, indicating a headshot. #stumped appears in red over the scope.

Cut back to Trump at the debates.

Trump: Only Rosie o'Donnell.

A second sniper rifle appears over the debate moderator's head.

The text +420 appears over the scope, followed by #stumped.

-- Comrade Stump, Sep 8 2015, You Can't Stump the Trump Vol.2. (https://www.YouTube.com/watch?v=vJhoLUgeIhc)

Note that unlike Mr. Bond and Moonman, it is still available on YouTube, containing little questionable material.

Hundreds of these videos, along with Trump parody songs and Trump memes of all kinds, were created throughout the Internet. The amazing part is that all of this support was entirely grassroots. At the very peak of Internet culture, at the very peak of the Internet's popularity with the younger generation, the Internet's greatest content creators all had organically decided to create what was essentially free campaign material for Trump simply for fun, thus using what was essentially the bleeding edge of culture and technology in Trump's service. This phenomenon became known by anon as "The Great Meme War of 2016."

The Great Meme War

The Great Meme War took place from June 16, 2015 - November 9, 2016 and was the Internet(primarily social media) battle between supporters of Donald Trump, Hillary Clinton, Bernie Sanders, Gary aka Aleppo Johnson, and Jill Stein. Attacks and battles took the form of arguments and memes in comment sections, threads, photos, videos and more. These memes were used to attack a candidate or sway their supporters. The War also included heavy shitposting, spam, copypastas, and dank memes. The War's fronts include Reddit, instagram, ifunny, YouTube, the news and media, and many others. -- UrbanDictionary.com (https://www.urbandictionary.com/define.php?term=The%20great %20meme%20war)

\

Hundreds, perhaps thousands of anon can claim the title of Great Meme War veteran. Many simply created and distributed Trump memes independently and at random, for fun. Others ran groupchats and more deliberate ops, especially as Hillary Clinton and Donald Trump became the official nominees and the race really heated up.

For example, one op was "draft our daughters."

> #DraftOurDaughters is a satirical social media hashtag launched by supporters of Donald Trump which encourages American women to register for Selective Service in preparation for hypothetical scenarios of United States military operations that would supposedly be launched by Hillary Clinton if she were elected as president of the United States.
>
> **-- Know Your Meme
> (https://knowyourmeme.com/memes/draftourdaughters)**

This op, organized on Twitter and 4chan, designed these memes to look like genuine Hillary ads, while also mocking Leftist social justice ideas like feminism in a way that was intended to "redpill normies" into questioning their assumptions.

Another tactic included hijacking topics trending on Twitter, creating satirical versions of them that would then appear in the feed next to other tweets with the same hashtag. This tactic also revealed a stark contrast between Trump and Hillary's social media strategy. The latter was deliberate and led by professional consultants and the mass media (which the Internet had by now dubbed the "dinosaur" or "legacy" media to highlight its irrelevance, as many Twitter accounts and independent YouTubers by now had larger audiences than professional news programs). The former was led by anon.

> "#HillarySoQualified she knows exactly which foreign dictators to hit up for slush fund contributions" **-- Ricky Vaughn @Ricky_Vaughn99
> (https://i.kym-cdn.com/photos/images/original/001/103/197/c85.png)**

Attached to the tweet is an infofgraphic, listing foreign donations to Clinton from countries such as Saudi Arabia and the UAE with the caption "These countries donated to Hillary Clinton's foundation, then got weapons deals"

Essentially, the Great Meme War was the culmination of Anonymous-style "hacktivism," utilizing weapons such as trolling, raiding, ops, memes, and anti-SJW humor that had been developed on the Internet over the last decade or so. In addition to getting Trump elected, and simply trolling for fun, it was intended to "redpill" ordinary people by exposing them to the same sorts of critiques of liberalism that had been developed by the Alt Right. It was often organized on sites like 4chan, but actually carried out on Twitter and Facebook, platforms considered more surface level and more popular with normies. The main front of the Great Meme War was Twitter. Not only was this the main platform where Trump himself reached his audience, but also one where anon freely mingled with normies and the two cultures met. Additionally, Twitter was home to mainstream news media, independent journalists, and celebrities -- all of whom could amplify the message.

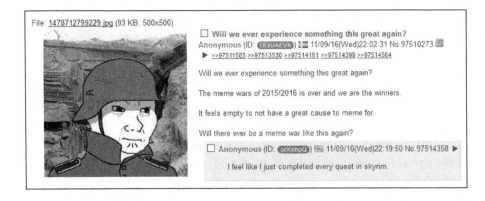

Social Media: Internet Culture goes Mainstream, Resulting in a Mass Redpilling

The Alt Right and Trump were the product of a very unique point in time, in which several trends happened to all converge at once. While Internet culture had been slowly developing over the course of the last decade, the nature of the Internet itself began to change due to advancements in technology. For almost this entire decade, the culture of the Internet was a subculture. Some people used the Internet heavily, while others did not. Increasingly, the counter-culture created from 4chan began to bubble up into IRL more and more. But there was still a barrier between offline and online. Right around the time of the 2016 election, two innovations changed this dynamic, explosively merging the two worlds.

The first was the invention of the smartphone.

> *"In contrast to the largely stationary Internet of the early 2000s, Americans today are increasingly connected to the world of digital information while "on the go" via smartphones and other mobile devices."*
>
> *-- Pew Research Center (https://www.pewresearch.org/Internet/fact-sheet/mobile/#:~:text=Mobile%20phone%20ownership%20over %20time,smartphone%20ownership%20conducted%20in%202011.)*

While the iPhone, one of the first successful smartphones, was released in 2007, it took some time for it to be adopted by the masses. This mass adoption was completed by about 2014. By that time, the smartphone had become standard on most cellular plans. I was actually a holdout, fearing that I would become addicted to the smartphone due to my already present addiction to the Internet, and put off getting a smartphone until 2013, when I was forced to get one by my cellular company. This is borne out in the official data from Pew Research.

In the U.S., 56 percent of adults are now smartphone owners, according to a study published Wednesday by Pew. This is the first time since Pew began tracking the numbers that the majority of the population owns a smartphone.

-- CNET, June 5 2013, "Smartphone Ownership Reaches Critical Mass in the US", (https://www.cnet.com/tech/mobile/smartphone-ownership-reaches-critical-mass-in-the-u-s/)

With everyone, even the normiest of normies, suddenly running around with an Internet-connected smartphone at all times, the Internet became less of a subculture and more of a fact of everyday life. Its omnipresence also meant that one never really "logged off," but instead had access to Twitter at all times. This was further facilitated by the rise of social media platforms such as Facebook, which were much more user-friendly to normies, designed to be used primarily on a smartphone rather than PC or laptop, and were based around simply connecting people into a social network and allowing them to share content or text-based information, rather than being based around some particular hobby or serving as a content creation platform such as YouTube.

As a result, normies flooded into an Internet ecosystem already populated by anon and dominated by the culture of 4chan, causing the two worlds to mix with each other and providing access to millions who could potentially be redpilled. The Internet was still the Wild West, censorship virtually unheard of, and it was not under the control of the establishment. Yet it now had a userbase which rivaled, and even eclipsed, the traditional mass media. This would be the state of affairs for roughly four years. It would end when Trump rose to power in 2017. After this, the establishment caught up to technology and realized that they had lost control of the narrative, leading to the Big Tech censorship that they would begin to roll out in 2017 in an effort to get the media back firmly within their control.

In other words, there was a small window between the rise of /pol/ around 2011 and the Censorship Era of the Internet which began in 2017. This small frame of 6 years was really the only time that you could be exposed to these heterodox ideas online without censorship. And it was maybe only four of those six years when the "means of information" was truly in the hands of the people and truly democratized, rather than in the hands of the establishment and their transmitters. If you were not "redpilled" during these 4-6 years, it is very difficult to become redpilled in the same way that people during this time period were.

"Based and Redpilled"

What does this word "redpilled" mean? Though we have been using the term throughout this text, we have never directly addressed its meaning. As with many Alt Right terms, people tend to get it very wrong. It does not mean being a fascist. It does not even mean being conservative or Right Wing at all. Essentially, it simply means understanding that "the world is not as it seems." That for example the media, rather than existing to inform, is in fact propaganda made to push a certain agenda and influence public behavior. Or that academia also has an agenda, rather than searching for the unbiased truth with an open mind, as they claim. Or that the country's politics do not work the way that you learn in a typical High School civics class, but instead follows a separate, non-explicit set of rules based around money, cronyism, and informal conventions.

The fact that this leads to a viewpoint that is considered Right Wing by the mainstream is purely incidental. That is because to be redpilled is to believe what people would believe organically if the means of information was in the hands of the people and there was no censorship, as there was not in the years 2011-2017. And because society has shifted so far to the Left, this is considered far-right. In contrast, to someone from 100 years ago, or really at any time throughout the majority of history, "redpilled beliefs" would probably be considered normal (outside of other extremely liberal time periods such as the late Roman Republic).

The term obviously originates with the film *The Matrix*. Thus, as you would expect, the opposite of the "redpill" is the "bluepill." A bluepilled person is someone who takes the world at face value and does not question it. A bluepilled ideology is one of the false ideologies of the liberal mainstream, such as feminism.

In addition to the red and blue pills of the film, anon created a few other variations. There is also the "blackpill," like the "redpill" except describing a more cynical and pessimistic mindset. The "whitepill" which is the opposite of the blackpill, an optimistic mindset. And the "clearpill" which is a stoic perspective of being neutral in regards to outcome.

Since then the word "redpilled" has changed in meaning over time, like all long-lived memes. Probably its most popular contemporary usage is in the so-called "redpill community," where influencers such as Andrew Tate and *Fresh & Fit* give "redpilled" dating advice to men. This "redpilled" advice usually involves a rejection of the tenants of feminism, and advice on how to pick up girls. It shares little in common with the original meaning of "redpilled" other than the fact that it sees feminism as a "bluepilled" ideology.

Another common Dissident Right term is "based." The word "based" is similar to the word "cool." It means that someone is their authentic self and speaks the truth, without worrying about political correctness or what others will think of them. It is often used to describe someone who has politically incorrect opinions and states them openly, as Trump did. Like someone who is "redpilled," it just so happens incidentally that someone "based" will inevitably have Right Wing beliefs according to mainstream society. This is again due to how far society has shifted to the Left due to the Left's capture of the means of information such as the media and academia.

The phrase "based and redpilled" used together was originally meant ironically, satirizing something that a typical Alt Right person, especially someone naïve and recently redpilled, might say. Eventually, over time it has evolved to be used both unironically or ironically depending on the context in which it was used (another example of "meta-irony").

Pepe the Frog

An entire book could also be written around Pepe the Frog, perhaps the most famous meme of all time, and a symbol that has now become synonymous with Internet culture. A documentary, actually, has already done that, *Feels Good Man (2020)*. In part this documentary is an attempt by its original creator, Matt Furie, to redeem Pepe the Frog after he became associated with the Alt Right.

Matt Furie was about as far away from Alt Right as one could possibly be. In fact he was a hippie, drawing strange Muppet-like cartoon characters, in his home city of San Francisco. I was a fan of his art in college, when Pepe was one of many obscure memes, much less well known than "rage comics" or "advice animals." I was happy that Pepe gave him exposure when I saw the meme briefly mentioned in an article about him in the art magazine *Juxtapoz*. A few years later I laughed at how horrified he must have been at what Pepe the Frog became.

So, how exactly did Pepe the Frog go from hippie Muppet cartoon character to mascot of the Alt Right? It all started in 2008.

On 4chan, another common type of thread were "scanslation" threads, where anon would post scanned copies of manga, or occasionally western indie comics (as in this case). They usually posted them slowly, one page per post, so that anon could comment on them and read them together in real time. In 2008, one of these comics happened to be Furie's *Boys Club*, a comic where Pepe the Frog and his Muppet-like monster friends hang out, eat pizza. and

do drugs
(https://i.kym-cdn.com/photos/images/original/000/937/799/6ad.jpg).

In one comic, Pepe the Frog pulls his pants down to his ankles in order to urinate, exclaiming "feels good man."
(https://i.kym-cdn.com/photos/images/original/000/095/218/feels-good-man.jpg)

The image, and sometimes just the phrase by itself, soon became a meme on 4chan.

In 2009, a variant of Pepe frowning with the text "Feels Bad Man" became the first Pepe variant, also known as "Sad Frog." (https://i.kym-cdn.com/photos/images/original/000/248/081/7d1.jpg). The final of the initial three variants was "Smug Pepe" created in 2011. (https://knowyourmeme.com/photos/862065-smug-frog).

Most memes tend to explode in popularity quickly, with hundreds of variations, and then die down. In contrast, Pepe was a very slow burn. There was a year between the initial and sad variants, and then two years between the sad and smug variations. Until 2014, for some reason, these were basically the only three variations used.

Then in 2014, Smug Pepe started becoming very popular, and people began making more Pepe variants including angry pepe ("REEE") (https://knowyourmeme.com/photos/913355-angry-pepe), Well Meme'd Pepe (https://knowyourmeme.com/photos/903981-well-memed), and others.

Soon Pepe would become one of the most popular memes on 4chan. "Smug Pepe" began to be associated with trolling, used by a troll in much the same way as the "trollface" of years earlier to indicate the troll's mischievous, aloof nature in contrast to the "triggered" person being trolled. Pepe in general, due to his role as a "blank slate," became easy to riff off of and apply to any situation or to express any emotion. Another meme, "rare Pepes" was created, where anon would pretend to trade different images of Pepe as if they were trading cards, leading to hundreds more variations. Eventually, Pepe came to be the new symbol of 4chan and underground Internet culture.

The next stage of Pepe occurred right around the same time as the rise of Trump and the Alt Right. By 2014, /pol/ and the proto-Alt Right had emerged as a prominent Internet subculture. Pepe was beginning to become popular on Reddit, which was seen as the dorky tag-along little brother of 4chan and a bridge between anon and normies. The perception was that memes created on 4chan would then cross over to Reddit, be dumbed down for mass consumption, picked up by normies on Facebook, and then thoroughly ruined. This was often in fact the case, and the evolution of "rage comics" and "advice animals" followed exactly this course.

In order to stop this process, anon had an idea. They would intentionally try to associate Pepe with Nazism and white nationalism in order to make it repellent to normies. Then they would no longer be interested in using it, therefore ensuring that it remained only for other based and redpilled anon. Anon got to work creating hundreds of Pepes dressed as Adolf Hitler or the KKK, throwing roman salutes, or covered in Swastikas. The strategy, apparently, worked. On April 13, 2017, a few months after Trump's successful election, *The Daily Beast* ran a story with the headline *"How Pepe the Frog Became a Nazi Trump Supporter and Alt-Right Symbol."*

> The green frog was behind the United States side of the metal fence at the country's southernmost border, smirking and holding a Donald Trump campaign button up to his chin.

A caricature of a Mexican couple—the man dressed in a sombrero and poncho, the woman with braided hair and an infant in her arms—looked out at him through the barricade and cried.

Then the frog was someplace else entirely, this time covered in Nazi insignia: above his smirk, the phrase "SKIN HEAD" and a swastika; over his left eyelid, "14," the numeric shorthand for "we must secure the existence of our people and a future for white children"; and over his right eyelid, "88," which stands for "Heil Hitler."

And there the frog was yet again, standing at a lectern stamped with the presidential seal, a red tie hanging from his green neck, Trump's iconic hair arranged on his head and an American flag at his back.

-- The Daily Beast, Apr 13, 2017, "How Pepe the Frog Became a Nazi Trump Supporter and Alt-Right Symbol" (https://www.thedailybeast.com/how-pepe-the-frog-became-a-nazi-trump-supporter-and-alt-right-symbol)

However, in the end, especially after the dissolution of the Alt Right, Pepe has once again become a symbol for Internet culture in general, rather than the Alt Right specifically. This appears to be his final and most enduring meaning. In 2019, he would be appropriated as a symbol of the Hong Kong protestors, many of whom, like Occupy Wall Street, used the Internet as a means to organize and share memes

To much of the world, the cartoon frog is a hate symbol. To Hong Kong protesters, he's something entirely different: one of them.

-- The New York Times, Aug 19 2019, "Hong Kong Protesters Love Pepe the Frog. No, They're Not Alt-Right." (https://www.nytimes.com/2019/08/19/world/asia/hong-kong-protest-pepe-frog.html)

However, the same year, Pepe, or at least a variant of him, once again became associated with far-right politics. By now, Pepe the Frog had spawned an extended family of other meme frogs, such as Apu Apustaja, a cuter, childlike version of Pepe (https://knowyourmeme.com/memes/apu-apustaja), and Groyper.

In 2019, during the "Groyper Wars," fans of far-right streamer Nick Fuentes would troll more mainstream political commentators such as Charlie Kirk of Turning Point USA (a pro-Trump organization aimed at college students) during Q&A panels on college campuses, criticizing him for his liberal stance on immigration and other issues where he was not seen as sufficiently far-right. Fuentes began referring to these trolls as "Groypers," a reference to Groyper being a popular avatar among anonymous far-right Twitter accounts at that time (https://knowyourmeme.com/memes/groyper). "Groyper" thus was coined as a word referring to a fan of Nick Fuentes and follower of his livestream/political movement, "America First."

The original popularizers of "Groyper" on Twitter (such as "Professor Groyper") who were not associated with Fuentes, complained that Fuentes had "stolen" Groyper. A fact that they were still seething about as of 2021, when I last interacted with their accounts on Gab (where they migrated to after being banned on Twitter). On Gab, they continue to complain about Fuentes and remind everyone about their hand in creating Groyper in their bio and all of their pinned posts, and basically make whining about stolen memes their entire personality.

Donald Trump Retweets Pepe, Hillary Clinton Cancels Pepe, Richard Spencer Gets Assaulted over Pepe

As the Trump campaign continued, the Internet's support for him grew stronger and stronger, and its influence over the election in general began to become more pronounced. Both Donald Trump and Hillary Clinton would end up addressing Pepe the Frog.

On October 13th, 2015, Donald Trump tweeted a picture of a Pepe version of himself standing at a podium with the caption "You Can't Stump the Trump"(https://i.kym-cdn.com/photos/images/original/001/028/964/4b3.jpg)

On September 9th, 2016, Donald Trump Jr would also post a rare Pepe. The meme featured Donald Trump, Pepe, Alex Jones, Roger Stone, Milo Yiannopoulos, and others with their faces photoshopped onto the poster of the 2010 action movie *"The Expendables"* but with the title *"The Deplorables,"* based on a speech in which Hillary used this term to describe supporters of Donald Trump (https://i.kym-cdn.com/photos/images/original/001/169/809/a2b.jpg).

The following day, NBC News published an article about the photoshop, which referred to Pepe the Frog as a "popular white nationalist symbol" based on a statement made by Southern Poverty Law Center's Heidi Beirich. That day, several news sites published articles referring to Pepe as a "white supremacist meme" and "white national symbol," including The Hill, Vanity Fair, Talking Points Memo and CNN . On September 12th, a post mocking the NBC article reached the front page of /r/KotakuInAction. **-- Know Your Meme (https://knowyourmeme.com/memes/pepe-the-frog)**

/r/KotakuInAction is an anti-SJW subreddit created during GamerGate. Its banner features Vivian James and the slogan "Gaming * Ethics * Journalism * Censorship." Yet another example of the information infrastructure built up after GamerGate, and employed to great effect during the election.

*The same day, the official Hillary Clinton presidential campaign blog published a post titled "Donald Trump, Pepe the frog, and white supremacists: an explainer," which labeled Pepe the Frog as "sinister" and a "symbol associated with white supremacy." Over the next 24 hours, posts about the Clinton campaign's reaction reached the front page of various subreddits, including /r/cringe, /r/politics,/r/OutOfTheLoop, /r/4chan and /r/The_Donald. In the comments sections, many Redditors mocked the Clinton campaign and the mainstream media for failing to understand the Pepe meme. Meanwhile, The Daily Dot published an article titled "Pepe the Frog is not a Nazi, no matter what the alt-right says," stating that "Pepe lacks political affiliation." -- **Know Your Meme** (https://knowyourmeme.com/memes/pepe-the-frog)*

Once again, in a sense, the Left was right. Some white supremacists *were* appropriating Pepe the Frog, quite intentionally. But the meaning of the symbol was ambiguous and hidden behind irony, as was much of the Alt Right, and had other legitimate meanings. Therefore, Hillary's response simply made her seem uncool, and "out of the loop" with the Internet savvy youth. Contrast this with the "based" Donald Trump, with a massive arsenal of young and enthusiastic supporters and a large, organic online following.

Hillary had previously addressed the "Alt Right" earlier that year, devoting an entire speech to it during a campaign stop in Reno, Nevada.

"From the start, Donald Trump has built his campaign on prejudice and paranoia.

He is taking hate groups mainstream and helping a radical fringe take over the Republican Party.

...

A man with a long history of racial discrimination, who traffics in dark conspiracy theories drawn from the pages of supermarket tabloids and the far, dark reaches of the Internet, should never run our government or command our military.

...

This is someone who retweets white supremacists online, like the user who goes by the name "white-genocide-TM."

...

The latest shake-up was designed to – quote – "Let Trump be Trump." To do that, he hired Stephen Bannon, the head of a right-wing website called Breitbart.com, as campaign CEO.

...

This is not conservatism as we have known it. This is not Republicanism as we have know it. These are race-baiting ideas, anti-Muslim and anti-immigrant ideas, anti-woman — all key tenets making up an emerging racist ideology known as the 'Alt-Right.'

Now Alt-Right is short for "Alternative Right."

The Wall Street Journal describes it as a loose but organized movement, mostly online, that "rejects mainstream conservatism, promotes nationalism and views immigration and multiculturalism as threats to white identity."

The de facto merger between Breitbart and the Trump Campaign represents a landmark achievement for the "Alt-Right." A fringe element has effectively taken over the Republican Party.

And this is part of a broader story -- the rising tide of hardline, right-wing nationalism around the world.

**– The Washington Post, Aug 25 2016, "Hillary's Alt-Right Speech, Annotated",
(https://www.washingtonpost.com/news/the-fix/wp/2016/08/25/hillary-clintons-alt-right-speech-annotated/)**

In a way, Hillary was again right. But by now, the Left had "cried wolf" too many times about "race-baiting", "anti-Muslim", "anti-immigrant" and "anti-woman" ideas. Americans were sick of hearing about it, and her pleas fell on totally deaf ears. People preferred Trumps bold, brash, "based" bravado to Hillary's shrill, stern scolding.

Instead of being lectured by their "betters" in Washington and the media, Trump was speaking directly to the people, assuring them that "I will be your voice." Instead of telling Americans what they must do or not do, say or not say, Trump was instead telling Americans what he could do for *them.* Such as ending the wars, re-industrializing the country, bringing jobs back to America, shutting down the border, and taking a tougher stance on America's rival, China. Americans were sick of the way the country was being run and wanted a radical change, and if that meant joining forces with the radicalism of the Alt Right in order to change it, then that was a concession they were willing to make. If that was *"race-baiting ... anti-Muslim ... anti-immigrant ideas, anti-woman,"* then so be it.

One of the last times Pepe made an appearance in American politics was on January 23, 2017. Richard Spencer appeared on ABC news wearing a Pepe pin on the breast of his suit jacket. A journalist accused him of being a Nazi, which Richard denied, and then asked him about the pin. *"Well, it's become sort of a symbol,"* Richard started to say, before a man clad in black ran up to Spencer and punched him in the face on live television. (https://www.youtube.com/watch?v=aFh08JEKDYk)

This event sparked a meme on the Left: "it's okay to punch Nazis." Again, the Alt Right acted as a provocateur that brought forth deeper questions, once hidden beneath the surface, into the light of day. Richard Spencer was perceived as a Nazi and considered to be a Nazi by many in society, but were those truly his views, since he denied it? Who gets to determine who is truly a "Nazi," and according to what basis? Was it appropriate to use violence against someone, simply over their beliefs? The traditional answer in America up until now had been "no." But this assumption was now being put to the test.

Meme Magic

There were many more pivotal moments in the Great Meme War. I have tried to stick to those that I think show the development of Internet politics and their intersection with technology, and not simply copypasta every single meme from that year from Know Your Meme. However, there is one one meme I would be remiss not to include. The god of the meme war, KEK. So stand back and stand by for even more excerpts and copypasta from Know Your Meme.

The story of KEK goes back to one of oldest memes of them all: lol or laugh out loud. Through time, this was corrupted into many forms on 4chan, including of course "lulz." Many more variations of lol would eventually be created on 4chan, most of them on the board /s4s/.

> *Shit 4chan Says was created on April 1st, 2013, as a parody of the Shit Reddit Says sub-reddit, with fake upvote/downvote arrows added on the board, before being changed back to the original 4chan board layout.*

> **-- Know Your Meme (https://knowyourmeme.com/memes/sites/s4s)**

/s4s/ was a late addition to 4chan, and basically became a board that was a satire of 4chan itself, with users making intentionally stupid posts and intentionally trying to force them to become memes, including "lel" which was essentially a parody of "lulz" (which itself was sort of a parody of "lol." This is typical of the very end of this era of Internet, with multiple layers of irony and self-referential meta jokes).

Eventually, posts seemed to have degenerated to users posting random three letter combinations such as "wew" (whose variation "wew lad" eventually came to express sarcastic exuberance and feigned interest) and "kek," which also indicated laughter in the same way as "lol," "lul," and "lel."

This is where I first encountered kek, anyways. But this is not the most popular etymology. Most anon say that "kek" actually came from the MMORPG *World of Warcraft,* and was used to indicate the laughter of Horde characters in the game. It then made its way to /s4s/ from there.

Since I never played *World of Warcraft,* I don't know if this is true. I do know that "kek" became one of /s4s/'s most popular memes, especially after a silly looking Turkish snack cake called "topkek" was discovered, and users began spamming pictures of topkek on the board (https://i.kym-cdn.com/photos/images/original/000/617/382/1d8.png).

This is only the first iteration of the meme.

Another component of what would become the god KEK were "dubs." On 4chan, every post would have a unique post number indicated at the top of the post. Since the beginning of 4chan, lucky strings of numbers, such as 12345678 or 22222222 were called "GETs." On /s4s/, anon started celebrating even minor posts such as a post number that ended in a single set of repeating digits (such as 12148677) calling these "dubs." Posters even went so far as to begin spamming posts with no meaningful content whatsoever, simply to try to get "dubs," a phenomenon that soon spread to other boards. At the height of the meme's popularity, these attempts to get "dubs" caused so much spam that for a time, moderators replaced the last digits of each post number with xs (ie 12148XXX), thus making dubs impossible. Dubs would soon become a key part of KEK worship.

Then, sometime during the Great Meme War, anon made a discovery. 5000 years ago, in ancient Egypt, the ancient Egyptians worshipped a god known as Kek. According to Wikipedia the god "is the deification of the primordial concept of darkness in ancient Egyptian religion." Kek was "depicted as a frog or frog-headed man." Anon posted his discovery to 4chan's history board, /his/.

"So a meme is 5000 years old"

-- 4chan responds to the discovery of KEK

Consequently, 4chan decided to adopt the god as its patron deity, given its association with chaos, frogs, and the word "kek." Anon even discovered that the word for kek in Egyptian hieroglyphics resembled a man sitting at a computer *(https://imgur.com/Wukb4TA)*.

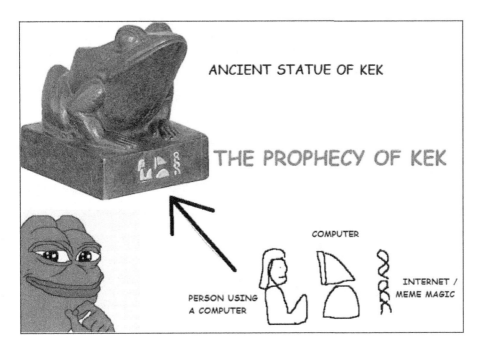

*On 4chan, the character Pepe the Frog is often considered a modern avatar of the diety [KEK], who uses ancient Egyptian meme magic to influence the world, often by fulfilling the wishes of posts that end in repeating numbers. Additionally, the deity is associated with the popular 4chan slang term "Kek", and is often embraced by supporters of 2016 Republican presidential candidate Donald Trump. Practitioners are known to frequently write "praise Kek," and jokingly refer to the church as a "religion of peace." **-- Know Your Meme (https://knowyourmeme.com/memes/cult-of-kek)***

The "cult of KEK" included anon creating "meme magic" or "KEK worship general" threads, and trying to roll "dubs" in order to invoke the will of KEK. Posts typically would follow the format *"if dubs, x will happen"* with x referring to an event (for example "Trump will win big on Super Tuesday") The culmination of this was the "77777777" GET for "Trump will win" posted on 6/19/16 (https://i.kym-cdn.com/photos/images/original/001/172/235/dc5.png)

In /pol/'s kek mythos, posts ending in sevens hold more weight than others, as seven is considered a lucky and/or holy number in many cultures, which increases in value for dubs and trips. Similarly, three sixes (666, the Number of the Beast) are considered to represent Satan and evilness. This received one of its highest points on June 19th, 2016, when a post reading "Trump will win" managed to get the 77777777 GET

-- Know Your Meme (https://knowyourmeme.com/memes/cult-of-kek)

The meme magic continued when 4chan discovered a song from the band *P.E.P.E.*, whose cover art featured an illustration of a green frog with a magic wand.

"Shadilay" is a 1986 Italo disco song by the Italian band P.E.P.E., which features an illustration of a green frog holding a magic wand in the album artwork for the single. After it was discovered by users on 4chan's /pol/ board in September 2016, many hailed the song as proof of meme magic and the Prophecy of Kek due to the band's name and frog illustration bearing similarities to Pepe the Frog.

-- Know Your Meme(https://knowyourmeme.com/memes/shadilay)

Henceforth, "Praise KEK! Shadilay, brothers" and similar expressions naturally became a part of the Cult of KEK. Anon created Vaporwave remixes of the song, interspersed with audio clips of Donald Trump. The song and its various remixes would be played in celebration on November 9, after Donald Trump's surprise victory — the ultimate proof that meme magic was real!

KEK also evolved into a fictional country called "Kekistan" which was related to the cult. But I am done reposting copypasta from Know Your Meme. You can look it up for yourself (https://knowyourmeme.com/memes/kekistan).

The cult of KEK is interesting for several reasons. In a way, it represents the zenith of the Internet subculture. It was a complex meme containing a long history and complicated allusions to other memes and board culture. "Meme magic" also represents the height of Internet culture's ability to influence IRL events, such as the election of Donald Trump, in their organized chaotic way. "Meme magic" is a great way to describe the optimistic, fun, invincible feelings of the Internet during 2016. One that, in the coming years, was about to be crushed into dust and annihilated — shoah'd, one might say — by Big Tech Censorship.

Trump Becomes President

> *Trump was the first president with neither prior public service nor military experience. This election was the first since 1908 where neither candidate was currently serving in public office. This was the first election since 1980 where a Republican was elected without carrying every former Confederate state in the process, as Trump lost Virginia in this election. Trump became the only Republican to earn more than 300 electoral votes since the 1988 election and the only Republican to win a Northeastern state since George W. Bush won New Hampshire in 2000 -- **Wikipedia (https://en.wikipedia.org/wiki/2016_United_States_presidential_electi on)**

On Tuesday, November 8, 2016 I did not vote. But, I did watch the election unfold. Every single major poll in America showed Hillary Clinton beating Donald Trump by a large margin, and there was no way to make the math add up in a way that would result in a win for Trump. After all, he would have to win the rust belt states like Wisconsin, Pennsylvania and Michigan, which had not been won by a Republican since the 1980s and in which polls predicted Clinton to be well ahead of Trump.

Up until the polls started closing, many mass media outlets predicted that Clinton had a "99%" chance of winning.

Scientist predicts 99% chance of Clinton win

-- MSNBC, Nov 4 2016 (https://www.msnbc.com/the-last-word/watch/scientist-predicts-99-chance-of-clinton-win-801634371744)

Survey finds Hillary Clinton has 'more than 99% chance' of winning election over Donald Trump

-- The Independent, Nov 5 2016 (independent.co.uk/news/world/americas/sam-wang-princeton-election-consortium-poll-hillary-clinton-donald-trump-victory-a7399671.html)

Clinton has 90 percent chance of winning: Reuters/Ipsos States of the Nation

-- Reuters, Nov 7 2016 (https://www.reuters.com/article/us-usa-election-poll/clinton-has-90-percent-chance-of-winning-reuters-ipsos-states-of-the-nation-idUSKBN1322J1)

The New York Times website even featured an animated infographic called "the needle," which updated these forecasts in real time (a version of the webpage from 2022 can be found here: https://www.nytimes.com/interactive/2022/11/08/us/elections/results-needle-forecast.html) *(Author's note: I do not know if it was exactly the same as this or if it was actually called "the needle" during 2016 but it was very similar)*, which showed the needle well over to the blue side at 99%. There was also a line graph of the "needle" as it changed over time, showing a blue line meandering across the top of the graph and a red line meandering across the bottom.

Then the polls began to close, moving from East to West: Florida – Trump. Pennsylvania – Trump. Ohio – Trump. Michigan – Trump. Wisconsin – Trump. Suddenly "the needle" did a 180 and jumped to the opposite side of the screen. The line graph backflipped into an X, with the red suddenly at the top at 90% and the blue line suddenly at the bottom.

4chan lost its mind. Threads of celebrating Pepes, Trumps with lazer eyes, and Shadilays flooded the board, causing threads to move at lightning speed. It was the greatest epic win in 4chan history. *"We did it, anon. We meme'd Trump into the White House!"*

The immediate response to Trump's election by Democrats was to accuse the election of being "rigged" somehow by Vladimir Putin, who had by now become a popular boogie man by Democrats due to his resistance to far-left social policies such as homosexuality, as well as establishment Republicans due to the power struggle between Russia and America over influence in Ukraine and other eastern European countries (especially after Russia annexed Crimea in 2014). This resulted in years of investigation by the intelligence agencies into the Trump campaign, which actually started before Trump was even elected, when Obama began to spy on his campaign. Trump accused them of spying on his campaign in March 2017, but the mass media vociferously denied this claim for years, calling Trump a liar. NBC called this accusation one of Trump's "biggest whoppers of 2017."

> *On March 4, Trump tweeted that his predecessor had wiretapped him. This is false.*
>
> *On March 5, former Director of National Intelligence James Clapper told NBC News in an exclusive interview that "there was no such wiretap activity mounted against the president, the president-elect at the time, or as a candidate, or against his campaign."*
>
> *Later, the Justice Department confirmed this in a lawsuit in September saying that the department and the FBI "have no records related to wiretaps as described."* **-- NBC News, Dec 24 2017, "Trump's Biggest Whoppers of 2017" (https://www.nbcnews.com/politics/donald-trump/trump-s-biggest-whoppers-2017-n830746)**

Later, it was revealed that the substance of what Trump said (that the Obama administration spied on his campaign) was right.

In collusion with the Clinton campaign, and with the complicity of national-security officials who transitioned into the Trump administration, the Obama White House deployed the FBI to undermine the new president, dually using official investigative tactics (e.g. FISA surveillance, confidential informants, covert interrogations) and lawless classified leaks — the latter publicized by dependable journalists who were (and remain) politically invested in unseating Trump.

— National Review, Aug 1 2020, "New Disclosures Confirm: Trump Himself Was the Target of Obama Administration's Russia Probe" https://www.nationalreview.com/2020/08/new-disclosures-confirm-trump-was-the-target-of-obama-administrations-russia-probe/

Attorney general William Barr says that American intelligence agencies spied on Donald Trump's 2016 campaign, and that he feels he needs to ensure that power is not abused in the US government.

"I think spying did occur," Mr Barr said during a Senate hearing. "But the question is whether it was adequately predicated and I am not suggesting that it wasn't adequately predicated. .... I am not suggesting those rules were violated, but I think it is important to look at that. And I am not talking about the FBI necessarily, but intelligence more broadly."

— The Independent, Apr 10 2019, "US intelligence agencies 'spied' on Trump 2016 campaign, says William Barr" (https://www.independent.co.uk/news/world/americas/us-politics/trump-2016-us-spying-william-barr-mueller-report-cia-nsa-fbi-senate-a8863736.html)

This attempt to disrupt Trump's administration through weaponizing the intelligence agencies and constantly investigating Trump for alleged Russian collusion would last for the majority of the Trump administration and has become known as "Russiagate."

The Left Wing on the Internet also tried to stop Trump, turning to "virtue signaling" by signing impotent Internet petitions to stop him from being inaugurated, or, later, impeach him:

> On the Internet, a number of online lobbying campaigns were launched in an attempt to prevent Donald Trump from being inaugurated in January 2017, most notably the Change.org petition urging the members of the Electoral College to ignore their states' electoral votes and honor the popular vote instead by electing Hillary Clinton. Started by Elijah Berg of North Carolina on November 10th, the petition garnered upwards of 2.59 million signatures within the first 24 hours, and by its fifth day, it had accrued more than four million signatures. Other notable petitions on the site include "Impeach Donald Trump," pleading the U.S. Congress to challenge the president-elect upon him taking the office, and "Steve Bannon's racist, anti-semitic, misogynistic views don't belong in the White House," which was created in response to Trump's appointment of Steve Bannon, the executive chairman of BreitBart News, as his administration's chief strategist on November 13th. **-- Know Your Meme (https://knowyourmeme.com/memes/events/notmypresident-anti-trump-protests)**

The inauguration on January 20, 2017 would be met with mass protests in Washington DC, often boiling over into far-left, Antifa-style riots which destroyed public property and injured a few police and civilians.

> Protests occurred during the inauguration ceremonies in Washington, D.C. The vast majority of protesters, several thousand in all, were peaceful. DisruptJ20 protesters linked arms at security checkpoints and attempted to shut them down. Some elements of the protesters were black bloc groups and self described anarchists, and engaged in sporadic acts of vandalism, rioting, and violence. Six police officers sustained minor injuries, and at least one other person was injured.

*A total of 234 people were arrested and charged with rioting, launching controversial trials that gave rise to allegations that the government was overreaching. Ultimately, 21 defendants pleaded guilty, and all other defendants were either acquitted or had charges dropped by prosecutors; the government failed to obtain a guilty verdict at any trial. In December 2017, the first six people to be tried in connection with the events of January 20 were acquitted by a jury of all charges. Twenty other defendants pleaded guilty and prosecutors dropped cases against 20 others. In January 2018, prosecutors dropped charges against 129 other defendants. In May 2018, prosecutors dropped charges against seven more defendants, after the court found that prosecution had intentionally made misrepresentations to the court and hidden exculpatory evidence from defendants in violation of the Brady rule, and prosecutors also reduced charges against others. Finally, in July 2018, the government dropped charges against all remaining defendants. -- **Wikipedia (https://en.wikipedia.org/wiki/Inauguration_of_Donald_Trump)**

These protests also became a source of "triggered liberal tears" for the anti-SJW movement. The most popular of these was "Luke crywalker," an androgynous, far-left protestor captured on ITV News crying in agony as they/them watched Trump inaugurated (https://knowyourmeme.com/memes/luke-crywalker), becoming a popular meme.

On the Internet, Left Wing Twitter users started the hashtag #NotMyPresident.

*On November 9th, 2016, shortly after the announcement of Donald Trump's victory in the election, the hashtag #NotMyPresident became the top trending topic on Twitter and elsewhere on social media, which effectively became the unofficial banner of anti-Trump protests in the days to follow. Throughout the day, dozens of marches and sit-in protests were mobilized in major cities across the country, led by a coalition of activist and advocacy groups for various causes like Black Lives Matter, gender equality and LGBTQ equality, as well as Muslim immigrants and many other minority communities. Also on November 9th, a Facebook event page titled "Trump is Not My President" was created for a march on Union Square, New York City on November 12th. -- **Know Your Meme (https://knowyourmeme.com/memes/events/notmypresident-anti-trump-protests)**

While this text has mostly focused on the Right Wing Internet, it's worth mentioning that the Left Wing also utilized the Internet for activism. They had their own ecosystem, particularly Independent media outlets such as *The Young Turks* and podcasts, typically of the Bernie Sanders-style democratic socialist variety, such as *Chapo Trap House*. They even had their own version of /pol/ on 8chan, /leftypol/ - a term that originated on /pol/ to describe Leftist posters on the board. This was during the earliest days of /new/ and /pol/, when ideologies were extremely diverse and there was no single set of ideas or culture yet associated with the board.

However, in a way this simply moved the already well-establish and mature activist ecosystem that the Left had created in the 1960s into the online world. It did not grow organically out of the Internet itself, but out of IRL. The IRL democratic socialist scene in Brooklyn was the real source of *Chapo Trap House,* not any Internet forum. In contrast, the Alt Right was simply another part of the Internet subculture. This made the online Right inherently much more counter-culture in nature than the online Left and inherently more cool, or perhaps more "based" is a better word.

This is of course because the online Right is part of the antithesis, and the antithesis occurs across many fronts, both cultural and aesthetic as well as ideological and political. The online Left is still part of the thesis, and carries with it an earlier set of cultural and aesthetic forms appropriate to that thesis, which were developed by the media of the age in which it was formed, not the media of the antithesis (the Internet, videogames, etc.).

Organizing a hashtag campaign such as #NotMyPresident is a very typical example of a Left-wing "op." It is deliberate, serious rather than ironic, wholly political rather than organic, contains no new ideas that are contrary to the status quo, is not particularly lulzy, and is not anything something from the Boomer generation could not have immediately understood.

The Trump inauguration remains the high-water mark of Dissident Right politics to this day, as of 2023. It can also probably be the considered the high-water mark of Internet culture as well, representing the peak of its influence in politics and mainstream culture as a whole.

> *A Golden Age of the Meme Culture: Say what you will about the current state of the memescape, but 2016 will soon be remembered as the year when memes broke through another great barrier and stepped into a new realm where no memes have gone before: The Beltway of Washington D.C. About six years ago, we began hearing references to Internet memes on network TV shows. In the next few years, we started seeing memes plastered on advertisement, films, and occasionally, headline news. In 2016, we saw President Obama dropping the mic during his speech and the First Lady doing the Mannequin Challenge with star-studded guests in the Blue Room of the White House. If that doesn't impress, relish the fact that for the first time ever, "memes" was looked up on Google Search more frequently than Jesus and God. So, yeah, memes are sort of a big deal.* **-- Know Your Meme's "The State of the Internets in 2016" (https://knowyourmeme.com/editorials/meme-review/the-state-of-the-Internets-in-2016)**

However, this victory would only last only about a year. Starting almost immediately, Trump would be undermined by the political establishment of both parties, as well as partially assimilated by the Republicans and in the end failed to enact most of his campaign promises. The Alt Right would start to suffer blows as it failed to make the transition from ironic Internet meme to serious political movement, finally imploding in the wake of Charlottesville. And, the most unthinkable of all, the Internet would begin to be the subject of coordinated, widespread censorship by Big Tech.

But before this final downfall, in the years of late 2016 and early 2017, the online Dissident Right would still get to enjoy a few more final victories.

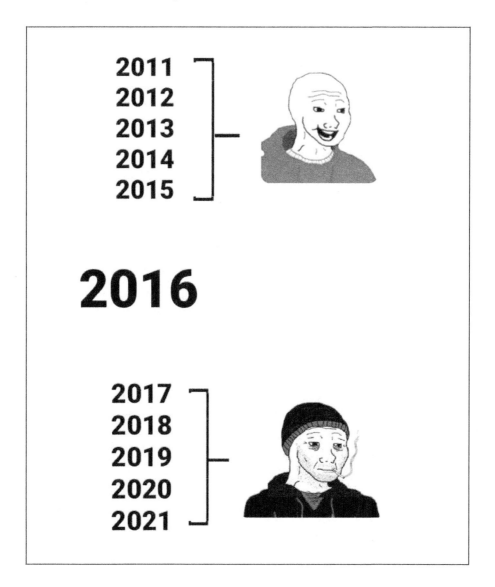

Chapter 4 - 2017 & 2018: CVille, HWNDU, Optics, Big Tech Censorship

Trump Becomes President, pt 2

I remember the day after Trump was elected quite clearly. I was living in Los Angeles at the time. All around me a strange, eerie sense of gloom hung in the air. Every person around me was feeling it, communicating it subtly in an unspoken way. When I was around others on the street, the atmosphere of gloom grew thick.

In the office, everyone was transfixed. Staring at the news screens. Here, there was no cloud of gloom, however. The people around me were in a somewhat conservative industry along the lines of finance. Many of them were normie Trump supporters. Instead of despair, it was an air of confusion. A dreamlike state. No one knew quite what to expect next. Would Trump really be inaugurated? Would he really be allowed to become President? Would he really build the wall? Would he really ban Muslims? Would he really be the next Hitler? Or would he really drain the swamp? The one thing I knew for certain is that no one would be working hard that day. Which meant I could spend my time browsing 4chan and soaking in their victory.

One person who did predict that Trump would win was comedian Sam Hyde, who claimed to have bet money that Trump would win and used the money to buy a motorcycle. However, like the rest of the Alt Right, this celebration would be short lived. Under a month later on December 5, 2016, *Million Dollar Extreme:World Peace* would be canceled due to Sam's political views, which resulted in a hit piece from Left Wing journalists and alleged internal sabotage at Adult Swim from liberal Tim Heidecker.

The Alt Right's Final Ops Pt 1 - OK

After successfully memeing Pepe, a smug cartoon frog, into becoming a hate symbol, anon wondered if they could do the same to other things. The idea was that, in theory, anything could be considered a "hate symbol," no matter how ridiculous. In a way this satirized the entire idea of a hate symbol in the first place. So anon decided to start a campaign to deliberately make the "OK" hand sign a hate symbol.

> *In February 2017, 4chan users launched Operation O-KKK to "flood Twitter and other social media websites" with posts claiming the OK hand sign was a "symbol of white supremacy," along with a picture of an OK symbol identifying the three up-turned fingers as a symbol for "W" and the thumb-and-forefinger circle as a symbol for "P"* – ***Know Your Meme (https://knowyourmeme.com/memes/ok-symbol-%F0%9F%91%8C)***

Some journalists took the bait, such as *Fusion* reporter Emma Roller, who tweeted a picture of conservative journalists Mike Cernovich and Cassandra Fairbanks doing the "OK" sign at a podium in what appeared to be the White House, with the caption *"Just two people doing a white power hand gesture in the White House"* and using the "white power" meme from 4chan as evidence.

Some savvier journalists, such as Tim Pool, didn't take the bait. Instead he posted a video entitled "4chan Has Become Too Powerful," explaining the origin of the meme as originating from a 4chan troll.

However, after enough Alt Right, Alt Lite, or Alt Right-adjacent personalities such as Milo posted pictures of themselves flashing the "OK" hand signal, eventually groups such as the ADL began to actually associate it with white nationalism, essentially making the campaign a success.

On April 30th, The Independent published an article claiming the "The Anti-Defamation League (ADL) characterises the symbol as a 'racist hand sign'," citing an entry in the ADL database of a woman holding a hand in the form of a "W" next to a hand formed to make the letter "P"

– Know Your Meme (https://knowyourmeme.com/memes/ok-symbol-%F0%9F%91%8C)

On September 14th, 2018 Twitter user @huppkels tweeted a video showing a member of the coast guard flashing the "OK" hand sign with the tweet *"Am I being crazy? Is anyone else seeing what I am here?"*

The video was widely circulated on Twitter, with some accusing the man of making a "white power" gesture. That evening, the official U.S. Coast Guard Twitter feed posted an announcement that the man had been identified and that they "removed him from the response"

– Know Your Meme (https://knowyourmeme.com/memes/ok-symbol-%F0%9F%91%8C)

"His actions do not represent the US Coast Guard" the Coast Guard tweeted.

In the optimistic days directly after the Great Meme War, 4chan felt invincible. It seemed like ops such as Operation O-KKK would simply go on forever. The success of the operation was further confirmation of this. So they continued to see how hard they could push the envelope. Next, anon decided to see if they could do the same thing to a Leftist symbol, re-appropriating it as an Alt Right symbol instead. They settled on the LGBT rainbow flag as their target.

The explanation for this one was that the different colored stripes represented the different races of people separated into their own countries. As with the OK hand sign, they began to produce memes and infographics warning of the dangers of the rainbow flag and its association with white nationalism. Unlike the OK hand sign, this operation was, for whatever reason, unsuccessful.

The Alt Right's Final Ops Pt 2 - Okay to be White

Another notable post-Trump op was "It's Okay to be White." This was another op that was intended to challenge the concept of a "hate symbol." Anon reasoned that since the media was anti-white, even the mildest form of sentiment that did not portray white people in a negative light would be considered a "hate symbol."

To prove this theory, 4chan designed a simple poster. It was a standard white piece of printer paper with the words "it's okay to be white" written in black text. This was about as mild and neutral of a statement as one could possibly make about white people. To disagree with it would be to imply that it was "not okay" to be white. That there was something inherently evil or wrong about white people based entirely on their race.

The plan was for anon to make copies of the poster and post it in public places, such as university campuses. When this inevitably caused the media to declare these posters as "white supremacist hate speech" surely this would wake up and redpill the normies.

Starting on October 31st, 2017, posts began circulating on 4chan calling for viewers to place posters with the slogan "It's Okay to Be White" in public places as a "proof of concept" that a "harmless message" would cause a "massive media shitstorm."

-- Know Your Meme (https://knowyourmeme.com/memes/its-okay-to-be-white)

In the thread where the posters were being designed, anon would of course create alternate variations of the poster. This is how memes evolved. This is what always happened during ops. People would post their ideas for what anon should do next, and anon would collectively follow the ideas that they approved of. However, in this case, anon was discouraged from riffing off of the initial poster design, knowing that some would begin to push things further to the extreme and include more material that could potentially be taken as offensive. They also feared that "shills" – Left Wing activists that had begun to infiltrate 4chan in order to undermine it – might try to sabotage the campaign. *"There is no phase 2!"* anon began to respond to any variations of the poster. Some anon responded by creating intentionally offensive and asinine variations of the poster, including those covered in swastikas and with links to *The Daily Stormer*. However, the vast majority obeyed the "there is no phase 2" command and posted the official version of the poster.

Whether the original trollers were white supremacist or not, actual white supremacists quickly began to promote the campaign—often adding Internet links to white supremacist websites to the fliers or combining the phrase with white supremacist language or imagery. This was not a surprise, as white supremacists had themselves used the phrase in the past—including on fliers—long before the 4chan campaign originated.

– ADL (https://www.adl.org/resources/hate-symbol/its-okay-be-white)

The posters more or less got the expected reaction. Police were called in to "investigate" the "hateful messages." Many people decried the posters as "racist" or "divisive," in spite of the fact that they did not even mention any other races. They also reacted by stressing their commitment to "diversity," in spite of the fact that the posters mentioned nothing about whether or not society should be diverse. As is typical of the media, they also used the tactic of "guilt by association," proclaiming the posters as hateful because 4chan was "hateful" while not addressing the content of the posters at all. This overwhelmingly negative reaction, along with the ADL officially listing the posters as a "hate symbol" was seen by anon as proof of a successful operation.

> The University of Regina declared the posters divisive. University President Vianne Timmons said: "Simply put, these signs have no place at our university."
>
> A spokesman for a Waterloo Region District School Board commented: "Our schools are safe spaces. We want to see them be safe for all of our children, so to see this kind of thing emerge is a worry."
>
> ...
>
> The University of Utah said: "If, indeed, these tactics are meant to silence our work in diversity and inclusion, please know we shall not be deterred." Concordia College said that their president was planning a meeting where students could discuss the matter.
>
> **– Wikipedia (https://en.wikipedia.org/wiki/It%27s_okay_to_be_white)**

Why were the posters "divisive"? Do people disagree with the statement? If this sentiment has "no place at our university" then are white people not welcomed at their university? How would the statement make people unsafe, and how would it "silence [their] work around diversity and inclusion? Are the efforts of diversity and inclusion invalidated by the inclusion of whites? Other statements were along similar lines.

> Posters that read "It's OK to Be White" have popped up in cities and schools across the country in recent days, including at Concordia College in Moorhead, Minn.
>
> ...

They have since been removed, but their brief appearance struck a chord with students who said the signs run counter to the school's values of inclusiveness and safety for all who work and study there.

"I was really shocked that someone had the guts to do this because we try to promote diversity so much, and seeing this is saying, "Hey, we still have students who aren't fully invested in this diversity message,' " senior Micah Ferden told WDAY-TV in Fargo.

...

Some have decried the posters as racist, and school President William Craft said he wanted to invite the campus community to engage in a more open conversation on the topic at a forum that he was working to facilitate.

...

"To be other than white is all too often to be subjected to discrimination, lack of opportunity, and even the threat and reality of violence," Craft wrote. "We must reject silences that demean and exclude, and we must engage open conversation about the experience of race on this campus and beyond."

– Star Tribune, Nov 4 2017 "Moorhead's Concordia College takes down 'It's OK to Be White' posters" (https://www.startribune.com/it-s-okay-to-be-white-posters-appear-at-moorhead-s-concordia-college/454977133/?om_rid=2048935369&om_mid=60882377)

Fliers saying "it's okay to be white" were found taped to the exterior doors of a Maryland high school Wednesday morning, apparently as part of an effort to spark racial division.

...

Johnson described the school community as "smart, diverse and inclusive" and said it would not "fall victim to attempts to divide us."

– The Washington Post, Nov 1 2017 "Signs saying 'it's okay to be white' found at Maryland high school" (https://www.washingtonpost.com/local/education/signs-saying-its-okay-to-be-white-found-at-maryland-high-school/ 2017/11/01/92013a26-bf3b-11e7-959c-fe2b598d8c00_story.html? utm_term=.35460d8feddb&itid=lk_inline_manual_4)

Not every single instance of the operation was a success. Some universities did react more neutrally:

Executive director of Washington State University's Office of Equity and Diversity responded to the posters by saying: "In my mind, it's a nonthreatening statement", further stating: "Sure, it's OK to be white. It's OK to be African-American. It's OK to be Latino. It's OK to be gay.

...

*Police were contacted regarding the flyers being posted at the University of California, Berkeley. A police department spokesperson said "the signs did not constitute a hate crime because they did not target a specific race and because no criminal act was committed".– **Wikipedia** (https://en.wikipedia.org/wiki/It%27s_okay_to_be_white)*

When Tucker Carlson defended the posters, saying, *"What's the correct position? That it's not okay to be white?"* he was criticized by *Newsweek* for *"Helping to Spread Neo-Nazi Propaganda"* (https://www.newsweek.com/neo-nazi-david-duke-backed-meme-was-reported-tucker-carlson-without-context-714655).

The *Washington Post* also responded to the incident:

The episode is indicative of the efforts white-nationalist groups have made to recruit in and around the nation's college campuses and other mainstream settings with claims of growing white maltreatment and expanding anti-white discrimination. The white victim construct is one that experts say, not so long ago, only had traction in avowed white supremacists, segregationists and neo-Nazi circles. But today, it animates open and anonymous public discussions of race and shapes the nation's politics.

— The Washington Post, Nov 3 2017 "'It's okay to be white' signs and stickers appear on campuses and streets across the country" (https://www.washingtonpost.com/news/post-nation/wp/2017/11/03/its-okay-to-be-white-signs-and-stickers-appear-on-campuses-and-streets-across-the-country/)

On October 15th, 2018, The Australian Senate almost passed a resolution officially condemning the phrase, but it was narrowly voted down.

In the Senate debate, the leader of the Greens, Richard Di Natale, noted that the slogan "'it's OK to be white' … has got a long history in the white supremacist movement". — The Guardian, Oct 15 2018, "'It's okay to be white' signs and stickers appear on campuses and streets across the country" (https://www.theguardian.com/australia-news/2018/oct/15/ok-to-be-white-australian-government-senators-condemn-anti-white-racism)

As of 2023, "It's Okay to be White" is still considered a hate symbol, and is still occasionally used by Right Wing protesters, including relatively moderate ones that I would not consider to be part of the Dissident Right or far-right at all. Such as in this article from Portland, Maine on February 2023.

Counterprotesters show up to condemn 'It's OK to be white' banner in Congress Square — Portland Press Herald, Feb 17 2023, "Counterprotesters show up to condemn 'It's OK to be white' banner in Congress Square" (https://www.pressherald.com/2023/02/17/counterprotesters-show-up-to-condemn-its-ok-to-be-white-banner-in-congress-square/)

While the most recent example I can find with a quick google search, this was in a small town. However, the slogan has been used all over the world, reaching as far as Scotland in 2019.

Racist 'It's Okay to Be White' Stickers Reappear in Scotland

— Newsweek, Dec 17 2019 (https://www.newsweek.com/ok-white-stickers-scotland-1477743)

In February 2023, *Rasmussen* ran a poll asking black Americans if they agreed that it was "okay to be white," directly referencing the meme. Only 53% of the black Americans said they agreed, while 47% indicated they either disagreed or were not sure (https://cbsaustin.com/news/nation-world/poll-finds-over-a-quarter-of-black-americans-dont-think-its-okay-to-be-white-scott-adams-dilbert).

Scott Adams, the creator of the *Dilbert* comic strip, was an early supporter of Donald Trump, starting an online political show "Real Coffee With Scott Adams" where he would often praise Trump's skills at "persuasion." In a February 2023 edition of the show, Scott Adams covered the *Rasmussen* poll, declaring black people "a hate group" since they did not think it was okay to be white.

> *So if nearly half of all Blacks are not okay with white people, according to this poll not according to me -- according to this poll -- that's a hate group, and I don't want to have anything to do with them.*
>
> *...*
>
> *The best advice I would give to white people, is to get the hell away from black people...There's no fixing this.*
>
> **– Scott Adams, Real Coffee With Scott Adams, Feb 22 2023, "Episode 2027 Scott Adams: AI Goes Woke, I Accidentally Joined A Hate Group, Trump, Policing Schools" (https://www.youtube.com/watch?v=K6TnAn7qV1s)**

As a result, *Dilbert* was canceled in many newspapers across the country.

This is the latest development as of 2023, when I am writing this. Who knows what tomorrow will bring. Half a decade after /pol/'s op, the ripple effects through society continue to be felt. As the antithesis continues to do battle with the thesis.

The phrase is in many ways the inverse of "Black Lives Matter." While they have almost an identical literal meaning, one is totally accepted by society and one is considered hateful. Both operate in a similar fashion, if you disagree with "Black Lives Matter" then do you think black lives don't matter? If you disagree with "it's okay to be white" do you think it's not okay to be white? Those who disagree with the phrase "Black Lives Matter" do not truly disagree with the statement but with the group it represents, or with the larger narrative around supposedly racist policing. This is the same argument made against "it's okay to be white," that the statement actually represents agreement with the entity it came from – 4chan or the Alt Right. Yet in the former case, the Left ignores this, while in the latter it is the focal point of their disagreement. The ADL lists one as "hateful" but not the other, although the concept of the two slogans is virtually identical.

The Alt Right's Final Ops Pt 3 - He Will Not Divide Us. One More Final: I Need You

Aside from maybe "memeing Trump into the White House," the most impressive display of the Internet's power was probably during "He Will Not Divide Us" (often referred to as HWNDU). It would also serve as a swansong of sorts, one last epic win before the fiery death of the Internet.

> *He Will Not Divide Us (HWNDU) is an anti-Trump online performance art project by actor Shia Labeouf and artists Luke Turner and Nastja Rönkkö, featuring a 24-hour livestream held in a variety of locations. While initially launched outside the Museum of the Moving Image in Queens, New York with a planned broadcast for the duration of Donald Trump's first term as president of the United States, the stream was moved several times after being disrupted by trolls from 4chan's /pol/ board and other online communities. –* **Know Your Meme**
> **(https://knowyourmeme.com/memes/he-will-not-divide-us)**

The initial "art project" was simply a camera mounted on one of the outer walls of the museum and pointed at eye level towards a parking lot opening to the city streets. Above the camera was printed the slogan "He Will Not Divide Us" ("he" referring to President Trump). Shia LaBeouf appeared facing the camera, repeating the words "he will not divide us" over and over again like a mantra. A mob of other Leftists (not sure if they were part of the project or random passersby) would join in Shia's "He Will Not Divide Us" chant. The stream was open to the public, and anyone walking by could stop and participate in the stream. Supposedly, the livestream was supposed to air 24/7 like this for the entire four years of Trump's presidency.

After discovering the campaign on 4chan, many anon visited the project to "troll" Shia, the project, and its Leftist participants.

> That day, YouTuber "I'm a fish" began uploading highlights from the stream in which /pol/ users praise Donald Trump, hold signs with Pepe the Frog, play the song "Shadilay" and write "KEK" on the museum wall.
>
> **– Know Your Meme (https://knowyourmeme.com/memes/he-will-not-divide-us)**

At one point in the stream, a black Leftist claimed milk was *"hate speech towards black people...like just purposely drinking milk outside very obnoxiously"* because racists *"try to say that black people are lactose intolerant"* (https://youtu.be/_p4h3jwJob0?si=2C_QFNmrcefepu9O&t=264). From this point, some anon began carrying quarts of milk at the event.

Among the trolls was New Yorker Brittany Venti, an Alt Lite game streamer who sometimes ironically pretended to be an air-headed hysterical feminist in order to mock SJWs. Venti at first ironically pretended to be one of the Left Wingers on the stream, giving a speech about how Barack Obama had *"saved Central Park's ice skating rink, in only four months and for only 2.5 million dollars after the city had failed to. Under budget and ahead of schedule. Barack Obama!"* (this was in fact true of Donald Trump, not Obama). This prompted the crowd on stream to break out in applause, one of them high-fiving Venti. Venti continued, *"I have one more thing to say. Donald Trump failed to support our allies, including Israel. The Jewish word for peace and unity is 'Shadilay.'"* Turning to the crowd, *"If everyone could say 'Shadilay' real quick, is that okay? It would mean a lot to me since I'm Jewish. Everyone say Shadilay?"* The crowd cried *"Shadilay!"* Venti continued, *"The Jewish word for 'to divide' is 'Soros.' Hashtag #NoSoros hashtag #Shadilay"* (a reference to Left Wing astroturfed hashtag campaigns such as #NotMyPresident). Later she would hold up pieces of paper with memes, chant *"he will nut inside us"* and scream *"fucking normies, get off of my stream! Reee!"* at the top of her lungs. (https://www.youtube.com/watch?v=wLnYxoDoToo) (https://www.youtube.com/watch?v=cmp9CcfJn3E)

In contrast to his monk-like chants, Shia grew increasingly "triggered" as he was successfully trolled by anon, getting up in anon's face and angrily yelling *"HE WILL NOT DIVIDE US!"* over and over again aggressively. At some point, Shia got into an altercation with the mob of trolls, forcing him to leave the vicinity.

> *On the evening of January 25th, 2017, Labeouf was arrested on stream on suspicion of assault. According to a New York Police Department spokesman, Labeouf allegedly grabbed a man's scarf and scratched his face, then pushed him to the ground after saying something that offended Labeouf on the livestream.* **– Know Your Meme (https://knowyourmeme.com/memes/he-will-not-divide-us)**

With Shia gone, HWNDU became simply a livestream camera pointing at the parking lot, where random anon would show up and create content. The event became a de facto meeting place for anon who wanted to meet each other offline, or who wanted to visit the stream to make content for the anon watching at home. This content included political debates between anon and the Leftists at the events, and in some cases anon simply giving stream of conscious monologues about whatever was on their mind at the moment.

You know something? I think for 70 years we've been divided. And I think it's been by people from both parties. I think it's been by people from both sides of the aisle. And I think what we really need is somebody to join people in saying, "we are middle America, and we need a person to represent us. Because for the last 60 years we haven't had somebody to represent us. We've had somebody from the 1%. Every. Single. Election. And they don't care what we think. They don't care at all, they care about their money and they care about making more of it. We need people from us. We need people from the people who are standing here. We're the ones that know what's going on. These people fuckin' don't give a shit. And they don't care at all. We need people from this parking lot. These are people who live here every single fuckin day. And we need these people to stand up. And take position, not the people who have been here for the last 80 fuckin years doin nothing but bullshit and jerkin' our chain.

– NewYorkDashCam, Feb 5, 2017, He will Not Divide Us Funniest Moments (*https://youtu.be/TOxo0REGhIA?si=aj9H5kgCIVii6K8w*)

Can I just honestly give my opinion on what this our project means? I don't think that this art project is meant to unite us. I feel like this art project divides us more than the "he" that it's referencing, because if you're going to demonize Donald Trump, who some people -- people on the Right – have elected as their president, and people on the Left haven't, then this art project is going to divide us more than this demonized version of Trump ever will. And I'm not even trolling I'm not even faking this. This is my own actual opinion on this. This...this is a shit art installation. This is gonna divide us more than Trump will.

– unknown HWNDU partipant, Feb 2, 2017, "hewillnotdivide.us meets /pol/ - Highlights, Day 6 Part 2" (*https://youtu.be/8MSnXaY9owl? si=OnaZAYXr-WUAdJwP&t=1015*)

Many of the highlights from this original HWNDU stream are still available online on the "I'm a fish/@HWNDU" YouTube channel (https://www.youtube.com/@HWNDU). It has also been covered by the

YouTube channel *The Internet Historian (*https://www.youtube.com/watch?v=_p4h3jwJob0*)*

Sam Hyde also crashed the event. He would be harassed by journalists, engage in a bit of trolling, and be swarmed by fans. Nick Fuentes, then a total unknown, attended the event and met Hyde, who he would later call one of his heroes. In 2020, by which time Fuentes had developed a large following, Hyde and Fuentes would collaborate for the video "*Q-Anon Exposed By Sam Hyde!!!*" *(https://www.youtube.com/watch?v=Mw7UqBuvDbc)* Hyde also made a guest appearance on Fuentes's show *America First with Nicholas J Fuentes* on DLive, during Fuentes's election night coverage of the 2020 presidential election.

A photo of Venti and other anon who had met IRL, all enjoying a meal together, has become a bittersweet symbol of the last days of the Alt Right and Wild West-era Internet culture.

However, the story does not end there. This was only phase one of HWNDU. The true demonstration of anon's power would be during the next evolution of HWNDU: Capture the Flag.

> On February 10th, 2017, Page Six reported that the Museum of the Moving Image would be shutting down the He Will Not Divide Us installation, citing violent altercations that had occurred on-site.

> **– Know Your Meme (https://knowyourmeme.com/memes/he-will-not-divide-us)**

The project was moved to Albuquerque, New Mexico, outside the El Rey Theater. It was basically identical to the previous format of the project, featuring a single livestreaming camera with the words "He Will Not Divide Us" printed above it. Anon showed up at this location as well, although far fewer in number, and their content was often less "trolling" and more akin to the monologueing of the later part of New York HWNDU. In spite of this, the new location lasted only three days before the camera was spray-painted by a masked vandal, ending the Albuquerque location of the project.

On March 8th, the livestream returned. This time, it consisted solely of a camera pointed up at a white flag with the words "He Will Not Divide Us" on it, against the backdrop of the sky in an unknown, "secret" location. With only these clues and the power of 4chan' collective autism, anon sought out to discover the location of the flag in order to continue trolling Shia.

> After defeat on the battlefields of New York and New Mexico, Shia headed to a new, hidden location. No more chanting or interaction, this latest exhibit would just be a flag waving arrogantly in front of a camera. There were no landmarks. No scenery. No clues at all to its whereabouts. It would be impossible to find and nothing could stop the broadcast. Check. Mate.

*And this would allow Shia to act smug for the next four to eight years. That is, unless /pol/'s agents could find away to track it down. Challenge accepted. It was to be the greatest game of capture the flag ever. — **The Internet Historian, Mar 15, 2017, "Capture the Flag | He Will Not Divide Us"**(https://youtu.be/vw9zyxm860Q?si=_97OLF75dOqhqkqi)*

Because the stream was 24/7, anon were able to use the time of sunset to determine that it was in the Eastern time zone. Anon also studied the stars during the night, as well as clouds and wind patterns near the location. Other anon scoured the news and social media, trying to determine Shia's whereabouts, and whether or not he was present at or near the site of the livestream. When planes flew over the location, anon monitored air traffic within the time zone. At one point in the stream, the croaking of frogs indicated the presence of water nearby – more meme magic.

Another major breakthrough came when a waitress posted about meeting Shia LeBeouf, with an article in *TMZ* confirming that Shia was in the vicinity of Greensville, Tennessee (which fell within the Eastern time zone).

However, it was ultimately the stars that would allow anon to locate the flag.

On March 9th, an unknown person was recorded taking down the flag and replacing it with a "Make America Great Again" hat and Pepe the Frog T-shirt

...

On March 10th, the news site Get Riced posted an article about how the location was discovered, claiming that viewers used triangulation techniques based on planes seen in the stream to determine the general area. A local then began honking their horn repeatedly while driving in the area, which were picked up by the webcam's microphone to further narrow the location. Finally, using star maps, 4chan users were able to identify the exact location of the flag on Google Maps.

*— **Know Your Meme** (https://knowyourmeme.com/memes/he-will-not-divide-us)*

After Shia removed the MAGA hat and shirt, he remained at the location, guarding the empty flagpole. According to *The Internet Historian*, Anon speculated ways of reattaching the hat to the poll using a drone. However, I have not been able to find evidence of if this was ever completed before the project was moved to its next location.

On March 22, the flag moved across the Atlantic, relocated to the top of the Foundation for Art and Creative Technology in Liverpool, England. It would be found by anon and taken down within 25 hours. Anon first tried forging a fake press pass in order to gain access to the roof where the flag was located, but was unsuccessful. Other plans involving drones fitted with contraptions such as weed-whackers, flamethrowers, and high wattage lasers. However, before these could be completed, anon had already scaled the building in an attempt to remove the flag.

> On March 23rd, as masked man appeared on the Liverpool stream. The stream was subsequently taken offline and photographs began appearing on both 4chan and 8chan of an empty flag pole on the building, with many speculating that it had been stolen by the masked man.
>
> ...
>
> Shortly after, a photograph of the masked man standing on a roof with a cohort was posted to /pol/, referring to the pair as "parkour autists" That day, the official @FACT_Liverpool Twitter feed announced that "on police advice" the installation was removed "due to dangerous, illegal trespassing" – **Know Your Meme**
> **(https://knowyourmeme.com/memes/he-will-not-divide-us)**

Next, the exhibit moved online, featuring a digital placard with the words "He Will Not Divide Us" overlaid across a digital HWNDU flag. *"HWNDU has been removed and relocated several times, but this one is here to stay"* the site claimed. A bold claim to make. The fact that they thought the exhibit would fare better online, on 4chan's home turf, seems a bit short-sighted.

Needless to say, the site would quickly 404 for several hours, supposedly due to a DDoS attack from 4chan.

For the next year and a half, the project would relocate to various locations across the world, including London, a remote cabin in Finland, and Nantes, France. In each case, anon was able to discover the new location and troll Shia. In France, a drone was finally employed in a HWNDU op. The drone, equipped with a flamethrower, attempted to burn the flag, but it was made of a fireproof material. By this time, many anon had grown bored with the campaign. The last HWNDU location was announced by Shia on May 8th, 2018, but I can find no other information regarding it.

Since 2018, Shia LeBeouf has converted to Catholicism, and seems to have become more based and redpilled.

> *LaBeouf also says, before his conversion, he did not initially feel compelled to have a relationship with Jesus because he only knew the "soft, fragile, all-loving, all-listening but no ferocity … meek" Jesus (Barron immediately offers the word "feminized"), and it was only when LaBeouf encountered what he considered to be "masculine" — "cape, dipped in blood, sword" — that Jesus felt "appealing."*
>
> *– Religion Unplugged, Sep 7, 2022, "Shia LaBeouf's Newfound Catholicism Part Of His Hollywood Redemption Story" (https://religionunplugged.com/news/2022/9/6/shia-lebeoufs-newfound-catholicism-part-of-his-hollywood-redemption-story#:~:text=The%20actor%20%E2%80%94%20who%20comes%20from,for%20the%20role%20of%20Pio.)*

The Alt Right and the Alt Lite

The unexpected victory of Donald Trump seemed like a great victory for the Alt Right and the inevitability of their ideology's ascension, but in fact it created a major problem: what *was* their ideology? A true answer to this would never be found, and instead the Alt Right would fall apart after the "Unite the Right" rally in Charlottesville.

The Alt Right had really never been intended to be a serious political movement, but instead more of a joke, or an "epic troll." Like Plankton from Spongebob, they "never thought they would get this far." As stated repeatedly throughout the text, the Alt Right was a big tent coalition loosely organized around a common opposition to political correctness and support of Donald Trump. Many "Alt Right" personalities were trolls like Sam Hyde, not true political figures. Some did not even care about politics but simply found "trolling the libs" funny.

Thus, the Alt Right began to fracture across ideological lines: those who wanted to be American nationalists versus those who wanted to include Europe, those who were pagan or atheist versus those who were Christian. These divisions would become very important after Charlottesville, during the "Optics Wars." However, for now, the greatest divide was between the "Alt Right" and the "Alt Lite."

The "Alt Lite" were more similar to the anti-SJW movement that arose after GamerGate. They were essentially liberals, libertarians, and moderate conservatives that were against the social justice Left and political correctness. They generally still believed in liberal assumptions about the world concerning racial equality, feminism, civic nationalism, etc. They might criticize Leftists because they were being "racist against white people." But that was because racism was wrong and we should all "judge each other on the content of our character not color of our skin." They might criticize feminists whenever they "held men and women to a double standard." But that's because they weren't truly treating men and women "equally." Or, as ShoeOnHead, an Alt Lite content creator often did, they might criticize a particular aspect of feminism, such as saying that the wage gap was a myth. At the same time, they would be fully supportive of women in the workplace. They might be against illegal immigration, but for immigration "as long as it was done legally." In spite of their more moderate stance, members of the Alt Lite would still use the frequently racist or anti-Semitic memes of the Alt Right, but did so strictly ironically or simply because they were popular at the time.

The "Alt Right" on the other hand, was more extreme. They were more willing to touch on "third rail" issues and directly contradict the assumptions of liberalism, which most Americans on all sides basically agreed on at the time. The Alt Right did not believe in equality. They believed that the races and genders differed from each other genetically, and thus there would always be disparate outcome between groups. They did not believe in colorblind civic nationalism. They believed white people had the right to their own homeland and to organize towards their own interests as a racial group. They did not believe in feminism, but that a woman's role was as a mother and wife. They were against immigration on a mass scale, whether legal or illegal, and wanted to retain a white majority in historically white nations.

And some members of the Alt Right went even further than this. Because the original idea of the Alt Right was based on "shock value," the trajectory was to become as offensive as possible and to become more and more extreme. There was no such thing as someone who was "too far-right" on the Alt Right. This was not a problem when it was all about making a statement about political incorrectness. But when the irony was stripped away and it was time to decide on one's true views, then it was necessary to draw the line somewhere.

This failure to draw the line somewhere brought people like David Duke and neo-Nazi skinheads into the big tent. This mistake is what lead to the eventual death of the Alt Right in August of 2017.

Charlottesville: the Fiery Death of the Alt Right

In 2017, the Alt Right was still riding off of the high of electing Donald Trump. Many had decided that it was now time to take the movement offline and turn to IRL activism. This culminated in a protest planned for August 11, 2017 called "Unite the Right" in Charlottesville, Virginia, which was organized to protest the city's decision to remove a statue of Robert E Lee (which the city saw as a racist celebration of slavery and Jim Crow).

The Unite the Right rally soon became a lightning rod, attracting many Alt Right organizations such as Identity Europa, the Rise Above Movement, the Traditionalist Workers Party, Vanguard America (the predecessors of Patriot Front) and Alt Right figures such as Mike Enoch of TRS, Richard Spencer, and Internet troll Baked Alaska. Some personalities within the Alt Lite, such as Brittany Venti, also decided to come to event, some merely out of curiosity. Other racist and neo-Nazi groups not associated with the Alt Right, such as David Duke (former Grand Wizard of the KKK), and neo-Confederate and neo-Nazi groups also attended the protest. Nick Fuentes, who had recently began his career as a streamer on *Right Side Broadcasting Network* (RSBN) earlier that year, also attended, although he was virtually unknown at the time. He did not participate in the infamous "tiki torch" march, having gone there mostly out of curiosity and because he had heard that others in the Alt Right and Alt Lite were going. He would be fired by RSBN as a result of his attendance.

Others thought that the rally was a bad idea. Gavin McInnes (a politically incorrect journalist, co-founder of *Vice Magazine* and creator of the Proud Boys) was invited to attend, but declined because he did not want "to be associated with explicit neo-Nazis." The Proud Boys themselves had been founded in September 2016 and were a fairly new organization. They were not a visible part of the rally, although some attended. In fact, Jason Kessler, the organizer of the protest, had been kicked out of the organization by McInnes personally, "once his racist politics became apparent." The "irony bros" such as streamer Beardson Beardly and Internet troll Paul Town also chose not to attend, the former sensing the potential for sabotage that would undermine the goals of the far-right. Mike Cernovich, an Alt Lite political commentator, also called the rally "a trap."

The Charlottesville rally was a disaster for the Alt Right. Trump was a charismatic celebrity billionaire, and could be beloved by Americans even when he said unpopular things. The Alt Right's trolling could also be seen as humorous, so long as they were a nebulous, anonymous bunch of Internet trolls. However, seeing a bunch of weirdos from the Internet emerge from their mother's basements and crawl into real life carrying fascist symbols and marching next to David Duke was far less palatable. The infamous "tiki torch" march was at once freakish and terrifying from one perspective, and buffoonish from another. The fiery faces of angry protesters lit up in the night recalled that of the KKK burning crosses on people's lawns, or a lynch mob. This was exactly the sort of image the media had tried unsuccessfully to attach to the Alt Right since the beginning. At the same time, the fact that instead of real torches, they were tiki torches, such as you might buy at Home Depot for a luau-themed barbecue party, combined with the assortment of Kekistan flags and Internet memes mixed with strange, esoteric, fascist symbols made the entire affair seem bizarre and comical to normies.

The violent street clashes between Antifa and counter protesters on one side and the Alt Right on the other, culminating with the death of Heather Heyer, fed perfectly into the media's narrative of an America about to succumb to a violent and dangerous fascist movement, which had just taken its first victim.

The myth of Charlottesville is that the rally was a big success for the alt-right. However, the organizers had two major political goals for the rally: firstly, to show the country that the alt-right is not just a social media phenomenon, and secondly, to bring various far-right groups together. Neither of these goals was realized.

Whether 500 or 1,500 people attended, Unite the Right was undoubtedly one of the largest explicitly extreme right rallies in recent US history. But while 1,500 people looks impressive in a town of 50,000, they came from all over the country, and constitute only a minuscule faction of the alt-right trolls on social media, let alone of the population of 325 million that live in the US.

– The Guardian, Aug 10 2018, "The far right hails 'Unite the Right' a success. Its legacy says otherwise"
(https://www.theguardian.com/commentisfree/2018/aug/10/unite-the-right-rally-alt-right-demise)

This violence (which included protesters and counter-protesters attacking each other with sticks and even homemade flamethrowers) was in a way the painful hangover from the "lulz" of 2016. It prefigured the chaos of 2020, a year in which running over protesters with cars became routine, as did street clashes between Proud Boys and Antifa.

After the events of Charlottesville, nearly every Alt Right faction hated every other Alt Right faction. People blamed Richard Spencer for the failure of the event, and Richard Spencer in turn burned bridges with everyone else. People began to dox one another out of spite. The movement had been humiliated in the eyes of the public. The lulz were over and the Alt Right was now a "dead meme." In the wake of Charlottesville, the Alt Right soured to the idea of IRL activism, and what remained of it would be an Internet-only phenomenon. The Dissident Right would not attempt to mobilize IRL again until Stop the Steal in 2020.

The Unite the Right 2 rally occurred on August 12, 2018, and saw low turnout, with up to 30 Kessler supporters while counter-protesters who demonstrated against the rally numbered into the thousands.

– Wikipedia (https://en.wikipedia.org/wiki/Unite_the_Right_rally)

The immediate consequences of Charlottesville forced the Dissident Right to abandon the Alt Right's strategy of being as offensive as possible for "shock" value. A line had clearly been crossed, and it was clear that the Dissident

Right was no longer being "ironic" but had evolved from trolling into a more serious political movement. Thus, the Alt Right began to dissolve, and the Dissident Right began a process of trying to determine what it actually believed in and what its identity would become. It began to distance itself from explicitly neo-Nazi and white supremacist groups, and no longer employ fascist or Nazi imagery such as the swastika. This process culminated in the "Optics Wars," which would ultimately replace the Alt Right with something closer to the Dissident Right that we know today.

Effects of the Alt Right on My Worldview

In 2016, I had still been something of a libertarian. I supported parts of the Alt Right, because I was against political correctness, but I did not support unironic fascism or Nazism. I thought there should be a peaceful pro-white advocacy group of some kind, similar to the NAACP but for white people, to prevent them from being discriminated against by the clearly anti-white Left. But that is a very different stance from supporting Nazis.

I still basically believed that people should not use the government to "force their beliefs on others." I originally supported Trump because I believed that since I opposed the Religious Right forcing their religion on others in the 2000s, I was a hypocrite if I did not oppose the SJWs for doing the same to Christians and conservatives in 2016. It was my hope that a victory for Trump would mean the end of "woke" Leftism, and a return to their older, more liberal form.

Around 2018 or 2019, my opinion began to change. I realized that a truly "liberal" government was just as much of a pipedream as an anarcho-Capitalist Utopia of pure "free markets" or the Communist's Utopia of "to each his ability, to each his need." The fact of the matter is that every individual could not simply choose for themselves. It was impossible to have a society without a set of shared norms with some mechanism of enforcement. All that liberalism did was create a vacuum in which the radical Left, or some other group, could come in and enforce their agenda.

To allow everyone to choose whatever rules they wanted for themselves would be like allowing everyone to use whatever currency they felt like or obey whatever traffic laws they felt like. The entire idea of society is that people give up a bit of their liberty in order to participate in society, and in turn reap the benefits of that society. These are benefits that the individual could not achieve on their own, but are possible only through organized and collective action. Therefore, it was inevitable that society would follow one ideology or another, one set of norms or another. In America in the current year, that either meant that the "Religious Right" would enforce their views on society, or else the "Woke Left" would enforce their views on society. Any other third alternative was entirely impractical.

Although not a Christian myself at the time, and still firmly an atheist, I decided that I preferred them to the Woke religion. This was primarily on two grounds:

1. The traditional morals of Christianity were closer to the norm than the Woke ideology. Christianity is closer to what was considered normal in most religions, and in most civilizations (including the Early Roman Republic, Islamic society, Buddhist and Confucian civilizations). The Woke ideology was based on ideas that had never been tried before and were entirely experimental, such as gay marriage or transgenderism. Any negative effects of traditional morality must have been discovered long ago. Meanwhile, it was totally unknown what a society shaped by the Woke ideology would be like.

2. The society that Christianity created was a great place to live. Christian Europe and the more religious America prior to the 1960s were places where there was a high quality of life, people treated each other with respect and manners, the streets were clean, society was efficient, and people cared about the sanctity of human rights and dignity. As society had become more liberal, things seemed to have indeed degenerated, becoming dirtier, poorer, more primitive, more rude, more miserable, etc.

Therefore, I decided to choose a side and support the side of tradition, based on Christian morality. However, the Alt Right was not a viable pathway towards creating this society. I hoped that, as I had predicted in 2016, their views would become more moderate and evolve into a more mature form as time went on and they continued to spread. Then perhaps there would be a movement that I could support.

The Weekly Sweat: Rise Of The Irony Bros

The Alt Right was a "big tent" movement, and it stressed unity between all factions of the Right against their common enemy, the Left. The basic assumption at the time was "don't punch right" and "no infighting." However, while one side of the Alt Right was drifting towards unironic and explicit white nationalism and fascism, resulting in the disaster of Charlottesville, another side of the Alt Right went in the opposite direction. This side of the Alt Right, having emerged victorious over the Left in electing Donald Trump, now set the same weapons of irony and trolling against the Alt Right itself. They became known as the "irony bros."

Infuriating other factions of the Alt Right, especially fans of TRS (a podcast network including *The Daily Shoah, Fash the Nation* and others) the "irony bros" critiqued the Alt Right from the Right, rather than the Left. Others eventually came to find this faction to be attractive, following the epic fail of Charlottesville.

The irony bros revolved around Beardson Beardly's livestream show *The Weekly Sweat,* part of the YouTube channel *Honeypot Productions,* which also included videos by content creator TVKwa and Twitter troll and influential Meme War veteran Paul Town. TVKwa's show was a surrealist, *Million Dollar Extreme*-esque parody of the news (which I cannot find anywhere but was very funny) featuring TVKwa dressed in a ski mask, sitting at a desk floating in a psychedelic void. Paul Town's content contained a humor that was racist but mostly nihilistic, misanthropic and extremely ironic and insincere (like a more dark triad version of Sam Hyde). *The Weekly Sweat* was a talk show hosted by Beardson Beardly, a gaming streamer, and Prince Hubris (also known as Shawn), a dakimakura-hugging NEET gym bro. It often revolved around drama within the Alt Right and mocking other Alt Right figures such as Richard Spencer and Mike Enoch.

Allied to the irony bros was Ricky Vaughn, Meme War veteran and one of the most influential Twitter accounts during the 2016 election.

> *The MIT Media Lab's quantitative analysis of social media and news influencers, which found the Ricky Vaughn Twitter account "was more impactful ... than several major media outlets and figures such as NBC News and The Drudge Report." –* **Vermont Public, April 10 2023, "Trump's 'Most Influential White Nationalist Troll' Has Vermont Roots"** *(https://www.vermontpublic.org/programs/2018-04-10/trumps-most-influential-white-nationalist-troll-has-vermont-roots)*

Nick Fuentes also was aligned with the irony bros and frequently called into the show as a guest.

Their biggest rivals were Richard Spencer and TRS, who would come to be emblematic of "wignats."

The Optics Wars: the Dissident Right Grows up, Finds Jesus

While the irony bros focused on mocking the Alt Right, Nick Fuentes offered the Dissident Right an alternative. Fuentes was a former student of International Relations at Boston University. Although originally a traditional Republican who supported Ted Cruz for President, Fuentes would become redpilled in college and change his allegiance to Donald Trump. At 18 years old, he dropped out of college to start his show *America First with Nicholas J*

Fuentes, which he hosted on RSBN out of a friend's dorm room. After attending Charlottesville, he was fired by RSBN and continued the show independently on his own YouTube channel.

Unlike many members of the Alt Right, who tended to be misfits and anti-social NEETs who locked themselves in their room browsing 4chan, Fuentes was a normal, well-adjusted kid. He had been Student Council President at Lyons Township High School, and had even been voted "most likely to be President."

On an episode of *Nationalist Review*, a far-right podcast Fuentes hosted with James Allsup, Fuentes would criticize an appearance on a college tour by Mike Enoch and others from TRS, calling it "bad optics." His criticisms included the schlubby, overweight and poorly dressed appearance of Mike Enoch, the lack of production quality of the event, the low level of audience turnout, and humiliating disruptions by hecklers.

Additionally, he criticized the Alt Right's use of fascist, Nazi and skinhead aesthetics, considering them to be "un-American" symbols of foreign, obscure ideologies of the past that would not resonate with conservative Americans. This difference in symbolism also applied to rhetoric. Fuentes emphasized making arguments in a very precise way and sticking to the facts of the matter in a way that would appear reasonable to the average person, rather than going for maximum shock value.

However, his largest criticism of the Alt Right was its lack of Christianity, which he said must play a prominent role in the Dissident Right movement. He harshly condemned and mocked both paganism and atheism.

Fuentes stressed that a distinction must be made between the Dissident Right and groups such as neo-Nazis, skinheads, and white supremacist organizations such as the KKK. Fuentes accused these organizations of being full of "wignats" or "white nigger nationalists." According to him, wignats were low IQ, violent, un-Christian, low-lives. Utterly spiteful, unsophisticated, and unsuccessful people who were as degenerate as those they criticized, and destined only for failure. In contrast, Fuentes promoted paleoconservatives such as Patrick Buchanan and white advocates such as Jared Taylor.

Fuentes accused wignats of having a similar attitude of self-victimization as black people who blamed all of their problems on white people, except that they blamed all of white people's problems on Jewish people instead. While criticizing Jews on certain points, such as their "dual loyalty" to Israel, as well as Jewish influence in the media and politics, Fuentes accused wignats of sounding "schizophrenic" and "obsessed with Jews" to the point that they appeared insane.

This new philosophy became known as "American Nationalism," and its adherents "amnats." The basic idea of it was to take the best ideas of the Alt Right, and merge them with the more mainstream conservative movement, thus shifting the Republican party away from the neocons and towards a truly oppositional Right Wing movement that was "actually conservative."

Fuentes was criticized by most of the Alt Right for his positions. They argued that the Dissident Right should be a "big tent movement" that included anyone who was "pro-white" including figures like David Duke. They also conflated the idea of "optics" with Fuentes's position on distancing themselves from certain symbols and rhetoric, referring to it as "optics cucking," and accusing Fuentes of "hiding his real views" in an attempt to deceive normies into supporting his actual, more fascist positions. They also attacked Fuentes for not being white enough (he is half Mexican) and not being concerned enough with race, accusing him of "civic nationalism."

Fuentes received support from Ricky Vaughn, who called into an early episode of *America First* and called it "the future." *The Daily Stormer's* Andrew Anglin, who himself might have been considered closer to a wignat in aesthetic, also praised Fuentes, seeing him as a useful and necessary compliment to his own strategy of over-the-top shock humor.

On the other hand, Murdoch Murdoch, a popular Alt Right show at the time, was anti-Fuentes, mocking him in two of their cartoons for being Mexican, his association with Baked Alaska (a personal friend of Fuentes at the time and seen as a buffoonish character by some in the Alt Right), depicting him as an immature Zoomer, and a gay "catboy." (Fuentes, who described himself as an "asexual incel" and associated with many "ex"-homosexuals, such as Milo, was often accused of being gay. He also appeared in a livestream with an edgy, racist livestreamer "Catboy Kami" during one of his livestreams in which Kami was dressed as a "catboy" for shock value). TRS and Richard Spencer were perhaps the biggest antagonists of Nick Fuentes, with amnats going out of their way to attack them, and being attacked back in turn.

The debate between the "wignats" and the "amnats" was known as the "Optics Wars." While ideological in nature, it also heavily involved many other areas. Aesthetics, with amnats excluding followers who used white supremacist or Nazi imagery (such as the swastika, 1488, and the black sun) while wignats embraced them. Rhetoric, with amnats being more deliberate and specific with their arguments and trying to appeal to the average conservative, while wignats preferred the extreme shock humor of the earlier Alt Right. Individual personalities, with amnats refusing to associate with neo-Nazi groups, skinheads, supporters of TRS, Patriot Front, David Duke, or Richard Spencer. Religion, with amnats being exclusively Christian (particularly Catholic), and wignats being pagan or atheist. And even race, with amnats accepting non-white members and wignats criticizing people in the movement not considered adequately white. Amnats also typically were supportive of Donald Trump and other Republican politicians, while the wignats started to become critical of Donald Trump and claimed there was "no political solution," instead favoring strategies such as dropping out of society to live in a remote place with like-minded people.

In addition to the "Optics Wars," Nick Fuentes also launched a "Thot War," accusing the Alt Right of simping for egirls such as Brittany Venti and Lauren Southern, not being sufficiently anti-feminist, and stressing that any political movement must be exclusively led by men due to the drama and security concerns that women brought with them, and the innate incompetency of women in politics. The irony bros assisted Fuentes in these "wars," especially the Thot War, which often included trolling or raiding female members of the Alt Right and Alt Lite.

The Alt Right continued to decline in popularity over time. This was not immediate, but rather a slow process. The wignats can be seen as the last vestiges of this movement, and they would remain for some time, especially on non-mainstream platforms such as /pol/, 8chan, Gab, and later federated instances such as poast. However, by about 2021 or 2022 they would lose whatever remaining relevancy they had. Richard Spencer would become a Biden supporter in 2020 and shill heavily for the Covid Vaccine while TRS faced financial lawsuits from Charlottesville and internal drama.

The amnats would effectively win the Optics Wars, becoming more and more popular, especially after the Groyper Wars in 2019 and Fuentes's rise in popularity. In my opinion, they offered a welcome change. It was more serious and reasonable, decried racial violence of any kind, promoted social conservativism and responsibility, advocated for white people while not being hostile to others races, and, most importantly, had a clearer and more positive message based on Christianity. I could not have supported a neo-Nazi or white supremacist movement, or one that associated itself with the KKK, but I did not see any problems with supporting a movement that was simply pro-white and followed something akin to Christian Nationalism. I certainly saw it as better than the alternative the Left was advocating for: a society hostile to whites and to God.

Then in 2022, Kanye West, assisted by none other than Nick Fuentes himself, would become the ultimate wignat, proclaiming "I love Hitler" to millions of viewers on *InfoWars,* thus definitively rendering the "Optics Wars" moot. It also fundamentally changed the trajectory of America First. It was no longer about synthesizing the best ideas of the Alt Right with mainstream conservatism. Instead, Fuentes would unveil a new ideology for America First, which he called "Christian Futurism." But, by that time, the landscape of both the Dissident Right and the nation had totally changed. The Alt Right was firmly in the rear view mirror and these sorts of disputes were no longer pertinent.

In addition to their organic loss of popularity of Charlottesville, as well as several Alt Right-inspired mass shootings that would occur in the following years, the Alt Right's demise would be accelerated by Big Tech censorship, which would begin in the same year.

Big Tech Censorship: the Fiery Death of the Internet

During the 2016 election, the establishment looked clueless and out-of-touch with the new Internet counter-culture that dominated the youth and was growing more popular by the hour. The Internet also allowed Trump's message to bypass the mainstream mass media, and narratives that contradicted them to proliferate unimpeded. There was only one solution: the Internet must be shut down.

> *A video recorded by Google shortly after the 2016 presidential election reveals an atmosphere of panic and dismay amongst the tech giant's leadership, coupled with a determination to thwart both the Trump agenda and the broader populist movement emerging around the globe.*

> *...*

> *Walker says that Google should fight to ensure the populist movement – not just in the U.S. but around the world – is merely a "blip" and a "hiccup" in a historical arc that "bends toward progress."*

...

> *CEO Sundar Pichai states that the company will develop machine learning and A.I. to combat what an employee described as "misinformation" shared by "low-information voters."*
>
> **– Breitbart, Dec 12 2018, "LEAKED VIDEO: Google Leadership's Dismayed Reaction to Trump Election"** (*https://www.breitbart.com/tech/2018/09/12/leaked-video-google-leaderships-dismayed-reaction-to-trump-election/*)

This resulted in the "Censorship Era" of the Internet, an era of increasing censorship of dissident views via a public-private partnership between the Big Tech companies and intelligence agencies such as the FBI (and sometimes even the White House directly). It was also facilitated by a new development in technology: machine learning, also known as AI.

With AI technology, it was possible for large tech platforms to censor tens of millions of users automatically, without the need for a human to be involved. It also allowed for a level of arbitrariness and opaqueness, which made it more difficult for people to circumvent by rephrasing their messaging to get past the censorship.

However, censorship was not relegated to machine learning algorithms. The government was also personally involved in Big Tech censorship. As the "Twitter files" revealed in 2022 (following the company's acquisition by Elon Musk) the government, including the White House, would "ask" Big Tech to censor specific narratives, specific posts, and specific accounts, and there were daily meetings between the tech platform and government entities.

> *Trust and Safety chief Yoel Roth not only met regularly with the FBI and the Department of Homeland Security, but with the Office of the Director of National Intelligence (ODNI). Also, Twitter was aggressively applying "visibility filtering" tools to Trump well before the election.*– **Twitter Files, Pt 3** (*https://www.racket.news/p/capsule-summaries-of-all-Twitter?r=5mz1&utm_campaign=post&utm_medium=web*)

The government was in constant contact not just with Twitter but with virtually every major tech firm.

These included Facebook, Microsoft, Verizon, Reddit, even Pinterest, and many others. Industry players also held regular meetings without government.– Twitter Files, "Twitter AND "OTHER GOVERNMENT AGENCIES" (https://Twitterfiles.substack.com/p/Twitter-and-other-government-agencies)

At the close of 2017, Twitter makes a key internal decision. Outwardly, the company would claim independence and promise that content would only be removed at "our sole discretion." The internal guidance says, in writing, that Twitter will remove accounts "identified by the U.S. intelligence community" as "identified by the U.S.. intelligence community as a state-sponsored entity conducting cyber-operations."

The second thread shows how Twitter took in requests from everyone — Treasury, HHS, NSA, FBI, DHS, etc. — and also received personal requests from politicians like Democratic congressman Adam Schiff, who asked to have journalist Paul Sperry suspended.– The Twitter Files Parts 11 and 12 (https://www.racket.news/p/capsule-summaries-of-all-Twitter?r=5mz1&utm_campaign=post&utm_medium=web)

In addition to leaks such as the "Twitter files," the government's engagement in censorship was legally found to be in violation of the 1st amendment in 2023.

The White House, health officials and the FBI may have violated the First Amendment rights of people posting about COVID-19 and elections on social media by pressuring technology companies to suppress or remove the posts, a federal appeals court ruled late Friday.

The decision from the conservative 5th Circuit Court of Appeals partly upheld an order from a Louisiana federal judge that blocked many federal agencies from having contact with companies like Facebook, YouTube and X, formerly Twitter, about content moderation

...

The 5th Circuit panel found that the White House coerced the platforms through "intimidating messages and threats of adverse consequences" and commandeered the decision-making processes of social media companies, particularly in handling pandemic-related and 2020 election posts.

"It is true that the officials have an interest in engaging with social media companies, including on issues such as misinformation and election interference. But the government is not permitted to advance these interests to the extent that it engages in viewpoint suppression," the judges wrote.

– USA Today, Sep 9 2023, Biden administration coerced social media giants into possible free speech violations: court",
(https://www.usatoday.com/story/money/2023/09/08/biden-administration-coerced-Facebook-court-rules/70800723007/)

"Today we reject the idea that corporations have a freewheeling First Amendment right to censor what people say," Judge Andrew Oldham, an appointee of former President Donald Trump, wrote in the ruling.

– Reuters, Sep 17 2023 , "U.S. appeals court rejects big tech's right regulate online speech"(https://www.reuters.com/legal/us-appeals-court-rules-against-big-techs-ability-regulate-online-speech-2022-09-16/)

However, while it is nice that a smoking gun has finally been uncovered in recent years, this was never necessary. The exact whys and wherefores never mattered. Everyone on the Internet felt the effects of Big Tech censorship almost palpably. They also correctly guessed its motivations, and the shape that would it take. Big Tech would operate by "boiling the frog." Banning the most controversial accounts first, and then slowly working their way up from there.

The first banned man was Andrew Anglin, founder of *The Daily Stormer*. This occurred shortly after Charlottesville. Anglin said that Heather Heyer did not die from vehicular impact, but instead from a weight-related heart attack. As a consequence, his site would begin to be censored.

On August 13, the website was informed by its domain registrar GoDaddy that it had violated the terms of service by mocking Heyer in an article by Anglin. He was given 24 hours to locate a new registrar for the site.

> The next day it moved to Google which almost immediately cancelled its registration for violation of terms, also terminating the website's YouTube account. The following day, the website registered with Tucows, who canceled it hours later for regularly inciting violence. On August 15, it was announced by "weev" that the site had moved to the dark web, and that it was now only accessible via Tor, while Facebook banned links to the site and Discord banned its server. On August 16, Cloudflare, the DNS provider and proxy service used to protect The Daily Stormer, also terminated their service.
>
> Cloudflare had previously refused to terminate sites based on their content, but CEO Matthew Prince made an exception, posting a public announcement and explanation on the company's blog. The Daily Stormer now receives DDoS protection from a content distribution network set up in March 2017, BitMitigate. The company's founder, Nick Lim, said that he found The Daily Stormer to be "stupid" but believed in freedom of expression. Several Twitter accounts connected with The Daily Stormer were also suspended. – **Wikipedia (https://en.wikipedia.org/wiki/The_Daily_Stormer)**

As of 2023, *The Daily Stormer* is only available on the tor network or "Dark Web," a part of the Internet that is inaccessible by normal browsers and requires the use of the anonymizing Tor browser to use.

In spite of the content of the site, at the time it was unthinkable and unprecedented that a site could be purged from the Internet in such as way. Publications such as the *Electronic Frontier Foundation, Slate, The Los Angeles Times, National Review* and even *NPR* wrote about the risks of opening the door to censorship of the Internet, warning that it could spread to censorship of other political views, including Left Wing ones.

The next target of censorship was Alex Jones. Alex Jones had been another high profile Trump supporter during the Great Meme War. He was syndicated on 129 stations, had a daily audience of five million listeners and his video streams topped 80 million viewers in a single month. *InfoWars* brought in tens of millions of dollars in ad revenue, allowing the production quality of his show to rival that of any mainstream media program. This created another avenue where the mainstream mass media narrative could be bypassed. On August 6, 2018, he was banned from YouTube, Apple and Facebook, "citing repeated violations of policies against hate speech and glorifying violence."

On September 6, 2018, he was banned from Twitter (https://apnews.com/article/2521ccbe3b5a43d68d66c21c030a7f2d).

> *"Apple does not tolerate hate speech," the company said in a statement. "We believe in representing a wide range of views, so long as people are respectful to those with differing opinions."*
>
> *...*
>
> *Early Monday, Facebook announced that it had permanently removed four Alex Jones-related pages — the Alex Jones Channel Page, the Alex Jones Page, the InfoWars Page and the InfoWars Nightly News Page.*
>
> *"We believe in giving people a voice, but we also want everyone using Facebook to feel safe," the company said in a statement. "It's why we have community standards and remove anything that violates them, including hate speech that attacks or dehumanizes others."*
>
> *– NPR, Aug 6 2018, "YouTube, Apple and Facebook Ban Infowars, Which Decries 'Mega Purge'"*
> *(https://www.npr.org/2018/08/06/636030043/YouTube-apple-and-Facebook-ban-InfoWars-which-decries-mega-purge)*

From this point on, censorship spread further and further. "Ban waves" on platforms such as Twitter and YouTube became common, where multiple accounts would be banned all at once, sometimes across multiple platforms, and usually with no explanation whatsoever. Aside from censorship initiated by the platforms themselves or at the behest of the government, advertisers would also initiate "ban waves" such as during YouTube's many "adpocalypses"

Organizations such as the ADL and SPLC would also use advertiser boycotts as a weapon. One such campaign, launched against Facebook in 2021, was called "#StopHateForProfit."

> *The report from the Anti-Defamation League (ADL)—one of multiple civil rights groups involved in launching the #StopHateForProfit campaign last June—analyzed the success of the boycott in realizing its goals a year later.*
>
> *...*
>
> *The #StopHateForProfit boycott was started last summer amid outrage over Facebook's content moderation policies, including its refusal to regulate a post from Trump in the midst of racial justice unrest that said, "When the looting starts, the shooting starts." After its June 17 launch, the boycott quickly drew the participation of "thousands" of companies, according to the ADL, including big-name brands like Pfizer, Best Buy, Ford, Adidas and Starbucks. Some of these companies pledged a short pause on advertising spending, while others vowed to cut off funding for the rest of the year or until Facebook made tangible changes.*
>
> *– Forbes, Jun 17 2021, "Last Year's Advertising Boycott Of Facebook Led To Change—But Not Where You Think, Report Finds" (https://www.forbes.com/sites/jemimamcevoy/2021/06/17/last-years-advertising-boycott-of-facebook-led-to-change-but-not-where-you-think-report-finds/)*

These boycotts put further censorship in the hands of organizations such as the ADL. As a result of these ADL-led advertiser boycotts, it became common practice to consult with these organizations when crafting terms of service, effectively putting these organizations in charge of such policies.

The era would reach its height in 2020 and 2021. During 2020, all information about the Covid-19 pandemic that contradicted the official narrative, including the inefficacy of masks, the theory that Covid originated in a lab rather than from a wet market, and side effects of the Covid vaccine, were either "fact checked" with automatic tags inserted onto the posts containing the establishment narrative, or the accounts spreading this information would be banned outright (even when it came from credible sources, such as doctors).

In the 2020 election, the contents of Hunter Biden's laptop leaked. It revealed both pictures and videos of Hunter Biden using racial slurs, smoking crack, and having sex with prostitutes, as well as using his father's name to enrich himself and general government corruption. The details of the story itself are really not important, but rather the attempt to censor it. A story about the laptop and its contents was published by the *New York Post* in the last months of the 2020 election. In spite of it coming from a reputable source, the story was banned on social media. Users were not even able to share the story in direct messages to one another. The mainstream mass media claimed the laptop story was "Russian disinfo."

Then, of course, in 2021, the sitting President of the United States, President Trump, would be banned from Twitter and Facebook.

By 2021, conservatives were not only being banned from social media platforms but other services such as AirBnb, payment processors such as Patreon and PayPal, and even banks. In the case of Lauren Southern and Michelle Malkin, even their families were banned from these services. On February 6, 2022, Michelle Malkin and her husband were both banned from AirBnb (https://prescottenews.com/index.php/2022/02/06/opinion-why-airbnb-banned-me-and-my-hubby-too-michelle-malkin/). Lauren Southern's parents were banned from AirBnb in 2023 (https://www.foxnews.com/media/conservative-activist-rejects-airbnbs-apology-banning-parents-something-more-nefarious-going-on).

In both cases, their family was not involved in their political activities.

Nick Fuentes, after the events of January 6th, would even be put on a no-fly list and have his money seized by the government (although it is unclear whether this was solely from his speech, or whether it was because of his refusal to wear a mask on a flight and because of a mysterious bitcoin donation around the time of J6. Still, these could simply be convenient excuses by the government). As of 2023, Nick Fuentes has been banned from every payment processor in the world, including those in Russia and China. He has been banned from most banks, having to move his money from one bank to another frequently. He is also banned from some crypto exchanges, such as Coinbase. He is also banned from several tech services, such as Github, in order to impede his ability to develop his streaming platform, Cozy.tv.

The entire time, Leftists dishonestly insisted that conservatives were not actually being censored by Big Tech at all, a fact that has now been debunked by leaks such as the Twitter files.

> *A video of Google's first all-staff meeting following the 2016 election has been published by Breitbart, revealing the candid reactions of company executives to Donald Trump's unexpected victory.*
>
> *...*
>
> *The video was characterized by Breitbart as evidence of Google's supposed partisan bias against Republicans – an allegation that has been made repeatedly by Trump, Republican lawmakers and conservative media outlets in recent months.*
>
> *...*
>
> *But the bombastic responses ignored the substance and true tenor of the meeting, which was more measured and less partisan than Breitbart implied.*

...

Nevertheless, the leaked video will probably only fuel the Republican narrative that major technology companies are biased against conservatives. Just last week, Twitter's chief executive, Jack Dorsey, faced four hours of questioning from a House committee, with Republican representatives focusing almost exclusively on specious allegations of anti-conservative bias. **— The Guardian, Sep12 2018, "Breitbart leaks video of Google executives' candid reaction to Trump victory" (https://www.theguardian.com/technology/2018/sep/12/breitbart-video-google-trump) This article was written in an attempt to do damage control for the Breitbart article cited at the beginning of this section. As is typical, it pretends that censorship was not happening and there was no bias against conservatives, in spite of this plainly being the case to any reasonable observer.**

Leftists also dishonestly claimed that, even if censorship was occurring, it was not a violation of the 1st amendment because, as a "private company" they could run their business "however they wanted." In addition to having been contradicted by the courts themselves in recent years, this is also contradicted by the Leftist's own stated beliefs. In no other case have Leftists ever asserted that "private companies can run their business however they want," instead favoring ever-increasing regulations on private companies. Additionally, Leftists do not believe in "freedom of association." If private companies are free to do business or not do business with whomever they want, then they could choose not to do business with black people or to not bake a cake for gay people. The first of these has been made illegal due to the efforts of Leftists via the Civil Rights movement, while the latter is contrary to the positions of the Left and also illegal in some jurisdictions due to Leftist activism.

The Censorship Era seems have ended in 2022. By this time, alt tech platforms such as Rumble had become popular enough to circumvent tech censorship. In the same year, Elon Musk bought Twitter, promising to turn it into a "free speech" platform and loosening censorship somewhat.

Chapter 5 - 2019 & 2020: Groyper Wars, Covid, BLM, 2020, J6

The Groyper Wars

In the fall of 2019, Kirk launched a college speaking tour with Turning Point USA titled "Culture War", featuring himself alongside such guests as Senator Rand Paul, Donald Trump Jr., Kimberly Guilfoyle, Lara Trump, and Congressman Dan Crenshaw.

In retaliation for the firing of St. Clair and the Politicon incident, Fuentes subsequently began organizing a social media campaign asking his followers to go to Kirk's events and ask provocative and controversial leading questions regarding his stances on immigration, Israel, and LGBT rights during the question-and-answer sessions, for the purpose of exposing Kirk as a "fake conservative".

At a Culture War event hosted by Ohio State University on October 29, eleven out of fourteen questions during the Q&A section were asked by Groypers. Groypers asked questions including, "Can you prove that our white European ideals will be maintained if the country is no longer made up of white European descendants?", and directed the question "How does anal sex help us win the culture war?" at Kirk's co-host Rob Smith, a gay black veteran of the Iraq War.

*Fuentes' social media campaign against Kirk became known as the "Groyper Wars". Kirk, Smith, and others at Turning Point USA, including Benny Johnson, began labeling the questioners as white supremacists and anti-Semites. -- **Wikipedia (https://en.wikipedia.org/wiki/Groypers)***

In 2019, during Charlie Kirk's "Culture War" tour's Q&A segment, two anonymous conservatives criticized Charlie Kirk about recent comments that he had made regarding his support for increasing immigration – saying he "wanted to staple green cards to the back of diplomas" – and for comments he had made during a speech in Israel where he said that America was simply "a placeholder for timeless ideas," but that Israel was not.

I reject this idea of dual loyalty. I have loyalty to ideas, and of course I love the Grand Canyon, I love the Rocky Mountains, and I love Boston, I love Chicago, but if all that disappeared and all I had was ideas and we are on an island -- that's America. But that's what people have to realize. That America is just a placeholder for timeless ideas, and if you fall too in love with you know oh the specific place, and all this, that's not what it is. Israel being the exception because there is a holy connection to this land.

– Charlie Kirk (https://www.youtube.com/watch?v=CZImGA8MvOw)

After the video of the Q&A went viral online, Nick Fuentes instructed his followers to continue going to Charlie Kirk events and pressing him on issues on which they felt he was not sufficiently conservative, such as his support for LGBT issues, support for increasing immigration (so long as it was legal), "civic nationalist" ideas, and unconditional support for Israel.

Turning Point USA was at the time one of the largest conservative organizations on high school, college, and university campuses. Earlier in 2019, they had fired TPUSA brand ambassador Ashley St. Clair, after she had appeared in a photo with Fuentes.

"TPUSA is a large national organization that touches hundreds of thousands of people all across the nation," the spokesperson said in a statement. "Ashley is no longer one of our thousands of volunteer activists and ambassadors. Charlie [Kirk] and TPUSA have repeatedly and publicly denounced white nationalism as abhorrent and un-American and will continue to do so."

...

[Ashley St. Clair said:] "I did attend a diverse dinner I was invited to in which I got to give voice to some of the anger I've had in the past," she said. "Some of the people pictured had been vicious to me online and I'm not above confronting people or forgiving people. I'm a strong Jewish woman and don't need to be told where I can and cannot go, I'm sick of guilt-by-association Twitter journalism that leaves out all context and meaning. The focus of the dinner was civility. I'm not accountable for anything anyone else posts online and I myself have been a victim of bigoted trolling. Attending a dinner for a civil conversation is not an endorsement for anybody's views."

– Washington Examiner, Oct 1 2019, "Turning Point USA 'brand ambassador' dumped after photo with white nationalists and anti-Semites surfaces"
(https://www.washingtonexaminer.com/news/turning-point-usa-brand-ambassador-dumped-after-photo-with-white-nationalists-and-anti-semites)

Nick's fans followed Kirk to each and every one of his events, as well as confronting other figures considered "neocons," "libertarians," or otherwise not conservative enough, such as Matt Walsh of the Ben Shapiro-owned *Daily Wire*, Republican Dan Crenshaw, and eventually even Donald Trump Jr.

On his daily livestream show *America First*, Fuentes would watch livestreams of the Charlie Kirk events, giving commentary after every question and instructing the Groypers on what rhetoric to use or not use, or how they should dress and present themselves. He stressed that they should "be optical." They should dress sharp, be physically attractive, speak with a clear and confident voice, avoid Internet memes such as Pepe which would allow people to disregard them as "trolls," avoid Nazi or white supremacist imagery of any kind, and wear rosaries and MAGA hats to identify them as true Christians and Trump supporters. After being banned by YouTube in the middle of the "Groyper Wars," Fuentes continued to stream, moving the show to DLive.

Fuentes began to refer to those asking the questions as "Groypers," after a variant of Pepe that had become popular online at the time (https://knowyourmeme.com/photos/1623958-*groyper)(*https://knowyourme me.com/photos/1684663-*groyper*). The title was meant to identify them as members of the online Dissident Right. Eventually, the name "Groyper" would be used for fans of Nick Fuentes and America First.

On Twitter, Fuentes wrote *"Turning Point is now making a concerted effort to slander critics of their bullshit fake conservatism as 'extremist trolls.' We are America First and you will be exposed as the frauds you are."*

Nicholas J. Fuentes ✅
@NickJFuentes

Turning Point is now making a concerted effort to slander all critics of their bullshit fake conservatism as "extremist trolls." We are America First and you are being exposed for the sellout frauds you are.

Benny ✅ @bennyjohnson
There were a number of trolls who sabotaged the Q&A portion of tonight's @tpusa event.

Many of the questions were abhorrent and were not asked in good faith....

8:38 PM - 29 Oct 2019

The Groypers asked questions such as:

> *"According to the US Census Bureau population projections, in 2045, whites will account for less than 50% of the population in the United States. Given that the Democrat Party's politics do not point to the maintaining of our ideals, and given that most groups other than whites overwhelmingly vote Democrat, how can we be sure that said ideals will be maintained when millions of immigrants come in with majority Democratic support. Can you prove that our white European ideals will be maintained if the country is no longer made up of white European decedents? … If not, should we support mass legal immigration?*
>
> *…*
>
> *When Kirk responded by calling this question "racist," there were shouts from the audience, and the bad mood continued to simmer throughout the remainder of the Q&A.*
>
> **– Daily KOS, Nov 1 2019, "Alt-right trolls make life miserable for Charlie Kirk and his Turning Point USA 'Culture War' tour" (https://www.dailykos.com/stories/2019/11/1/1896408/-Alt-right-trolls-make-life-miserable-for-Charlie-Kirk-and-his-Turning-Point-USA-Culture-War-tour)**

At Ohio State University, Charlie Kirk appeared next to Rob Smith, an openly gay black man who advocated for acceptance of homosexuality. Fuentes tuned into the event on stream and provided commentary. Kirk was asked *"how does anal sex help win the culture war?"* by one of the Groypers, an Idaho-based conservative activist Dave Reilly. Charlie Kirk appeared shocked by the question, while Rob Smith was agitated and immediately began to defend himself *"Do you have the balls to ask the gay man on the stage that question?"* Dave Reilly repeated the question to Rob Smith.

Rob Smith shook his head back and forth before loudly chastising Reilly:

> **Rob Smith:** *"This is America--"*
>
> **Fuentes** (commentary): *"AMERICA'S GAY!"*

Rob Smith: *"--this is the greatest country in the world. America is great because we have Western values."*

Fuentes: *"Western values are gay values!"*

Rob Smith: *"Do you know that gays and lesbians are able to contribute to American society?"*

Fuentes: *"No, they're not. Get em out! Get em out!"*

Rob Smith: *"And let me tell you--"*

* The audience begins booing *

Fuentes: *"They're being booed! They're being booed!"*

After beginning to change the subject to his service in the military, Reilly repeated his question a third time before Smith finally gave up and said *"It's a BS question."* Charlie Kirk took over, *"Honestly, I don't care what two consenting adults do, and your hyper-focus on it seems kinda weird."* They then started to accuse Reilly of secretly being gay. (https://rumble.com/v2vfz7q-groyper-war-ohio-state-highlights.html) Note that this is virtually indistinguishable from how a Left Winger would respond to the same questions.

Benny Johnson, the organization's chief creative officer, noted the following on Twitter:

There were a number of trolls who sabotaged the Q&A portion of tonight's @tpusa event.

Many of the questions were abhorrent and were not asked in good faith.

White nationalism and anti-gay hatred have no place in our movement.

This is what the Left wants.

It's time to Wake Up

— Benny (@Benny)

Smith — a gay, black conservative who served in the Iraq War and notes in his Twitter bio that he's "proudly despised by leftists AND the alt-right!" — helped Kirk slap down a number of inappropriate questions.

There's a difference between asking genuine questions & trolling "How does Anal Sex help win the Culture War" isn't a serious question. It's homophobic & disgusting

In America, what happens between two consenting adults is their business

They're the New Westboro Baptist Kids

— Benny (@Benny)

Another questioner asked Kirk and Smith how America could maintain "white" values, and Kirk decried the premise, telling the individual, "I find that to be a racist question" and "I do not think that America should become a white ethno-state," adding he considers such a view a "fringe perspective."

– The Blaze, Oct 30 2019, "Turning Point USA blasts white nationalist, homophobic 'trolls' who 'sabotaged' event Q&A" (https://www.theblaze.com/news/turning-point-usa-blasts-white-nationalist-anti-gay-trolls-who-sabotaged-event-q-a)

At another event, a Groyper asked Kirk if he would support a policy "that benefited the United States, to the detriment of Israel," and Kirk responded by calling it a "false choice" and said that such a scenario was "impossible." Soon, virtually every single Q&A question was a Groyper, with only a few sparse non-Groyper questioners.

Charlie Kirk struggled to give acceptable answers to these questions, as he could not give an answer so extreme that it would get him in trouble with TPUSA or its donors, nor could he give an answer too "cucked," and thus appear too weak and alienate his base of conservative, Christian Trump supporters. They also could not shut down the Q&A part of the event entirely, or he would be seen as running from the questioners and being against "free speech."

He tried to deal with the Groypers in several ways. First, TPUSA stopped streaming the events. The Groypers responded by livestreaming the events from their phones. At another event, they announced that "Left Wing" and "Right Wing" questioners would have to form separate lines, allowing them to only call on the Left Wing questioners and ignore the Right Wing questioners. Groypers responded by getting in the Left Wing line, although some were moved, especially if they were seen with rosaries or looked like Groypers. Kirk even resorted to shouting over questions he said were "anti-

Semitic conspiracies," such as questions dealing with the USS Liberty (which Groypers said was an intentional attack on the United States by Israel) and even cutting questioner's mics.

At the tour's final event, Charlie Kirk unveiled a small LCD monitor that was hidden beneath a blanket next to him. He struggled to get the monitor to work at first. Finally, after successfully configuring the monitor, he aired a very old episode of *America First* in which Fuentes criticized Trump and defended Ted Cruz. However, this tactic did not work, and Kirk was heckled and booed off of campus.

At an event on the tour with Donald Trump Jr., they announced that there would be no Q&A portion of the event. The audience erupted in boos and chants of "Q! AND! A!" resulting in Don Jr.'s girlfriend Kimberly Guilfoyle shouting back at the Groypers in a shrill voice, *"You're not making your parents proud by being rude and disruptive and discourteous!"* and accusing them of looking like *"people who engaged in online dating."* At another point Guilfoyle bragged about how *"women are better off under President Trump and this economy"* to boos from the crowd. After failing to control the irate crowd, Don Jr. and Guilfoyle were heckled off of the stage. (https://rumble.com/v2vhkr3-groyper-war-ucla-highlights.html)

At Stanford University in November, Ben Shapiro devoted An entire 45 minute speech to condemning Fuentes and the Groypers and calling them "Alt Right," but refused to mention Fuentes by name. In the speech, he read the infamous "cookie joke," a superchat donated to Fuentes that seemingly denied the holocaust by comparing it to baking cookies. Although this was a statement by a superchatter and not Fuentes himself, Fuentes had played along with and riffed on the message after receiving it. Shapiro did not offer a Q&A portion, and any audience members who appeared to be Groypers were barred from entering the speech. Fuentes covered the speech on his show and accused Shapiro of strawmanning his beliefs, and hypocritically presenting himself as a free speech warrior who will "debate anyone" while refusing to

debate Fuentes or allowing him to defend himself.
(https://rumble.com/v2yfpx6-nick-fuentes-reacts-to-ben-shapiros-stanford-speech.html)

In December, Fuentes "confronted" Ben Shapiro outside of SAS (a conservative conference) after being banned from the event. Fuentes was discussing his views with passersby when Shapiro suddenly appeared with his family. Fuentes heckled Shapiro, asking him why he refused to interact or debate with him.

> Many criticized Fuentes for "heckling" Shapiro with his family by his side. While Fuentes supporters accused Shapiro of using his family as a "human meat shield," as some dubbed it.
>
> "It's great to see you. Why did you give a 45-minute speech about me at Stanford? And you wouldn't even look at my direction," Fuentes yells at Shapiro while crossing the street.
>
> Shapiro doesn't respond to Fuentes' remarks.
>
> "That's our free speech warrior," Fuentes states.
>
> **– Daily Dot, Dec 21 2019, "Nick Fuentes trying to bicker with Ben Shapiro riles up the Internet " (https://www.dailydot.com/debug/ben-shapiro-nick-fuentes/)**

Fuentes seemed to have collaborated with Identity Europa and its leader Patrick Casey at some point during the Groyper Wars, as many members of the organization appear to have participated in the Q&A, including Patrick himself. At Ohio State, Casey grilled Kirk over the firing of Ashley St. Clair:

You do run TPUSA and TPUSA did remove its relationship with Ashley St. Clair—and all she really did was take a picture with Nick Fuentes, she was in the same room, so my question to you, Charlie, is: as someone who purports to be pro-debate, -free speech and the exchange of ideas, do you support blackballing people based on having controversial opinions or being even in the same room when a photograph is taken with someone who has controversial opinions?

– Daily KOS, Nov 1 2019, "Alt-right trolls make life miserable for Charlie Kirk and his Turning Point USA 'Culture War' tour" (https://www.dailykos.com/stories/2019/11/1/1896408/-Alt-right-trolls-make-life-miserable-for-Charlie-Kirk-and-his-Turning-Point-USA-Culture-War-tour)

Around the same time, Patrick became a "Groyper general" (an informal name for close allies of Fuentes) and began to take an active role in America First. In addition to Casey, Fuentes would gain other close allies from the Dissident Right, including Jake Lloyd, musician and "self help guru" Steve Franssen, and political commentator Scott Greer. Jaden McNeil, leader of Kansas State University's Turning Point chapter, would also defect to Fuentes. In January 2020, McNeil would start a new organization, *America First Students* at Kansas state. McNeil would become a streamer like Fuentes, and seemed poised to be Nick's successor.

The Groyper Wars would lead to Fuentes receiving his first ally in the mainstream right, Michelle Malkin. A contributor to Fox News and Newsmax, Malkin had long been a critic of the country's lax immigration policies. She had been a part of the conservative movement since 1992. An accomplished writer and speaker, she was exactly the kind of "optics" that Fuentes was looking for. Over the years she had worked for or been featured on many mainstream and prestigious publications, including *The Seattle Times, The Daily Wire, The O'Reilly Factor* and *National Review,* and was well connected. In October 2019, she joined Fuentes's attack on Charlie Kirk and defended the Groypers:

"I was flabbergasted to hear Turning Point USA founder Charlie Kirk telling students at a university campus lecture last week that 'We should staple a green card behind your diploma,'" Malkin declared. "He repeated this nonsense at Ohio State University during a 'Culture War' tour stop this week, asserting that any foreign national who graduates from any 'four-year college' should get a green card if any 'American employer' needs to fill a job."

"So much for America First," she continued, adding, "Kirk's proposal is even more extreme than Silicon Valley tech lobbyists' pet project," because the Turning Point USA founder "doesn't just want to inundate the IT job market with low-wage Chinese, Indians, Koreans, Sudanese, 'or whatever.' He wants to open the floodgates in all labor markets, whether or not there is a purported labor shortage."

Malkin went on to call out Kirk's "cluelessness about immigration policy and law," and wrote, "So American students get screwed. Social Security and Medicare get cheated. Foreign spies and jihadists get another entry point. Universities get control over immigration policy. Corporatists get cheap labor. Where's the benefit to the conservative audiences Charlie Kirk entertains on the lecture circuit?"

– Mediaite, Oct 31 2019, "Michelle Malkin Tears Into 'Slow Learner' Charlie Kirk In Scathing Article"
(https://www.mediaite.com/politics/michelle-malkin-tears-into-slow-learner-charlie-kirk-in-scathing-article/)

In a later speech at UCLA, Malkin again defended Fuentes, calling him "one of the New Right leaders." After posting a video of her speech on Twitter, she was fired by Young America's Foundation and removed as one of their speakers. (https://reason.com/2019/11/18/young-americas-foundation-michelle-malkin-nick-fuentes/)

The heckling of Donald Trump Jr. at UCLA made national news (https://politicalresearch.org/2021/01/15/america-first-inevitable) and Fuentes rose to national prominence for the first time following this event, roughly 2 years after beginning his career. He capitalized on this opportunity by starting his own political conference, AFPAC.

When the Groypers were barred from attending the annual national gatherings of TPUSA and the Conservative Political Action Conference (CPAC), they held their own suit-and-tie America First conferences outside both events, presenting themselves as a credible counter-hegemonic alternative to establishment conservatism. "The America First movement has basically taken the initiative as the central challenger to conservative inc," Fuentes gloated on the alternative social media site Telegram on March 1, 2020. "We are consolidating the dissident Right sphere behind America First against conservative inc….increasingly this is becoming a central and defining fault line."

– PoliticalResearch.Org, Jan 15 2021, "America First Is Inevitable" (https://politicalresearch.org/2021/01/15/america-first-inevitable)

The first AFPAC (America First Political Action Conference) was organized by Patrick Casey and was a relatively modest affair, featuring Casey, Greer and Malkin as its inaugural speakers. However, Fuentes planned to gradually grow the event over time until it became a rival to CPAC. When the location was leaked by Antifa, Casey panicked and instructed everyone that the event needed to be dispersed. Fuentes did not like this reaction. He wanted to create a movement that was above ground, using people's real identities, out and in the open, and one that would not retreat in the face of Antifa. Casey would not organize any of the future AFPACs.

Nick Fuentes also capitalized on his newfound notoriety by founding a non-profit, "The America First Foundation" and starting an internship program.

There would be no Groyper Wars in subsequent years, Fuentes reasoning that he did not want to be a one trick pony and following Saul Alinsky's 7th rule for radicals: *"A tactic that drags on too long becomes a drag."*

From the end of the Groyper Wars, America First would become the most important faction within the Dissident Right. In time, even the wignats would become defined, not by their political positions, but by their opposition to

Nick Fuentes. While other factions of the Dissident Right were still present in the period of 2019-2023 and may be touched on from time to time, the majority of the rest of this text will prominently feature America First and Nick Fuentes. This is because Fuentes during this period was the main driving force in synthesizing the antithesis of the Dissident Right with the liberal thesis, somewhat deliberately and self-consciously. As of 2023, the main antagonists of the Groyper Wars, including Charlie Kirk and Matt Walsh, have now adopted Fuentes's positions on all topics except for criticisms of Israel (*Author's update: as of December 2023, Charlie Kirk has also began to criticize Israel somewhat, insinuating that they had advance knowledge of the October 7 attacks by Hamas)*. They all support an immigration moratorium, are anti-LGBT, support traditional gender roles, at times are anti-feminist, and speak openly against anti-white racism and the demographic replacement of whites with non-whites.

On August 23 2023, Charlie Kirk would tweet *"Whiteness is great. Be proud of who   you are."* (**https://twitter.com/charliekirk11/status/1694386955143020768**). Dinesh D'Souza would go even further:

> *Virtually every IQ study over the past half century shows that blacks, who are the rock-solid base of the Democratic Party, have the lowest IQ of any ethnic group, one standard deviation below whites and Asian Americans.*
>
> *– Dinesh D'Souza, May 29 2023 (https://Twitter.com/DineshDSouza/status/1663216798764875779?lang=en)*

While not involved in the Groyper Wars directly, D'Souza is a prominent mainstream conservative. This comment shows just how far to the right the conservative party has moved in just four years, in no small part as a result of the influence of America First.

Clown World

I suppose now is as good a time as any to introduce another meme that will pop up from time to time in this text, "Clown World." While, according to Know Your Meme, the meme was created in 2018, and did not truly become popular until 2019, the concept predates the actual meme. Rumblings of the "Clown World" timeline began in 2016, and it is in this year that we are considered to have entered Clown World. It refers to us entering a timeline in which absurd and difficult-to-believe events started to occur, such as Donald Trump the reality TV star becoming President of the United States. In fact, Trump was not the only unbelievable event that happened that year. It was also the year of destabilizing events such as Brexit, as well as other events that were simply bizarre. Such as the 2016 clown sightings.

The 2016 clown sightings was a case of mass hysteria fuelled by reports of people disguised as evil clowns in incongruous settings, such as near forests and schools. The incidents were reported in the United States, Canada, Australia, England and subsequently in other countries and territories starting during August 2016. The sightings were first reported in Green Bay, Wisconsin, in what turned out to be a marketing stunt for a horror film. The phenomenon later spread to many other cities in the US. By mid-October 2016, clown sightings and attacks had been reported in nearly all U.S. states, 9 out of 13 provinces and territories of Canada, and 18 other countries.

...

According to The New York Times, the clown sightings resulted in at least 12 arrests across the United States and one death. In Reading, Pennsylvania, a 16-year-old boy was fatally stabbed during an incident that could have been provoked by a prowler wearing a clown mask. The charges related to the sightings included making false reports, threats, and chasing people.

...

On October 12, the Russian Embassy in London issued a warning for Russian and British citizens because of the clown scare.

On October 13, Fijian police warned people against involvement in the events.

...

*Students at Pennsylvania State University and Michigan State University were involved in mobs that searched for clowns on campus after reported sightings.Campgrounds floated with rumors of clown attacks. – **Wikipedia (https://en.wikipedia.org/wiki/2016_clown_sightings)***

It also refers to a world in which things are in general absurd, backwards and upside-down.

The current state of global society: women are men, men are women, the schools teach propaganda instead of classes, left is right and right is left so basically, the reverse-world in steroids. You can see this effect in any collectivist movement like Fat acceptance, these people literally tell people that morbid obesity is healthy for example.

*– **UrbanDictionary.com (https://www.urbandictionary.com/define.php?term=Clown %20World**)*

"Clown World" is also personified by a clown version of Pepe the Frog, known as Honkler or pepoclown: a small, short Pepe wearing clown makeup and a rainbow wig. (https://knowyourmeme.com/photos/1459543-clown-pepe-honk-honk-clown-world)

As with other memes, there was an attempt to appropriate this meme as a racist symbol (like the OK hand sign) using the logic that HH could mean Honk Honk or Heil Hitler. This resulted in the meme being banned on several platforms.

> On June 8th, 2019, Twitter user @GarbHum posted a screenshot of a Facebook notifcation that a post using the word "Honk" had been removed for not following the site's "Community Standards"
>
> ...
>
> On July 1st, 2019, the /r/honkler subReddit was banned for violating the platform's "content policy against violent content". Shortly after, Reddit RibosomalTransferRNA submitted a post titled "/r/honkler has been banned" to the /r/AgainstHateSubReddits community, where it garnered more than 2,100 points (92% upvoted) and 230 comments within 48 hours. The following day, The Daily Dot published an article titled "Alt-right subReddit that used clowns to promote white nationalism has been banned."
>
> **– Know Your Meme (https://knowyourmeme.com/memes/clown-pepe-honk-honk-clown-world)**

2020 in Hindsight

In 2016, I predicted that Trump would be assimilated into the Republican party and become essentially just another Republican, albeit an unorthodox one. In some ways, this prediction would be fulfilled, but in other ways it would not. 2020 would be a year in which both sides of Trump — Trump the Republican, and Trump the revolutionary — would be on full display. 2020 would be the next year in which history would re-assert its presence. It was one of the most pivotal years in American and world history, even more so than 2016. It was in 2020 that any hope of returning to the pre-2016 world was irreversibly shattered and Clown World was firmly established as the new normal. Censorship, political division, the erosion of American constitutional rights, racial conflict, and the destabilizing force of Donald Trump, would all boil over in just one year.

Covid Crashes the Party

It was New Years Eve 2019. I was at a coffee shop, watching the ball drop on TV, while scrolling through Twitter and Facebook. On Facebook, normies were posting about "putting the turmoil of the 2010s behind us, getting a brand new start, and making the 2020s like the roaring 20s part two!"

Meanwhile, on the Internet, Mr. Metokur, the YouTuber of GamerGate fame, was making video after video about Covid's increasing spread through China, warning of a future global pandemic and growing more and more hysterical. Meanwhile on *America First*, Nick Fuentes was warning, "*one day, we may look back in hindsight and refer to these days as the pre-Covid world.*" Disturbing images from China were floating around the Internet, showing people passing out in the streets from the disease, and Chinese authorities dressed in full-body yellow hazard suits, spraying down Chinese streets with disinfectant and barricading citizens in their rooms. Rumors spread online of a disease that would attack people's brains and liquefy their lungs.

Few people remember, but in the early days before Covid, roughly between November 2019 and March 2020, it was the conspiracy theorists on the Right who feared the disease and the Left who downplayed it. For example, the Right wanted a travel ban for China, while the Left called such a proposal "racist" and Nancy Pelosi had a photoshoot in Chinatown to prove how safe it was and how there was nothing to worry about.

Then, in early March, people began to panic-hoard groceries, disinfectant items, and, infamously, toilet paper. Large entertainment events such as concerts began to slowly be canceled, one by one. By the second week of March, the lockdowns suddenly started. Everyone was terrified of the new disease. The world felt post-apocalyptic.

At first, I took the disease very seriously. Not only did I wear an N95 mask to get groceries, but also plastic gloves. Another reversal was that in the early days of the pandemic, the Left was against facemasks, with health officials at the time claiming they could not protect from Covid. Later, it was revealed that this was done only to prevent people from panic-buying the masks, so that the government could buy them and replenish their own supply. I didn't know what to think about masks, but I figured the less exposure to the outside world the better.

The grocery store had become an eerie place. It was nearly empty. The few people who were there, clad in protective gear, avoided each other as much as possible. Because of the panic buying and supply chain disruptions, the shelves became bare. It was impossible to get some items, such as beans, rice, and toilet paper. It was utterly socially taboo to pick an item up off of the shelf, and then change your mind and put it back on the shelf.

One time, I took my dog to the park and was extremely annoyed when a stranger started to pet it. I was extremely meticulous about my exposure to others. Meanwhile, the Left did a 180 and began mandating facemasks. Some boomers considered this an infringement on their rights, which I laughed at and mocked. *"Typical libertarian Boomers"* I thought. The Dissident Right at the time was talking about having the military throw anyone in jail who dared defy Covid restrictions. They also speculated about how Covid would disrupt society. What would happen when truck drivers started dying like flies, and there was no one to transport the food? What would happen when people ran out of food, and started forming gangs and going house to house and taking supplies by force?

I hoarded food and supplies, calculating that they would last for about 6 months. I also gathered all of the firearms in the house and took inventory, making sure I had plentiful ammunition and that they were all in working order. I began to run several scenarios in my mind, such as what I would need to do if I had to barricade the house, if I ran out of food, if the house became unsafe and I needed to leave, etc. I even slept with a shotgun near my bed for most of 2020.

However, as the data about Covid came in, I slowly became convinced that the Boomer libertarians had gotten one right this time. The news ran a live ticker every day, tracking the spread of the disease. This tracked both Covid cases, as well as Covid deaths. Every day, I took the two numbers and did the math. Eventually, I realized that the chance of dying from Covid was about the same as dying from the flu. This was the opposite of the information that was stated at the beginning of the pandemic, when it was claimed that it was about 100 times more deadly. Furthermore, the people dying tended to be old, sickly, or overweight. In other words, people that could also die from a normal flu. Young, healthy people like me simply were not dying.

Eventually, the Dissident Right also began to change its tune. By about April or May, Covid had become a firmly partisan issue, with the Left supporting the government's draconian Covid response, and the Right firmly opposing it.

By this time, I stopped taking any Covid precautions whatsoever. I simply did not care if I got the disease. I would follow whatever regulations were in place, such as wearing a mask, simply to avoid trouble. I did not think that wearing the mask was a big deal or a serious infringement on people's rights. I only began to oppose the masks later, when the vaccine mandates began. When this started I began to think, *"is this what the mask mandates were about? Were they boiling the frog, getting us to agree to something reasonable so that they could introduce these vaccine mandates later?"* from that point on, I militantly refused to follow any Covid guidelines, including wearing a mask. But that would not be until 2021.

Eventually, I did catch Covid in October 2021. By this time, people had developed a homegrown medical regiment they could use to avoid going to the hospital. Not only were the hospitals crowded, but they would push the vaccine on you, or kill you by putting you on a ventilator. This home regiment consisted of several vitamins and supplements, such as Quercetin and Vitamin D, and also the anti-parasite medicine Ivermectin. The medical establishment decried Ivermectin as "horse de-wormer" and told people the drug was dangerous to take and that they should get their vaccine instead. They forbid doctors from prescribing it to patients, forcing people to go to veterinary and farm supply stores to get the version of the drug made for horses. This version of the drug was identical to the human version, the only difference was the recommended doses. The human doses for Ivermectin had to be calculated by the person taking the drug. It was also possible to get the human version of Ivermectin on the black market. Although medical articles about Ivermectin from before the pandemic were buried by the Big Tech algorithms to prevent people from reading them, I managed to dig up one from the CDC published years before the pandemic. This article confirmed that Ivermectin was one of the safest drugs out there, with few side effects, and little chance of overdosing or adverse effects from mixing it with other medication. So, I reasoned that even if it did not help with Covid, it would not hurt either. I was bedridden for about a week and a half with a nasty cough, drank lots of water, and took this DIY drug regiment. Two weeks later I was back at work and my usual schedule. This proved to me that I was right about not needing to take the vaccine.

The government's response to Covid was probably planned far before it was put into action in 2020. It bears a striking resemblance to "Event 201," an event hosted by The Johns Hopkins Center for Health Security in partnership with the World Economic Forum and the Bill and Melinda Gates Foundation in 2019. "Event 201," like similar events held in the past and going back to the early 2000s, "war-gamed" the spread of a global pandemic, and how the government should respond.

Event 201 was a 3.5-hour pandemic tabletop exercise that simulated a series of dramatic, scenario-based facilitated discussions, confronting difficult, true-to-life dilemmas associated with response to a hypothetical, but scientifically plausible, pandemic. 15 global business, government, and public health leaders were players in the simulation exercise that highlighted unresolved real-world policy and economic issues that could be solved with sufficient political will, financial investment, and attention now and in the future.

The exercise consisted of pre-recorded news broadcasts, live "staff" briefings, and moderated discussions on specific topics. These issues were carefully designed in a compelling narrative that educated the participants and the audience.

– Center For Health Security (https://centerforhealthsecurity.org/our-work/tabletop-exercises/event-201-pandemic-tabletop-exercise#about)

The Event 201 pandemic exercise, conducted on October 18, 2019, vividly demonstrated a number of these important gaps in pandemic preparedness as well as some of the elements of the solutions between the public and private sectors that will be needed to fill them. The Johns Hopkins Center for Health Security, World Economic Forum, and Bill & Melinda Gates Foundation jointly propose the following:

1. *Governments, international organizations, and businesses should plan now for how essential corporate capabilities will be utilized during a large-scale pandemic.*

2. *Industry, national governments, and international organizations should work together to enhance internationally held stockpiles of medical countermeasures (MCMs) to enable rapid and equitable distribution during a severe pandemic.*

3. *Countries, international organizations, and global transportation companies should work together to maintain travel and trade during severe pandemics.*

4. *Governments should provide more resources and support for the development and surge manufacturing of vaccines, therapeutics, and diagnostics that will be needed during a severe pandemic.*

5. *Global business should recognize the economic burden of pandemics and fight for stronger preparedness.*

6. *International organizations should prioritize reducing economic impacts of epidemics and pandemics.*

7. *Governments and the private sector should assign a greater priority to developing methods to combat mis- and disinformation prior to the next pandemic response.*

Accomplishing the above goals will require collaboration among governments, international organizations and global business. If these recommendations are robustly pursued, major progress can be made to diminish the potential impact and consequences of pandemics.

We call on leaders in global business, international organizations, and national governments to launch an ambitious effort to work together to build a world better prepared for a severe pandemic.

– Center For Health Security (*https://centerforhealthsecurity.org/our-work/tabletop-exercises/event-201-pandemic-tabletop-exercise#recommendations*)

The full text of these scenarios leaked online in 2020, as did similar plans concerning the 2020 election. However, by this time Big Tech censorship was in full force. Unlike in 2016, the normie and dissident spheres of the internet were separated, creating two separate ecosystems of information.

While most of the Dissident Right, including the Groypers, were firmly against the Covid regime, this was not totally universal. Among the wignats, opinion was mixed. Several "race realist" Twitter accounts, such as Nemets, supported the Covid restrictions, and got vaccinated. Richard Spencer, who was by now an outspoken Biden supporter, also supported the government's crackdown against Covid and the vaccine. This would lead to a low point in Spencer's online popularity, and further reinforced the split between wignats and the Groypers *(Author's update: Spencer and Fuentes made amends on November 29, 2023, putting their previous differences behind them, but leading to a break in the alliance between Anglin and Fuentes)*.

The Fiery But Mostly Peaceful Protests

I don't want to give a play-by-play of the events of 2020, because that is not the focus of this text. The focus of this text is to give an account of the history of the online Dissident Right and its effects on the Trump Era.

However, here is a quick rundown of the 2020 BLM protests and riots (I will use both terms interchangeably, the former is preferred by Leftists and the mainstream mass media, and the latter the Dissident Right. In fact, both occurred).

On May 25, 2020, George Floyd was arrested for trying to spend a counterfeit twenty dollar bill. Floyd, who was high on a cocktail of drugs, including fentanyl and methamphetamine, resisted arrest. At 6 foot 4 inches tall and 223 pounds, Floyd was able to fight off three officers, including white officer Derek Chauvin, and prevent them from putting him in a police car (https://en.wikipedia.org/wiki/George_Floyd). In an effort to restrain him, two officers pinned Floyd to the ground and Derek Chauvin placed his knee on Floyd's neck for 9 minutes and 29 seconds, asphyxiating him (according to the medical examiner and official autopsy). Throughout the ordeal, Floyd would cry, insist "you got the wrong guy," plead "don't do me like that," and cry out "I can't breathe" (including before the officers had pinned him to the ground or put their knee on his neck).

If you dispute my depiction of these events, the full bodycam footage can be found on YouTube, including on the channel @PoliceActivity, "Full Bodycam Footage of George Floyd Arrest", August 10 2020 (https://www.youtube.com/watch?v=XkEGGLu_fNU) and on the alt tech video platform odysee on channel @yogisworld, (https://odysee.com/@yogisworld:a/george-floyd-death-full-bodycam-footage:e)

As the incident occurred, pedestrians surrounded the officers, berating them and filming them. One of them posted footage of the event, which they had shot with their smartphone camera. This video was only 48 seconds long (the full bodycam video of the encounter is 30 minutes and 11 seconds long) and shows only Chauvin with his knee on Floyd's neck, as he cries and pleads "I can't breathe" and calls out for his mom, with no other context.

As a result of this, a series of protests broke out in Minneapolis, eventually escalating into looting, arson, and in some cases even murders. These protests and riots then spread to every major city in the United States, and even to smaller cities and suburbs, such as Kenosha, Wisconsin. The riots went on for weeks, from roughly May 26 to June 8, according to Wikipedia (although some lasted well into July, and violent clashes between Antifa/BLM and Trump supporters such as the Proud Boys would continue for the rest of the year). Although no evidence for a racial motive in the event has ever been found, the media decided to fan the flames of racial hatred by presenting the incident in racial terms.

The killing of George Floyd was shocking. But to be surprised by it is a privilege African Americans do not have. A black person is killed by a police officer in America at the rate of more than one every other day. Floyd's death followed those of Breonna Taylor, an emergency medical technician shot at least eight times inside her Louisville, Ky., home by plain-clothes police executing a no-knock warrant, and Ahmaud Arbery, killed in a confrontation with three white men as he jogged through their neighborhood in Brunswick, Ga. Even Floyd's anguished gasps were familiar, the same words Eric Garner uttered on a Staten Island street corner in 2014: "I can't breathe." **– TIME, Jun 4 2020, "Why The Killing of George Floyd Sparked an American Uprising" (https://time.com/5847967/george-floyd-protests-trump/)**

In fact, only 18 unarmed black people were shot by police in 2020. And 26 unarmed white people were shot by police (https://www.washingtonexaminer.com/opinion/most-of-the-people-killed-by-police-are-white).

The riots also occurred as Covid restrictions, such as social distancing, were still in full force. While protests against Covid restrictions and Trump campaign rallies were reported in the media as "superspreader events" (https://www.newyorker.com/news/letter-from-trumps-washington/donald-trumps-2020-superspreader-campaign-a-diary) the same could not be said of these state-sanctioned BLM demonstrations.

There has been a lot of concern on how the protests over the past several days may produce a wave of coronavirus cases. This discussion is often framed as though the pandemic and protests in support of black lives are wholly separate issues, and tackling one requires neglecting the other. But some public health experts are pushing people to understand the deep connection between the two.

...

Facing a slew of media requests asking about how protests might be a risk for COVID-19 transmission, a group of infectious disease experts at the University of Washington, with input from other colleagues, drafted a collective response. In an open letter published Sunday, they write that "protests against systemic racism, which fosters the disproportionate burden of COVID-19 on Black communities and also perpetuates police violence, must be supported."

...

Protests address "the paramount public health problem of pervasive racism," the letter notes.

...

By Tuesday afternoon, more than 1,000 epidemiologists, doctors, social workers, medical students, and other health experts had signed the letter. The creators had to close a Google Sheet with signatures to the public after alt-right messages popped up, but they plan to publish a final list soon, says Rachel Bender Ignacio, an infectious disease specialist and one of the letter's creators. The hopes for the letter are twofold. The first goal is to help public health workers formulate anti-racist responses to media questions about the health implications. The second is to generate press to address a general public that may be concerned about protests spreading the virus.

– Slate, Jun 2 2020, "Public Health Experts Say the Pandemic Is Exactly Why Protests Must Continue" (https://slate.com/technology/2020/06/protests-coronavirus-pandemic-public-health-racism.html)

The media also downplayed the violence of the riots, even as it egged them on. Calling them "mostly peaceful protests," and even (as on the now-infamous CNN chyron) "fiery but mostly peaceful" (https://thehill.com/homenews/media/513902-cnn-ridiculed-for-fiery-but-mostly-peaceful-caption-with-video-of-burning/). However, the fact is that the 2020 BLM riots were the most violent riots in American history.

*Arson, vandalism, and looting that occurred between May 26 and June 8 caused approximately $1–2 billion in insured damages nationally, the highest recorded damage from civil disorder in U.S. history, and surpassing the record set during the 1992 Los Angeles riots. – **Wikipedia (https://en.wikipedia.org/wiki/George_Floyd_protests)***

They also resulted in at least 25 deaths (https://www.theguardian.com/world/2020/oct/31/americans-killed-protests-political-unrest-acled).

Meanwhile, the protests were livestreamed 24/7 on the ground by the people actually there, such as @UnicornRiot and others. These livestreams were posted on Twitter, YouTube, DLive, and others. On DLive, channels such as Ethan Ralph's *The Killstream* ran 24/7 protest coverage, circumventing the mass media and allowing people who had the time to sit around watching livestreams all day an unfiltered look into the events. These painted a very different story from the mainstream mass media, including rioters burning down and looting fast food restaurants, police precincts, apartment complexes, car parks, shopping malls, banks, department stores, and basically entire city blocks. In Long Beach, where I had once resided for many years, my local grocery store was looted and put to the flame.

The protesters even took over six city blocks in downtown Seattle, barricading the streets around the area and declaring it the "Capitol Hill Autonomous Zone" or CHAZ. The borders of this area were protected by the protesters by armed guards carrying assault weapons. CHAZ was allowed to remain under the control of the protesters for around a month, from June 8 to July 1. The area began to fall under the control of what essentially amounted to a warlord, rapper "Raz Simone." Finally, after five shootings occurred within the zone, police removed the protesters.

The BLM riots in 2020 give us a great opportunity to look at the difference between how the mainstream mass media covered the event, versus how the

Internet covered the event. It also gives us ample examples on how the mainstream media tried to push a particular narrative, which the Internet could undermine.

Consider this article about the BLM protests, which was very popular at the time:

> The vast majority of Black Lives Matter protests—more than 93%—have been peaceful, according to a new report published Thursday by a nonprofit that researches political violence and protests across the world.
>
> The Armed Conflict Location & Event Data Project (ACLED) analyzed more than 7,750 Black Lives Matter demonstrations in all 50 states and Washington D.C. that took place in the wake of George Floyd's death between May 26 and August 22.
>
> Their report states that more than 2,400 locations reported peaceful protests, while fewer than 220 reported "violent demonstrations." The authors define violent demonstrations as including "acts targeting other individuals, property, businesses, other rioting groups or armed actors." Their definition includes anything from "fighting back against police" to vandalism, property destruction looting, road-blocking using barricades, burning tires or other materials. In cities where protests did turn violent—these demonstrations are "largely confined to specific blocks," the report says.
>
> **– TIME, Sep 5 2023, "93% of Black Lives Matter Protests Have Been Peaceful, New Report Finds" (https://time.com/5886348/report-peaceful-protests/)**

Taken at face value, this may seem innocuous. But let's examine the claims more carefully, taking into account both the source and the content of the study.

First, the study comes partially from the state department itself, as well as foreign governments, and the Leftist academic establishment:

U.S.-based ACLED is funded by the State Department's Bureau of Conflict and Stabilization Operations as well as foreign governments and other organizations, including the Dutch Ministry of Foreign Affairs, the German Federal Foreign Office, the Tableau Foundation, the International Organization for Migration, and The University of Texas at Austin. It relied on data collection from the U.S. Crisis Monitor—a joint project led by ACLED and Princeton University's Bridging Divides Initiative—that tracks and publishes real-time data on political violence and demonstrations in the U.S in order to "establish an evidence base from which to identify risks, hotspots and available resources to empower local communities in times of crisis."

– TIME, Sep 5 2023, "93% of Black Lives Matter Protests Have Been Peaceful, New Report Finds" (https://time.com/5886348/report-peaceful-protests/)

The study also seems to sympathize with the protesters, and repeats debunked narratives about other police shootings such as Breonna Taylor (which were contradicted by the facts of the official legal case), using only the media as its source.

While Floyd's killing ignited the demonstrations, the protest movement has also organized around other victims of police violence and racism across the country. In August 2019, police officers confronted Elijah McClain while he was walking home from a convenience store in Aurora, Colorado. McClain died after authorities reportedly tackled him, put him in a carotid hold, and had first responders inject him with ketamine (The Cut, 11 August 2020). At the start of 2020, Ahmaud Arbery was shot and killed by a former police officer and his son while out jogging in south Georgia (New York Times, 24 June 2020). The assailants claim they suspected him of breaking into nearby homes. In Louisville, Kentucky, police raided the wrong home3 while attempting to serve a warrant and exchanged gunfire with one of the occupants; his partner, Breonna Taylor, a 26-year-old paramedic who was sleeping at the time,4 was shot and killed by the officers (New York Times, 1 September 2020).

*Demonstrations over Floyd's killing have also called for justice in these cases and other past incidents that remain unresolved. In many local communities, protests marking Floyd's death have doubled as acts of remembrance for people like Michael Brown, Eric Garner, Freddie Gray, and Trayvon Martin — whose killing in 2012 originally sparked the BLM movement (CNN, 26 February 2017). Even amid the current round of demonstrations, new cases have been added to the list, from Rayshard Brooks, an unarmed Black man killed by police in Atlanta, Georgia (CNN, 15 June 2020; New York Times, 22 June 2020), to Jacob Blake, an unarmed Black man shot seven times by police in Kenosha, Wisconsin (CBS News, 26 August 2020).– **ACLED, Sep 3 2020, "Demonstrations and Political Violence in America: New Data for Summer 2020" (https://acleddata.com/2020/09/03/demonstrations-political-violence-in-america-new-data-for-summer-2020/)**

The report even defends the violent demonstrators, implying that they only became violent because of "white supremacist" agent provocateurs. Once again, they use only mainstream media reports to support these claims. It seems that they are not content simply to make excuses for violent black demonstrators, but they must also push the narrative that any wrongdoing in the world is the fault of white people.

Despite the media focus on looting and vandalism, however, there is little evidence to suggest that demonstrators have engaged in widespread violence. In some cases where demonstrations did turn violent, there are reports of agents provocateurs — or infiltrators — instigating the violence.

During a demonstration on 27 May in Minneapolis, for example, a man with an umbrella — dubbed the 'umbrella man' by the media and later identified as a member of the Hells Angels linked to the Aryan Cowboys, a white supremacist prison and street gang — was seen smashing store windows (Forbes, 30 May 2020; KSTP, 28 July 2020). It was one of the first reports of destructive activity that day, and it "created an atmosphere of hostility and tension" that helped spark an outbreak of looting following initially peaceful protests, according to police investigators, who believe the man "wanted to sow discord and racial unrest" (New York Times, 28 July 2020).

> *In another example on 29 May in Detroit, a number of non-residents reportedly traveled to the city to engage in violent behavior during a demonstration, leading to multiple arrests (MLive, 2 June 2020).*– **ACLED, Sep 3 2020, "Demonstrations and Political Violence in America: New Data for Summer 2020" (https://acleddata.com/2020/09/03/demonstrations-political-violence-in-america-new-data-for-summer-2020/)**

However, simply because it comes from an official government source with a clear agenda to push, this does not mean that we should simply disregard it out of hand. We should also examine the argument being made. There are two misleading parts of the content of the article's argument. First, the data can be manipulated to show us any percentage desired. Secondly, the entire premise is ludicrous to begin with.

The data can be manipulated simply by manipulating how many demonstrations are tracked. If the number of "violent demonstrations" is constant, then the broader the definition of "demonstration" and the more demonstrations we have in the denominator, the lower percentage of "violent" demonstrations. Likewise, the more narrowly we define what counts as a demonstration, the fewer demonstrations we have in the denominator, and the higher percentage of them will be violent. A narrow definition might only count official demonstrations that have a paper trail of some kind (such as demonstrations organized by official organizations) while excluding smaller, informal demonstrations that have no official documentation. A broad definition might count all demonstrations, both formal and informal. In the latter case, presumably we would also need a way to confirm that the informal demonstration did in fact occur in order to track it accurately, otherwise the data is even more spurious.

The ACLED has written a lengthy and at times opaque article about its data collections, saying they "review over 2,800 sources" but only listing a few of them buried deep in the article, and detailing various methods of how they weigh these sources in order to filter out "fake news" (allowing another possible opening for manipulation). They also seem to source much of their data, again, from the mainstream media (which then reports on the findings of this "report." A circular, incestuous relationship. This in itself should be a red flag). However, after a lot of digging, I managed to track down this bit of information:

> *ACLED codes all physical congregations of three or more people (single-person demonstrations are not coded) as a demonstration when they are directed against a political entity, government institution, policy, group or individual, tradition or event, businesses, or other private institutions.*
>
> *This includes demonstrations affiliated with an organization (e.g. NAACP), a movement (e.g. Black Lives Matter), or a political party (e.g. Republicans), as well as those affiliated with identity groups (e.g. LGBTQ+, women, Native Americans). Whenever such salient identities exist, they will be coded as an 'Associated Actor' to the respective primary actor (for more on coding decisions, see the ACLED Codebook). In addition, ACLED also codes demonstrations around a certain topic, even if not associated with a specific identity group or organization (e.g. against climate change, anti-vaxxers, COVID-19 restrictions, etc.).*
>
> *– ACLED, "FAQs: ACLED United States Coverage"*
> *(https://acleddata.com/acleddatanew/wp-content/uploads/dlm_uploa ds/2023/03/ACLED_US-Coverage-FAQs-March-2023.pdf)*

This seems to indicate that they used a broad definition of "demonstration," including informal demonstrations with as few as three people present. This is exactly what you would expect them to do if they wanted to push the narrative of the "peaceful protest" by raising the number of total demonstrations in the denominator as much as possible.

Funny how this is what you always seem to find. Intentional manipulation by a collaboration (one might say a conspiracy) between media, NGOs, and academia in order to push a particular narrative, that coincidentally always happen to be a Leftist and anti-white narrative. Realizing that this is what is going on in nearly every case is the true meaning of what the "redpill" actually is.

Of course, the entire premise of the article is ridiculous to begin with. It is utterly inconsequential what percentage of the demonstrators were violent. It does not matter how many buildings were *not* burned down by violent protesters. That would be like defending a murderer by saying he did *not* murder 99% of people. So it is actually totally unnecessary to dive into the numbers. What is more interesting is watching the collaboration between these different spheres of the establishment that led to this report and article.

Meanwhile, on *The Killstream* and other livestreams, viewers watched with their own eyes (unfiltered by various journalists, the state department, and NGOs) what can only be described as anarchy unfold for weeks on end:

At cost of $350 million, approximately 1,300 properties in Minneapolis were damaged by the civil unrest, of which nearly 100 were entirely destroyed. Saint Paul suffered damages that totaled $82 million and affected 330 buildings, including 37 properties that were heavily damaged or destroyed, with most destruction along the University Avenue business corridor.

...

Looting and property destruction were widespread in Minneapolis overnight from May 27 to May 28, with the heaviest destruction occurring in the vicinity of the third precinct police station near Minnehaha Avenue and East Lake Street. Looting, which first began at a Target store in the Minnehaha Center shopping district, spread to a nearby Cub Foods grocery store, and then to several liquor stores, pharmacies, and other businesses across the city. The fire at the AutoZone store that was damaged earlier in the evening led to a series of other acts of arson. Among the losses to fire was Midtown Corner, an under-construction, $30 million redevelopment project for 189 units of affordable housing, which was destroyed by fire. Across the street from the apartment building, the manufacturing facility for 7-Sigma, a local high-tech company, also suffered extensive fire damage and part of the factory building collapsed. The response from firefighters in the area was delayed as crews required police escorts for protection from rioters.The Minneapolis fire department responded to approximately 30 fires overnight.

...

Multiple large, mobile crowds and chaos were reported across the city by nightfall. A crowd of 1,500 protesters were marching through a downtown shopping district in Minneapolis where there were 400 state troopers present. The tension escalated when another large crowd advanced on the city's first police precinct station near Hennepin Avenue and 5th Street. A Minneapolis police officer that drove near the crowd rolled down her window and indiscriminately fired Mace at protesters, bystanders, and journalists; the incident was caught on a viral video. Later, demonstrators downtown shot off fireworks and stood off against a line of Minneapolis police officers who fired tear gas.

protesters marched on the Interstate 35W highway. Smaller crowds gathered elsewhere. "We were defending an entire city with 600 officers against thousands and thousands of protesters," Frey later said of the events.

...

*As the intensity of demonstrations increased the night of May 28, dozens of businesses were looted and set on fire on East Lake Street in Minneapolis near the city's third police precinct station. Looters broke into the Minnehaha Lake Wine & Spirits liquor store across the street from the police station, passed out bottles to the crowd, and then set the store on fire. Looters broke into the nearby Max It Pawn store on East Lake Street. Montez T. Lee Jr. of Rochester, Minnesota, poured liquid accelerant around the shop and lit it on fire. Bystanders discovered that a person— later revealed as Oscar Lee Stewart Jr. of Burnsville, Minnesota —was trapped inside the building, but were unable to help guide him out after frantically removing some plywood from windows and shining flashlights inside. Fire crews that arrived later found the building too unstable for a rescue operation into the structure. Stewart became the second person to die during the riots as he succumbed to inhalation and burn injuries. His remains were left in a pile of rubble and were not recovered until nearly two months later. – **Wikipedia**
(**https://en.wikipedia.org/wiki/George_Floyd_protests_in_Minneapolis%E2%80%93Saint_Paul**)*

Stuck in my house during lockdown with little else to do, I would watch multiple streams on multiple monitors of my computer. In addition to the raw carnage of looting, arson, and the occasional murder, there were other scenes from the riot that were simply bizarre (although some turned out later to be fake). These included: protesters breaking into the zoo and releasing animals, including a hippo (this was fake), protesters hijacking a bulldozer (this was fake), protesters attacking firetrucks as they attempted to respond to the fires (real), protesters with chainsaws (https://fukkot.com/riots/americas-weirdest-riot-videos/2020:05:28-03:03:00-Theres-a-dude-with-a-fuckin-chainsaw-in-Minneapolis.mp4), an old man emerging from a pickup truck with a bow and arrow and pointing it at the protesters who then form a mob around the man and attack him (https://fukkot.com/riots/americas-weirdest-riot-videos/2020:05:31-00:56:18-Salt-Lake-City-riots.mp4), a naked man fighting protesters (https://fukkot.com/riots/americas-weirdest-riot-videos/2020:06:03-04:26:38-Location-unknown.mp4), an old man attacking protesters with a strange weapon that looks like Wolverine's claws (https://fukkot.com/riots/americas-weirdest-riot-videos/2020:06:03-20:09:02-Wolverine-trumps-chainsaw-right%3f.mp4), protesters stealing a delivery truck from a parking lot (https://fukkot.com/riots/all/2020:05:28-22:17:19-They-just-stole-a-truck-from-furniture-barn-in-St-Paul.mp4), and appearances by Spiderman and the Joker (https://www.polygon.com/comics/2020/6/4/21280274/spider-man-punisher-joker-batman-black-lives-matter-protests)

An archive of livestream footage can be found at https://fukkot.com/riots/ as of 2023.

Throughout the riots, the Dissident Right was extremely adamant that Trump must call in the military to crush the riots with force.

While Trump threatened to do so on multiple occasions, this never came to fruition. It was later revealed that Trump wanted to act, but was sabotaged by his subordinates.

Former Defense Secretary Mark Esper said there would've been active-duty troops with "rifles and bayonets" on American cities' streets amid 2020 protests over police brutality had he and chairman of the Joint Chiefs of Staff Mark Milley not challenged former President Donald Trump, per ABC News correspondent Jonathan Karl's new book.

...

Trump threatened to deploy the military during the height of nationwide anti-racism protests following the May 2020 police killing of George Floyd in Minneapolis. In some places, there was looting, rioting, and violence in connection to the demonstrations.

...

On June 3, Esper took his opposition to Trump invoking the Insurrection Act a step further by declaring it publicly.

It was seen as a direct contradiction of the president.

...

Trump was livid with Esper for expressing opposition to the Insurrection Act, Karl wrote, and lambasted his defense secretary during a White House meeting that also included Milley.

Trump told Esper that the president alone had the power to invoke the Insurrection Act. Pushing back, Esper told Trump that he'd simply declared he was opposed to invoking the law and hadn't explicitly defied the president.

Esper was sending a "clear but unstated" message that he would resign rather than carry out that order, according to Karl.

*– **Business Insider, Nov 15 2021, "Esper said he and Milley stopped Trump from sending soldiers with 'rifles and bayonets' into US cities amid George Floyd protests: book"** (https://www.businessinsider.com/trump-george-floyd-protests-wanted-to-deploy-troops-rifles-bayonets-2021-11)*

However, his failure to act made Trump appear weak to the online Right that had once fought in the Great Meme War on his behalf. Wignats considered Trump simply another pawn for Israel, no better than George W Bush. Amnats reluctantly voted for him in 2020, feeling that he had been assimilated into the GOP but was better than the alternative, and praising recent staffing changes under John McEntee and the beginning of construction of the border wall.

However, this attitude would change during 2020, with the stolen election. While the increasingly irrelevant wignats played little part in Stop the Steal, considering it just another "retard rally" like Charlottesville, Nick Fuentes would call his Groypers to arms in service to the rightfully elected President.

The Election Is Fortified Pt.1: The Secret History of the Shadow Campaign That Saved the 2020 Election

Beginning in early 2020, conservatives such as Donald Trump and Darren Beattie of Revolver news, continuously warned Republicans that the Democrats were planning to steal the election.

This is because the 2020 election would be held like no other election had been before in American history. Instead of voting in person, Americans, for the first time ever, would be mass mailed unsolicited ballots, which they would then drop off at completely unmonitored "drop boxes."

Instead of an election day, there would be several days in which Americans could drop their ballots off. Instead of getting the results of the election as soon as the polls closed, the ballots would slowly be counted over the course of many days. In several states, these laws would go into effect as ordered by state judges, something which is unconstitutional, as only the legislative branch is supposed to determine how elections are conducted. In Pennsylvania, when these unconstitutional election procedures were challenged in court, conservative Supreme Court Justice Amy Coney Barret recused herself from the case, resulting in a divided court.

Trump himself was among the first to cry foul play.

> *At a Sept. 23 press briefing, the president said "we're going to have to see what happens," when he was asked if he would commit to a peaceful transfer of power. "Get rid of the ballots," he said, and there would be a "very peaceful … continuation" of power.*
>
> *"The ballots are out of control," he said of mail-in ballots. "You know it. And you know who knows it better than anybody else? The Democrats know it better than anybody else." He doubled down the next day, saying mail-in ballots are "a whole big scam" when asked if he would only accept the election results if he wins.*
>
> *…*
>
> *"We want to make sure the election is honest, and I'm not sure that it can be," he told reporters on Sept. 24. "I don't know that it can be with this whole situation — unsolicited ballots. They're unsolicited; millions being sent to everybody. And we'll see."*
>
> *…*
>
> *On Sept. 10, we wrote about the president's false claim that Democrats are mailing out "80 million unsolicited ballots" so they can "harvest" votes to elect Democratic presidential nominee Joe Biden in November.*
>
> *…*
>
> *The president has made at least 14 claims in the past two weeks about "unsolicited ballots."* **– FactCheck.org, Sep 25 2020, "Trump's Repeated False Attacks on Mail-In Ballots" (https://www.factcheck.org/2020/09/trumps-repeated- false-attacks-on-mail-in-ballots/)**

At the same time Jon Podesta, of the famous Podesta email leaks of 2016, was war-gaming this very scenario. This was known as the "Transition Integrity Project":

> *Transition Integrity Project (TIP) was a series of political scenario exercises in the United States at the beginning of June 2020, involving over 100 current and former senior government and campaign leaders, academics, journalists, polling experts and former federal and state government officials. The exercises examined potential disruptions to the 2020 presidential election and transition. TIP is not an organization, but rather a short-term project run under the auspices of the organization Protect Democracy.*
>
> *...*
>
> *In the summer of 2020, TIP conducted a series of war-gaming exercises. The scenarios examined by TIP included:*
>
> *Game One: Ambiguous. The first game investigated a scenario in which the outcome of the election remained unclear from election night and throughout gameplay. The results from three states are in contention and ballots are destroyed in one of the states, making it unclear who should have won that state. Neither campaign is willing to concede.*
>
> *Game Two: Clear Biden Win. Biden wins both the Electoral College and the popular vote. Trump alleges fraud and takes steps to benefit himself and his family but ultimately hands the White House over to Biden.*
>
> *Game Three: Clear Trump Win. The third scenario started with an Electoral College victory for President Trump (286 to 252), but a popular vote win (52% to 47%) for former Vice President Biden. In this scenario Biden refused to concede, convinced the Democratic governors of two states that Trump won to send separate slates of electors to the Electoral College, encouraged three states to threaten secession, and convinced the House of Representatives to refuse to certify the election and declare Biden the victor.*

*Game Four: Narrow Biden Win. The final scenario explored a narrow Biden win where he leads with less than 1% of the popular vote and has a slim lead at 278 electoral votes. The Trump campaign sows chaos but Senate Republicans and the Joint Chiefs of Staff eventually signal that they accept Biden's win. Trump refuses to leave and is removed by the Secret Service. – **Wikipedia (https://en.wikipedia.org/wiki/Transition_Integrity_Project)**

Another interesting aspect of this is that it appears that the Democrats were planning to contest the election themselves under dubious pretenses (winning the popular vote) even if Trump clearly won the electoral college vote

For the past several months, a number of articles on what awaits us in November have referenced war games conducted by the Transition Integrity Project, a kind of pop-up think tank on the election. It counts over 100 academics, political operatives, government officials, and pundits as members, including former Republican National Committee Chairman Michael Steele, former Democratic National Committee Acting Chair Donna Brazile, Weekly Standard founder Bill Kristol, and Hillary Clinton's former campaign manager John Podesta.

– The New Republic, Sep 14 2020, "The Ridiculous War-Gaming of the 2020 Election" (https://newrepublic.com/article/159352/war-gaming-2020-election-trump-biden)

This article reveals the scope of the operation. Nothing about the 2020 election happened by accident. Everything was planned far in advance by the most powerful people in the world, who were very determined to remove Trump from power, and had the means to do so. This included both Democrats, Bill Kristol (the mother of all neocons), and billionaire gatekeepers of the media such as Mark Zuckerberg.

"We assess with a high degree of likelihood that November's elections will be marked by a chaotic legal and political landscape," the Transition Integrity Project, which organized the "war games," said in a report this week. "The winner may not, and we assess likely will not, be known on 'election night' as officials count mail-in ballots," the report said. "This period of uncertainty provides opportunities for an unscrupulous candidate to cast doubt on the legitimacy of the process and to set up an unprecedented assault on the outcome." – USA Today, Aug 6, 2020
"Experts held 'war games' on the Trump vs. Biden election. Their finding? Brace for a mess"
(https://www.usatoday.com/story/news/politics/elections/2020/08/06/election-2020-war-games-trump-vs-biden-race-show-risk-chaos/5526553002/)

As seen in the USA Today article, the media repeated over and over again the "Red Mirage" narrative, that Trump would appear to win on election night only for the results to change in subsequent days, seeding this idea in the minds of the American people. In September, Mark Zuckerberg said in an interview with Axios:

"What we and the other media need to start doing is preparing the american people that there is nothing illegitimate about this election taking additional days or weeks to make sure all the votes are counted."

-- Mark Zuckerberg, Sep 7 2020
(https://Twitter.com/Perpetualmaniac/status/1303097486437879808)

Darren Beattie ran articles for months, trying to warn the American people of the coming election rigging. He called what was about to come to pass in November a "color revolution" on American soil, and drew attention to the fact that many of the people involved were the same people responsible for color revolutions in other countries, such as Ukraine.

One of the most frustrating features of the Trump Administration is its tendency to hire, and even promote, personnel who are either indifferent or actively opposed to President Trump and the America First agenda he ran on in 2016.

Although the Administration remains crawling with such subversives, saboteurs, and so-called "Never Trumpers," one especially interesting case is State Department employee George Kent.

George Kent was a star witness at the Trump impeachment hearings, in which he described Trump's actions in Ukraine and the United States as "injurious to the rule of law."

...

But once one takes a look at what George Kent's job actually is at the State Department, the story becomes far more suggestive—even explosive. Kent just happens to be Deputy Assistant Secretary in the European and Eurasian Bureau. This bureau is generally known as the State Department hub for so-called "Color Revolutions," through which the State Department, together with covert agencies and a constellation of allied NGOs influence, and at times overturn, elections in foreign countries. Indeed, one former senior state department official has told Revolver News that Kent is a "color revolution expert" — a designation that has been corroborated to Revolver by two current senior State Department sources.

...

What is relevant here is not whether Yanukovych rigged the election, or whether he would have been a better ruler for Ukraine. What is relevant is that the State Department's preferred candidate did not win, and the State Department, with the help of its constellation of friendly NGOs, helped to facilitate the overthrow of Yanukovych by contesting the legitimacy of the election, organizing mass protests and acts of civil disobedience, and leveraging media contacts to ensure favorable coverage to their agenda in the Western press — all tactics eerily similar to those used against President Trump beginning the day after he was elected.

...

The similarity between the Atlanticist-backed Belarus riots and the way the organized Antifa and BLM protests operate in the United States is impossible to ignore. Indeed, many of the Color Revolution experts currently fixated on Belarus have explicitly made this comparison in relation to the United States. The Transatlantic Democracy Working Group (more about them later) is a deeply anti-Trump so-called "bipartisan" group that is essentially a Who's Who of every influential Color Revolution regime-change NGO in the World.

...

Many have noticed theoretical parallels and similarities between how US State Department and associated Atlanticist NGOs run color revolutions in foreign countries, and the sustained operations targeted against Trump in the United States. The case of George Kent — and many others to be exposed in this series — demonstrates that these similarities are not merely theoretical—they literally involve the same people! The very same people running cover revolution operations in Ukraine and Eastern Europe have been using the very same playbook to overturn 2016 and destroy the legitimacy of President Trump's election.

And guess who runs the Belarus station at the State Department? If you guessed George Kent, the "color revolution professional," you might be right.

– Revolver News, August 16 2020 "The Curious Case of George Kent: State Department's Belarus "Color Revolution" Expert and "Never Trump" Impeachment Witness" (https://revolver.news/2020/08/george-kent-never-trump-state-department/)

In our previous report on Never Trump State Department official George Kent, Revolver News drew attention to the ominous similarities between the strategies and tactics the United States government employs in so-called "Color Revolutions" and the coordinated efforts of government bureaucrats, NGOs, and the media to oust President Trump.

This follow-up report will focus specifically on how the "contested election scenario" we are hearing so much about plays into the Color Revolution framework — indeed, sowing doubt about the democratic legitimacy of the target and coupling it with calls for massive "mostly peaceful" demonstrations comes straight out of the Color Revolution playbook. And this is precisely the messaging we've seen from by those same key players in media, government, and the Democrat Party machine, most prominently from a shadowy George Soros-linked group known as the Transition Integrity Project — more about them soon.

...

It would be disturbing enough to note a coordinated effort to use these exact same strategies and tactics domestically to undermine or overthrow President Trump. The ominous nature of what we see unfolding before us only truly hits home when one realizes that the people who specialize in these Color Revolution regime change operations overseas are, literally, the very same people attempting to overthrow Trump by using the very same playbook. Given that the most famous Color Revolution was the "Orange Revolution" in the Ukraine, and that Black Lives Matter is being used as a key component of the domestic Color Revolution against Trump, we can encapsulate our thesis at Revolver with the simple remark that "Black is the New Orange."

...

We can start to get a sense that a curiously high percentage of key Trump opposition figures, especially those involved with the impeachment of the President, have or have had some kind of professional role overseeing Color Revolutions in Eastern Europe. The people most viciously and effectively targeting Trump today are regime change professionals of the Color Revolution variety, whose preferred playbook involves a combination of attacking the legitimacy and electoral integrity of their target, mobilizing mass demonstrations of "mostly peaceful protesters," and using any effort to crack down on said protests to further escalate the offensive against the target regime.

...

Now that we are armed with the Color Revolution framework, and the specific role that electoral legitimacy plays in that model, we are in a strong position to evaluate the true agenda behind the Transition Integrity Project's "War Game" scenario suggesting that Trump won't concede the election. The title of Rosa Brooks's Washington Post piece is suggestive, prompting us to wonder whether it is a prediction or a threat: "What's the Worst that Could Happen: The Election Will Likely Spark Violence and a Constitutional Crisis:"

A landslide for Joe Biden resulted in a relatively orderly transfer of power. Every other scenario we looked at involved street-level violence and political crisis.

Translation: vote for Biden, or else.

Soon, Attorney General William P. Barr opens an investigation into unsubstantiated allegations of massive vote-by-mail fraud and ties between Democratic officials and Antifa. In Michigan and Wisconsin, where Biden has won the official vote and Democratic governors have certified slates of pro-Biden electors, the Trump campaign persuades Republican-controlled legislatures to send rival pro-Trump slates to Congress for the electoral college vote.

Translation: despite severe problems with mail in voting, any effort by the Justice Department to ensure the integrity of a mass mail-in system will be interpreted in advance as part of an authoritarian coup on the part of Trump. In other words, if Trump takes any reasonable measures to prevent the Color Revolution coup against him, he will automatically be acting in an authoritarian manner justifying said Color Revolution against him. Funny how that works, isn't it?

In every exercise, both teams sought to mobilize their supporters to take to the streets. Team Biden repeatedly called for peaceful protests, while Team Trump encouraged provocateurs to incite violence, then used the resulting chaos to justify sending federalized Guard units or active-duty military personnel into American cities to "restore order,"

Translation: No matter how violent these "peaceful protests" become, any effort by Trump to establish authority will be used to confirm the pre-determined conclusion that he is an authoritarian and that extraordinary measures must be taken to remove him from office.

Social media platforms can commit to protecting the democratic process, by rapidly removing or correcting false statements spread by foreign or domestic disinformation campaigns and by ensuring that their platforms aren't used to incite or plan violence.

Translation: Social media must be fully censored leading up to the election. Facebook is already doing its part, for instance, by aggressively censoring any mention of Kyle Rittenhouse that suggests he acted in self-defense (he did).

...

Which leads us to the next passage from Rosa Brooks:

Mass mobilization is no guarantee that our democracy will survive — but if things go as badly as our exercises suggest they might, a sustained, nonviolent protest movement may be America's best and final hope.

Translation: Just in case Biden isn't able to win fair and square, they have introduced a mail-in voting system that dramatically increases the likelihood of some type of contested election scenario. If that occurs, the outcome of the election will no longer be in the realm of democratic choice, where perhaps the forces against Trump have a disadvantage. Instead, the election becomes an issue of sustained mass mobilization of demonstrators capitalizing on every opportunity for escalation, a full court press by media demonizing every effort by Trump to restore order as authoritarian, and a transmission of the electoral process to court battles which disadvantage Trump.

...

After 2016, a critical mass of ruling class factions in the national security apparatus, state bureaucracies, Big Tech, and media decided that they would never allow the American people to meddle in their own elections again. And as a result of this contempt for the will of the people, our country is closer to an existential crisis than it has been at any period since the Civil War.

In an age of mandated masks there is one metaphorical mask that is slipping—that is the mask of pretty illusions that covered up the true nature of the American power structure with phrases like "liberal democracy." As this mask slips and we confront both the face and the fist of evil, we must do everything in our power to prevent the complete transformation of this country into the brutal, soulless tyrannies our would be overlords imagine for us and our posterity. **– Revolver News, Sep 4 2020, "Transition Integrity Project: Is this Soros Linked Group Plotting a "Color Revolution" Against President Trump?" (https://revolver.news/2020/09/transition-integrity-project-is-this-soros-linked-group-plotting-a-color-revolution-against-president-trump/)**

On February 4 2021, with Trump by now firmly out of power, Leftists were so proud of how smoothly their plans to rig the 2020 election had been successfully executed that they could not help bragging about it. They did so in an article in *TIME* entitled, "The Secret History of the Shadow Campaign That Saved the 2020 Election." (https://time.com/5936036/secret-2020-election-campaign/)

A weird thing happened right after the Nov. 3 election: nothing.

...

A second odd thing happened amid Trump's attempts to reverse the result: corporate America turned on him. Hundreds of major business leaders, many of whom had backed Trump's candidacy and supported his policies, called on him to concede. To the President, something felt amiss. "It was all very, very strange," Trump said on Dec. 2. "Within days after the election, we witnessed an orchestrated effort to anoint the winner, even while many key states were still being counted."

In a way, Trump was right.

There was a conspiracy unfolding behind the scenes, one that both curtailed the protests and coordinated the resistance from CEOs. Both surprises were the result of an informal alliance between left-wing activists and business titans. The pact was formalized in a terse, little-noticed joint statement of the U.S. Chamber of Commerce and AFL-CIO published on Election Day. Both sides would come to see it as a sort of implicit bargain–inspired by the summer's massive, sometimes destructive racial-justice protests–in which the forces of labor came together with the forces of capital to keep the peace and oppose Trump's assault on democracy.

The handshake between business and labor was just one component of a vast, cross-partisan campaign to protect the election–an extraordinary shadow effort dedicated not to winning the vote but to ensuring it would be free and fair, credible and uncorrupted. For more than a year, a loosely organized coalition of operatives scrambled to shore up America's institutions as they came under simultaneous attack from a remorseless pandemic and an autocratically inclined President. Though much of this activity took place on the left, it was separate from the Biden campaign and crossed ideological lines, with crucial contributions by nonpartisan and conservative actors.

...

Their work touched every aspect of the election. They got states to change voting systems and laws and helped secure hundreds of millions in public and private funding. They fended off voter-suppression lawsuits, recruited armies of poll workers and got millions of people to vote by mail for the first time. They successfully pressured social media companies to take a harder line against disinformation and used data-driven strategies to fight viral smears. They executed national public-awareness campaigns that helped Americans understand how the vote count would unfold over days or weeks, preventing Trump's conspiracy theories and false claims of victory from getting more traction. After Election Day, they monitored every pressure point to ensure that Trump could not overturn the result. "The untold story of the election is the thousands of people of both parties who accomplished the triumph of American democracy at its very foundation," says Norm Eisen, a prominent lawyer and former Obama Administration official who recruited Republicans and Democrats to the board of the Voter Protection Program.

...

That's why the participants want the secret history of the 2020 election told, even though it sounds like a paranoid fever dream—a well-funded cabal of powerful people, ranging across industries and ideologies, working together behind the scenes to influence perceptions, change rules and laws, steer media coverage and control the flow of information. They were not rigging the election; they were fortifying it. And they believe the public needs to understand the system's fragility in order to ensure that democracy in America endures.

...

Protecting the election would require an effort of unprecedented scale. As 2020 progressed, it stretched to Congress, Silicon Valley and the nation's statehouses. It drew energy from the summer's racial-justice protests, many of whose leaders were a key part of the liberal alliance. And eventually it reached across the aisle, into the world of Trump-skeptical Republicans appalled by his attacks on democracy.

– TIME, Feb 4 2020, "The Secret History of the Shadow Campaign That Saved the 2020 Election" (https://time.com/5936036/secret-2020-election-campaign/) The paper alo reveals, among other things, that Leftists planned BLM-style violent riots if Trump was declared the winner, although obviously these were never carried out

For more information on this, I suggest reading the article in its entirety. Explaining the inner-workings of 2020 election is out of the scope of this text.

Whatever you may believe about it, at a minimum the 2020 election was entirely unprecedented. In every single US state except for Oregon and Washington, "*States and territories with at least one local, state, or federal primary election date or method of voting [was] altered as of August 5, 2020.*" (https://en.wikipedia.org/wiki/2020_United_States_presidential_election#Issues_unique_to_the_election).

Additionally, when one looks at the data from the election, the results are totally anomalous.

Biden became the first Democrat to win the presidential election in Georgia since 1992 and in Arizona since 1996, and the first candidate to win nationally without Florida since 1992 and Ohio since 1960, casting doubt on Ohio's continued status as a bellwether state.

...

Almost all counties previously considered reliable indicators of eventual success in presidential elections voted for Trump instead of Biden, meaning that they did not continue their streaks as bellwether counties.

– Wikipedia (https://en.wikipedia.org/wiki/2020_United_States_presidential_election#Statistics)

New research of mine is forthcoming in the peer-reviewed economics journal Public Choice, and it finds evidence of around 255,000 excess votes (possibly as many as 368,000) for Joe Biden in six swing states where Donald Trump lodged accusations of fraud. Biden only carried these states – Arizona, Georgia, Michigan, Nevada, Pennsylvania, and Wisconsin – by a total of 313,253 votes. Excluding Michigan, the gap was 159,065.

...

Recounts haven't been useful in resolving fraud concerns, as they merely involve recounting the same potentially fraudulent ballots.

...

First, I compared precincts in a county with alleged fraud to adjacent, similar precincts in neighboring counties with no fraud allegations. Precincts tend to be small, homogeneous areas, and many consist of fewer than a thousand registered voters. When comparing President Trump's absentee ballot vote shares among these adjacent precincts, I accounted for differences in Trump's in-person vote share and in registered voters' demographics in both precincts.

While precincts count in-person votes, central county offices are responsible for counting absentee or mail-in ballots. A county with systemic fraud may count absentee or mail-in ballots differently from a neighboring county. We can try to detect this fraud by comparing the results in bordering precincts that happen to fall on opposite sides of a county line. These precincts will tend to be virtually identical to each other – voters may simply be on the other side of the street from their precinct neighbors.

In 2016, there was no unexplained gap in absentee ballot counts. But 2020 was a different story. Just in Fulton County, Georgia, my test yielded an unexplained 17,000 votes – 32% more than Biden's margin over Trump in the entire state.

With the focus on winning the state, there is no apparent reason why Democrats would get out the absentee ballot vote more in one precinct than in a neighboring precinct with similar political and demographic characteristics.

...

*Finally, artificially large voter turnouts can also be a sign of vote fraud. This fraud could come in the form of filling out absentee ballots for people who didn't vote, voting by ineligible people, or bribing people for their votes. – **Real Clear Politics, Mar 28 2022, "New Peer-Reviewed Research Finds Evidence of 2020 Voter Fraud"** (https://www.realclearpolitics.com/articles/2022/03/28/new_peer-reviewed_research_finds_evidence_of_2020_voter_fraud_147378.html)*

As the Trump campaign seeks to overturn results in key states alleging various types of electoral fraud as covered in my last post, today I will focus exclusively on statistical anomalies in the 2020 Presidential race that at the very least raise questions and likely point to targeted election fraud.

...

House of Representative results anomaly. *The party whose candidate wins a Presidential election normally increases its representation in the House of Representatives thanks to the campaign momentum of the winning candidate at the top of the ticket. I've analysed the net House seat gains in each Presidential election since 1964 and the party winning the Presidency gains on average of net 16 House seats. Biden appears at this stage to be the 2020 winner however the Democrats are on track to lose a net of 12 House seats. This is a swing of -28 seats from the norm which is a huge statistical anomaly because normally a winning Presidential candidate has down ballot coattails that benefit House candidates for their party.*

...

Senate results anomaly. *Anomalies even extend to the Senate where voting swings are less pronounced than the House due to the 6 year term and only 33% of Senate seats being up for re-election in a given Presidential election. Because so many Senate races involve incumbents who fundraise and campaign aggressively in addition to their party's candidate at the top of the ticket, on average the number of votes cast for a Senate candidate of a party is more than the votes cast for the winning Presidential candidate of the same party.*

I have analysed the Senate voting patterns for 17 swing states since 1964 concentrating on the Senate races in states where the candidate for Senate is in the same party as the WINNING candidate for President. The numbers of races caught in this analysis ranges between 6 and 9 races per each Presidential election. The average vote differential between the Senate candidate and the winning Presidential candidate of the same party is 4.4% more votes for the Senate candidate over the Presidential candidate.

The 2020 election bucks this trend with votes for Biden in the swing states exceeding his own party's senate candidates votes by on average 2.5% (provisional results only of course). This is a statistically significant 7% swing which may not sound much but given Biden holds leads of 1% or less in four states (AZ, GA, WI, and PA), this differential is consequential.

...

***Thousands of precincts all reporting significant over vote in Michigan.** Russell Ramsland of Allied Security Group, LLC of Dallas, TX swore an affidavit concerning a detailed audit his company did on voting machines in Texas in 2018. He wrote in detail of the many serious security inadequacies of the software and then examined the 2020 Presidential vote count in a number of counties in Michigan. He reported that over 3,000 precincts in the state of Michigan reported a vote count between 80 and 350% of registered voters. He lists a number of precincts in his report and in some cases a massive over vote. The vast majority of the precincts on the list were on or about 100%.*

...

Biden underperforms Obama in 80% of Wisconsin counties but hugely overperforms in just 5 counties.

...

***Wayne County, Michigan anomaly.** On Tuesday attempts were made to certify the vote in Democrat heavy Wayne County in which Detroit Michigan sits. Initially the decision was deadlocked 2 -2 but after various online attacks, doxxing and threats on a Zoom call the two Republicans on the County Elections Board caved and certified. They have since reversed their decision and filed affidavits alleged intimidation and bullying tactics.*

One of the Democrats on the Board in his rant on Twitter to heavy his colleagues, uttered some inadvertent but important truths that shed light on yet another anomaly, that of the fact that in fully 71% of precincts in the county, the tally of absentee ballot of those who requested ballots and those who cast ballots was unable to be reconciled because the number of actual absentee ballots counted exceeded the number legally requested.

...

Anomaly of hugely lopsided Biden votes added in minutes in the dead of night.

...

Pennsylvania's mail in ballot anomaly. *Democrats will say that Trump lost Pennsylvania because the mail in ballots went so heavily to Biden. Trump won in-person voting in PA 70/30 and had a 900,000 vote lead on election night but as the night wore on and mail in ballots were counted, his lead was whittled away and over the next week, he ended up being 40,000 votes behind.*

The trouble is that when you look at the margin that Biden beat Trump in the mail in ballots broken down by each county, the margin at which Biden won was at or around 40% in each county. That defies logic in that Biden would be expected to lead Trump strongly in the Democrat stronghold counties and lead less strongly or trail Trump in the Republican stronghold counties, much as was the pattern with the in-person voting on election day.

This result is statistically impossible and has never been replicated anywhere.

...

Mail in ballot rejection rates in 2020 defy historical norms.

Mail in ballots have been a feature of the US political landscape in various states for a number of election cycles. For obvious reasons they are subject to some rejection as voters fail to validate the ballot with a signature on the envelope or the signature submitted does not reflect the signature held on file at the time of registration.

In 2016, mail in ballot rejection rates were around on average 1% and in some states as high as 6%. In Georgia they were over 6% in 2016 and yet an unbelievably small 0.2% in 2020.

During the 2020 primary season, being the first voting to take place after some states switched to the mass mailing of ballots to ALL voters on the roll as opposed to posting only to voters who specifically requested a mail in ballot.

In New York state during their primary in June this year, a whopping 20% of mail in ballots were rejected primarily because of the confusion and errors in sending ballots to not fully accurate voter rolls. Thus, it came as a big surprise to observers to see the rejection rate of mail in ballots in the swing states that Trump appears to have lost to have minute rejection rates of 0.3%. This flies in the face of the statistical experience of prior Presidential elections and the chaos seen only months ago with mass mail in ballots being sent during the spring/summer primary elections.

A partial explanation is that the cure rate of flawed ballots is higher but that is because state and county courts have arbitrarily expanded the time allowed to cure defective mail in ballots from the usual statutory 3 days to as long as 8 additional days without any amendment of the relevant statutes by state legislatures who alone are tasked in the US Constitution with the job of setting election rules. This issue is the subject of some of the Trump campaign lawsuits.

– KiwiBlog, Nov 21 2020, "Statistical anomalies in the 2020 Presidential Election"(https://www.kiwiblog.co.nz/2020/11/statistical_anomalies_i n_the_2020_presidential_election.html). This source is admittedly obscure. If you don't like it, that's ok, it is not the only source for these anomalies. You can research them for them for yourself. I chose this source because it collects them all in one convenient place.

However, it is ultimately futile to rehash the 2020 election. By now, people have likely already made up their own mind. In the next section, I will simply describe my own subjective experiences.

The Election Is Fortified Pt.2: Trump Wins the Election

On election night, November 3 2020, Trump had an un-surpassable lead over Joe Biden, taking Florida, Ohio, and important swing states such as Pennsylvania and Georgia.

> *"You may have gone to bed thinking this election was headed one way, and then you woke up and saw things were different, and maybe trending, increasingly, in another direction."* **– CNN, Nov 4 2020, "Map shows how election results shifted toward Biden"(https://www.YouTube.com/watch?v=hw_icilWISY)**

Somehow, CNN had read all of our minds. As usual on election night, I stayed up and watched the polls close, as slowly each state was called throughout the night, moving from east to west, one by one. Florida – Trump. Ohio – Trump. Iowa – Trump. Then suddenly, the counting stopped. I waited for hours for more states to be called, but to no avail. Still, Trump was leading in so many states by such a wide margin that his victory was assured. At 3 am in the morning, I finally decided to go to bed.

But, it was a restless night. Unable to sleep, I scrolled through Twitter, keeping an eye, half-awake, on the election coverage. Suddenly I began to see strange tweets. In Fulton county, Georgia, a water pipe had burst at a ballot processing site, causing everyone to be sent home. Then, a skeleton crew returned to the ballot processing site and continued counting votes. Surveillance footage from that night showed workers pulling suitcases full of votes out from under a table. Later it would be reported that no water pipe had burst after all. After the videos were published to Twitter, the media claimed "it was part of normal ballot processing and there was no evidence of improper ballots" and that "It's true that there was a brief period where observers were not present...however this is not a breach of protocol. Georgia law permits observers to stay in the room the whole time, but doesn't require them to be there for counting to take place." (https://apnews.com/article/fact-check-trump-indictment-fulton-suitcases-pipe-654281257169)

There were also videos of Trump-aligned poll observers being harassed, shouted down, and removed from polling locations by Biden-aligned poll workers. Videos posted by observers on Twitter showed polling locations placing poll observers too far away from the ballots to see anything, and even using pieces of cardboard to cover windows and obstruct the ballot "processing" from the public. These were later attested to, under oath, by whistleblowers during a series of state senate hearings.

Over the next few days, the "red mirage" played out exactly as the "Transition Integrity Project" had predicted months earlier. Trump was leading Biden by 675,000 votes on November 4. In the coming days, mail-in ballots would continue to be counted until the media called every important swing state for Biden. As soon as Biden had a sufficient lead, suddenly there were no more ballots to count.

> *Democratic nominee Joe Biden is gaining on President Donald Trump in the key battleground states of Georgia and Pennsylvania.*
>
> *Trump's lead in Georgia narrowed to just 463 votes, with 99% of total estimated votes counted. The state carries 16 Electoral College votes.*
>
> *With 95% of estimated votes counted in Pennsylvania, Trump leads with 18,229 votes. The state has 20 electoral votes.*
>
> *– CNBC, Nov 7 2020, "Election 2020 results: Biden chips away at Trump lead in Pennsylvania, Georgia margin razor thin"(https://www.cnbc.com/2020/11/05/election-live-results-updates-trump-biden.html)*

According to the media, this was the "most secure election in history" (https://www.vox.com/2020/11/13/21563825/2020-elections-most-secure-dhs-cisa-krebs) and there was nothing to be suspicious of whatsoever in spite of, at minimum, an unprecedented election process in 48 out of 50 states. According to this narrative, Trump was simply declaring victory because he was a "tyrant," trying to end democracy in America, and his followers were fools who took everything he (their elected representative) said as fact (instead of taking everything that their unelected media said as fact).

The Dissident Right, watching the events that they had predicted for months unfold, wanted only one thing from Trump: defy the mass media and the establishment and claim victory. Say that the election was stolen, and don't let them win without a fight. This time, he would do exactly that, delivering a victory speech on November 4.

> *"Millions and millions of people voted for us tonight. And a very sad group of people is trying to disenfranchise that group of people.*
>
> *And we won't stand for it. We will not stand for it.*
>
> *...*
>
> *We were winning everything, and all of a sudden, it was just called off.*
>
> *...*
>
> *This is a fraud on the American public.*
>
> *This is an embarrassment to our country. We were getting ready to win this election, and frankly, we did win this election"*
>
> **– President Donald J Trump, November 4, 2020**
> **(https://www.YouTube.com/watch?v=duE8tnrSmNc)**

On November 7, 2021, Biden was declared the winner of the 2020 election. Of course not by any elected representative, but by the media.

By this time "Stop the Steal" protests had broken out in every swing state in the country. I myself was present at Stop the Steal in Phoenix, where figures such as Alex Jones, Baked Alaska, and a number of Groypers were present. Charlie Kirk, in spite of living in Arizona not far from the event, inexplicably failed to make an appearance. The establishment Right, like Bill Kristol, was in on the steal, and did not send its leaders to fight for Trump. Instead, the task fell to the Dissident Right. For the first time since Charlottesville, the movement would move offline, this time led by Ali Alexander (one of the main organizers of Stop the Steal), *InfoWars*, the Proud Boys (who by now had become numerous, and acted as bodyguards against Antifa and BLM attacks), libertarian militia groups such as the 3 percenters, and other grassroots organizations such as "Women for America First" (previously a part of the "Tea Party" movement).

These leaders were supported by millions of normie Trump supporters. Due to this, the optics of these IRL events were not tarnished in the way that Charlottesville was. Fascist symbols, what few of them appeared, would be heckled away by militant Groypers, who instead chanted *"America First"* and *"Christ Is King."* Instead of being a movement of fringe Internet weirdos, it was a mainstream, mass movement mostly represented by ordinary people (although led by some dissident leaders). This is another key turning point in the evolution of the antithesis. It was the first event in which the mainstream and Dissident Right spheres began to mingle freely together, and the barriers between them dissolve. From this point on, the Dissident and mainstream Right would grow more and more into a single movement, with Trump as their leader, and it would be the anti-MAGA establishment that would become increasingly fringe. In a few years, your average conservative would sound much more like Nick Fuentes than Bill O'Reily.

After the media had selected Biden as their new leader, the Dissident Right tried to launch an information counter-insurgency against the mainstream mass media. However, since 2016, the tables had turned. Platforms like Twitter and YouTube had strict policies against challenging the results of the election, and were not shy about banning accounts. Even if you were not banned, Twitter, Facebook, Instagram, and a variety of other platforms would hide your post as "sensitive," or automatically affix a label linking to official "fact checker" articles "debunking" your claims with the establishment narrative. Therefore, most normies tended to side with the media, and only the extremely online people who knew how to dig for information on alt tech platforms like DLive could access Dissident narratives.

The perception of the movement was also not helped by Lin Wood and Sydney Powell. These attorneys acted as con men, leading high profile lawsuits challenging the election, such as "The Kraken." However, instead of attacking the main facilitator of voter fraud (the change in election laws and mass mail-in ballots) they concocted elaborate "Boomer conspiracy theories" alleging fantastical tales of Venezuela hacking voting machines. Naturally, the Left Wing media boosted these ridiculous lawsuits in order to discredit more reasonable ones, a common disinfo tactic. And just as naturally, Boomers (who absolutely suck at conspiracy theories) loved "The Kraken" and fell for the bait.

However, there were more reasonable challenges to the election. This is where Trump supporters put their faith. Leftists love to point out that all of Trump's legal challenges were dismissed by the legal system. In typical Leftist fashion, this is technically true, but intentionally ignores the greater context (a tactic known as "context denial"). Most of these legal challenges would not be thrown out on the basis of evidence presented in the case, but rather on legal technicalities such as "laches" and "lack of standing."

Trump v. Biden (Wis. Dec. 14, 2020) – In a 4-3 decision, the Wisconsin Supreme Court dismissed three of Trump's four claims under the doctrine of laches. However, it decided on the merits Trump's claim that voters wrongfully declared themselves indefinitely confined. Ultimately, the court ruled against Trump on this claim because Trump challenged the status of all voters who claimed an indefinitely confined status, rather than individual voters. Trump petitioned to the U.S. Supreme Court for writ of certiorari on Dec. 29, 2020 with a motion for expedited consideration, but the court denied his motion to expedite on January 11. – **CampaignLegal.org, "Results of Lawsuits Regarding the 2020 Elections"(https://campaignlegal.org/results-lawsuits-regarding-2020-elections). One example of a Trump election lawsuit. This article claims it was eventually decided "on the merits," not only on laches. However, here too, we see that this is based on a technicality (Trump challenged the status of voters in the wrong way).**

This culminated in *Texas v Pennsylvania.*

Filed by Texas State Attorney General Ken Paxton on December 8, 2020, under the Supreme Court's original jurisdiction, Texas v. Pennsylvania alleged that Georgia, Michigan, Pennsylvania, and Wisconsin violated the United States Constitution by changing election procedures through non-legislative means – thus violating the independent state legislature theory.

*The suit sought to temporarily withhold the certified vote count from these four states prior to the Electoral College vote on December 14. The suit was filed after about 90 lawsuits arising from disputes over the election results filed by Trump and the Republican Party had failed in numerous state and federal courts. – **Wikipedia** (**https://en.wikipedia.org/wiki/Texas_v._Pennsylvania**)*

In the days to come, *Texas v Pennsylvania* would be seen as the last hope of stopping the steal. Unlike "The Kraken," this lawsuit seemed legit. Trump himself called it "the big one." As the days went on, more and more states hitched their wagon to the suit. But the Supreme Court ultimately dismissed the case as "lacking standing."

Within one day of Texas's filing, Trump, over 100 Republican Representatives, and 18 Republican state attorneys general filed motions to support the case. Trump referred to this case as "the big one" of the election-challenging lawsuits. Attorneys general for the defendant states, joined in briefs submitted by their counterparts from twenty other states, two territories, and the District of Columbia, urged the Court to refuse the case, with Pennsylvania's brief calling it a "seditious abuse of the judicial process".

...

On December 11, in an unsigned ruling, the court ruled that Texas lacked standing and denied the suit.

The State of Texas's motion for leave to file a bill of complaint is denied for lack of standing under Article III of the Constitution. Texas has not demonstrated a judicially cognizable interest in the manner in which another State conducts its elections. All other pending motions are dismissed as moot.

Justice Alito, joined by Justice Thomas, disagreed with the ruling denying leave to file a bill of complaint, but did not otherwise find for the plaintiffs. He wrote that the Court is duty-bound to hear the case, referencing Thomas's dissent in Arizona v. California, 589 U. S. ___ (Feb. 24, 2020):

*In my view, we do not have discretion to deny the filing of a bill of complaint in a case that falls within our original jurisdiction ... I would therefore grant the motion to file the bill of complaint but would not grant other relief, and I express no view on any other issue. -- **Wikipedia (https://en.wikipedia.org/wiki/Texas_v._Pennsylvania)***

I am unaware of any of Trump's legal challenges in which the court actually examined ballots or audited the vote, which were the demands of the Stop the Steal protesters. However, given the number of cases filed, it is possible that one is out there. Whatever the case may be, the impression of Trump supporters was that they never received a fair hearing in court. They were expecting a situation similar to *Bush v Gore* in 2000.

In the eyes of Trump supporters, after years of being abused or ignored by an establishment who had nothing but contempt for them, who governed only for the 1%, who would pursue the same policies no matter whether the president was Bush or Obama, they had *finally*, against all odds, against the mass media and the establishment of both parties, elected a president who would represent them, and sent him to Washington. In return, the establishment thwarted him at every turn: with two impeachments, with spying on him during Russiagate, with denying that he had won in 2016 and blaming it on Russian interference, with harassing him with the intelligence agencies on dubious charges, and finally by launching a color revolution and rigging the election against him in 2020. And then, when they stood shoulder-to-shoulder next to their President to try to fight it, the mass media and the legal system, including their own "conservative" Supreme Court, just laughed at them.

So instead of sending Trump to Washington, now the American people themselves would go to Washington. Now the American people would knock on the doors of Congress. And then tear them down.

The Fiery But Mostly Peaceful Insurrection

As part of the greater "Stop the Steal" movement, there were three "MAGA marches," held in Washington DC. The first was the "Million MAGA March" on November 14 (which I attended), then the second "Million MAGA March" on December 12, and then the final "Million MAGA March" (also known as the "Save America March") announced by none other than President Trump himself, on January 6, 2021. The latter of these would go on to be called simply "J6."

Before heading to the Million MAGA March, in addition to my MAGA hat and Trump 2020 flag, I packed a suitcase full of pepper spray, goggles, and a hard hat. Since the BLM riots, there had been numerous and sometimes lethal street fights between Antifa/BLM and MAGA (particularly Proud Boys), so this was a real concern. As it turned out, I would not be needing them. The police erected barricades between Antifa and the MAGA March, Proud Boys were plentiful and knew how to fight, and Trump supporters outnumbered Antifa/BLM by about 1000 to 1. Trump supporters were so numerous that I would believe it if there were literally a million people at the event, although official numbers from Left Wing media estimate only thousands or tens of thousands. Meanwhile, only a few dozen Antifa were on the other side of the barricades. Whatever the exact number, the entirety of DC became MAGA country. The streets, still lined by burned and boarded-up buildings from BLM and sparsely inhabited by Covid-masked liberals, would be bursting to the seams with Trump flags and the stars and stripes. All of the planes into and out of the city were full of nothing but Trump supporters.

During the event, I ran into both Proud Boys and Groypers. The Proud Boys were very much frat-boyish in nature. They had a gym-bro, tough-guy aura about them, and were clad in the black and yellow Proud Boy colors. They were not afraid to be aggressive and get into counter-protester's faces. Although they had been called white supremacists in the media, they were much darker than than the Boomer Trump supporters around them. All of the races seemed about equally represented, with as many hispanic, Asian and black Proud Boys as white ones.

The Groypers had gathered around a raised platform, waiting for Fuentes to arrive and give a speech. Already on stage were his close allies, Patrick Casey, Jaden McNeil, Vincent James, and Steve Franssen. The Groypers I would describe as rambunctious Sunday school kids. They were fond of heckling others in the march, including a lone wignat clad in fascist regalia whom they chased away from the platform. They booed and chanted "shame" at Lady MAGA, a Trump-supporting drag queen. They chanted "Fuck Charlie Kirk" (who was once again nowhere to be found). They were not fans of "journos."

> When asked why he decided to come out to the march, one groyper told the Daily Dot, "journalists suck" before walking away. Attendees exhibited similar disdain for the media, including Fox News. **– Daily Dot, Nov 15 2020, Groypers, Proud Boys, other far-right groups rally for Trump at 'Million MAGA March' (https://www.dailydot.com/debug/million-maga-march/)**

The Groypers were covered in Pepes, America First flags and pins (which were often homemade), crucifixes, Bibles, saints, rosaries and other Catholic regalia. One of them had created homemade business cards with Nick Fuentes on them that had a link to his DLive channel and * End the Foreign Wars * End Free Trade * printed underneath it. He was distributing them to the MAGA Boomers and Proud Boys as they passed the platform. Unlike the

Proud Boys, probably about 95% of them were white males, although
Tenryo, who is black, appeared on stage next to Fuentes and his closest allies.
The overwhelming majority of Groypers were under the age of 25. They
were very courteous, genuine, and friendly to me, striking up a conversation
even though I was shy.

As darkness fell, Antifa/BLM would stalk DC, looking for small groups of
protesters to attack. Patrick Casey sent out a message on Telegram warning
people to travel in groups or hide their Trump gear and try to blend in. But
some of the Groypers, Proud Boys, and *InfoWars* fans were prowling the
streets and partaking in after-rally festivities. Back in my hotel room, I
watched them on Baked Alaska's DLive stream. In the livechat people
couldn't imagine how many people were at the rally and how animated they
were. The Boomers in particular seemed on the edge of "fedposting" at all
times (the term "fedposting" refers to making violent threats, especially
towards the government or politicians. It is generally discouraged on the
Internet, under the assumption that it might land someone in legal trouble).
Due to their no-fucks-given militant attitude, they were dubbed the
"*Boomerwaffen.*" A crowd of Trump supporters, including Baked Alaska, met
at the Washington Monument, surrounding it with 100s of people in MAGA
hats chanting "Stop the Steal" and cheering for Trump. In the livechat, people
began to comment "there's so many of us here. I bet we could take this city if
we wanted to."

I considered going back to DC in January. I felt pressured to do so since I had
been summoned directly by my President, but ultimately I decided not to. I
had already attended the Million MAGA March in November, so I felt I had
done my duty. Also, by that time it was a moot point. The steal had won. But,
of course, I had to attend the event virtually, on DLive. Most agreed that the
Stop the Steal movement was over, and Biden would be the next President.
But there were rumors of "The Pence Option," a legal theory that stated that
Pence could refuse to count some of the electoral college votes in the
disputed states. Ali Alexander, one of the main Stop the Steal organizers, also

claimed that *"three Republican members of the House as allies were planning 'something big': Gosar, Biggs and Brooks."* On the night before J6, I had been watching Baked Alaska's livestream. A typical Boomer, later identified as Ray Epps by *Revolver News*, urged people, *"tomorrow, we need to go inside the Capitol."* Baked and others would chant *"fed, fed, fed!"* at the time. But, ultimately this was considered typical *Boomerwaffen* fedposting. Nothing more was thought of it.

As I was accustomed to doing since the 2020 BLM riots, I had multiple monitors set up. On one, Trump was giving a speech to his supporters, on another I scrolled through Twitter, and on another was *The Killstream* covering a set of protesters in front of the Capitol. As Trump was in the middle of his speech, Mike Pence tweeted that he would not be invoking "The Pence Option." This is when all hell broke loose. Protesters in front of the Capitol broke down barriers separating themselves from the building, and overwhelmed the police guarding it. We all know what happened next.

> *These are the things and events that happen when a sacred landslide election victory is so unceremoniously & viciously stripped away from great patriots who have been badly & unfairly treated for so long.*
>
> **– President Donald J Trump**

At the time of the attacks, the Dissident Right couldn't believe what was happening before their eyes. It was a moment of overwhelming rage, laughter, and ecstasy. An epic raid, but in real life.

Baked Alaska broke into Nancy Pelosi's office and started playing with her phone, pretending to make a call: *"Hello? Congress? I'd like to report a stolen election. Yah we need to get our boy Donald J Trump into office. Yah can we do that real quick?"* Other protesters would take pictures of themselves stealing Nancy Pelosi's lectern, or putting their feet up on her desk.

Meanwhile, Congress evacuated the building, scurrying into underground tunnels beneath the capitol, and hyperventilating into plastic bags.

> *President Donald Trump sided with his supporters after they stormed the U.S. Capitol on Wednesday, saying of the violence: "These are the things and events that happen when a sacred landslide election victory is so unceremoniously & viciously stripped away from great patriots who have been badly & unfairly treated for so long." Earlier, rather than denouncing the violence, he empathized with his supporters, telling them in a video, "I know how you feel" and that they were "very special." In the same breath, he called for them to "go home peacefully." He did not condemn their actions or call for their arrest, as he has numerous times for his political opponents. He complained again of a "fraudulent election," the cause his supporters in the federal building were ostensibly fighting for.*
>
> *...*
>
> *Twitter clamped down on the video almost immediately, barring users from sharing it except with a comment or a direct link. –* ***The Daily Beast, Jan 6 2021, "Trump Justifies Violence at Capitol: These 'Things' Happen When No One Recognizes My 'Sacred Landslide'"*** *(https://www.thedailybeast.com/trump-to-supporters-as-they-storm-the-capitol-the-election-was-stolen-from-us)*

Twitter would then ban the President from their platform.

Chapter 6 - 2021 & 2022: The GAE strikes back, The Trumpism Without Trump Moment, MDE Never Dies, Kanye The Wignat, Elon the Redditor Saves The Internet

The Globalist American Empire Strikes Back: The Aftermath of J6

After J6, the protesters who entered the Capitol were locked away for years, often in solitary confinement and in poor conditions. They, in effect, became political prisoners. Ban waves swept through the Internet. Groypers were arrested.

> *Five people who federal investigators say are associated with the far-right group America First have been arrested in connection with last year's attack on the U.S. Capitol.*
>
> *– NBC News, Sep 20 2022, "Members of far-right group America First charged in connection with Jan. 6 riot" (https://www.nbcnews.com/politics/justice-department/members-far-right-group-america-first-charged-connection-jan-6-riot-rcna48664)*

Baked Alaska would serve two months behind bars (https://www.theguardian.com/us-news/2023/jan/10/baked-alaska-anthime-gionet-sentenced-capitol-attack#:~:text=Anthime%20Gionet%2C%20a%20far%2Dright,%E2%80%93%20participation%20he%20live%2Dstreamed). This was perhaps not surprising, given that he livestreamed himself trespassing inside the capitol. But so was *InfoWars* host Owen Shroyer, who had gone no further than the capitol's steps (https://apnews.com/article/owen-shroyer-InfoWars-capitol-riot-sentencing-11cb087e9716061591fd46b6861c4c1c)

Even Meme War veteran Ricky Vaughn, who had largely disappeared from the Internet after being doxed in 2017 by wignats, would be prosecuted for a meme he made in 2016.

> *A Florida man was arrested this morning on charges of conspiring with others in advance of the 2016 U.S. Presidential Election to use various social media platforms to disseminate misinformation designed to deprive individuals of their constitutional right to vote.*
>
> *Douglass Mackey, aka Ricky Vaughn, 31, of West Palm Beach, was charged by criminal complaint in the Eastern District of New York. He was taken into custody this morning in West Palm Beach and made his initial appearance before U.S. Magistrate Judge Bruce E. Reinhart of the Southern District of Florida.*
>
> *"According to the allegations in the complaint, the defendant exploited a social media platform to infringe one the of most basic and sacred rights guaranteed by the Constitution: the right to vote," said Nicholas L. McQuaid, Acting Assistant Attorney General of the Justice Department's Criminal Division. "This complaint underscores the department's commitment to investigating and prosecuting those who would undermine citizens' voting rights."*
>
> **– Office of Public Affairs, Jan 27 2021, US Dept of Jusrtice, (https://www.justice.gov/opa/pr/social-media-influencer-charged-election-interference-stemming-voter-disinformation-campaign)**

Like "Draft Our Daughters," the meme was created to look like a real Clinton campaign ad. In the meme, it told voters they could vote "from home" by posting "Hillary" and the hashtag "#PresidentialElection." Prosecutors said this was "Election Interference."

"Protecting every American citizen's right to cast a legitimate vote is a key to the success of our republic," said William F. Sweeney Jr., Assistant Director in Charge of the FBI's New York Field Office. "What Mackey allegedly did to interfere with this process – by soliciting voters to cast their ballots via text – amounted to nothing short of vote theft. It is illegal behavior and contributes to the erosion of the public's trust in our electoral processes. He may have been a powerful social media influencer at the time, but a quick Internet search of his name today will reveal an entirely different story."

The complaint alleges that in 2016, Mackey established an audience on Twitter with approximately 58,000 followers. A February 2016 analysis by the MIT Media Lab ranked Mackey as the 107th most important influencer of the then-upcoming Election, ranking his account above outlets and individuals such as NBC News (#114), Stephen Colbert (#119) and Newt Gingrich (#141).

As alleged in the complaint, between September 2016 and November 2016, in the lead up to the Nov. 8, 2016, U.S. Presidential Election, Mackey conspired with others to use social media platforms, including Twitter, to disseminate fraudulent messages designed to encourage supporters of one of the presidential candidates (the "Candidate") to "vote" via text message or social media, a legally invalid method of voting.

– Office of Public Affairs, Jan 27 2021, US Dept of Jusrtice, (https://www.justice.gov/opa/pr/social-media-influencer-charged-election-interference-stemming-voter-disinformation-campaign)

However defenders of Mackey say that the meme was obviously meant to be satire. Indeed, people on both sides often make similar jokes, such as sarcastically telling voters to vote on a date that is after election day. For example, comedian Kristina Wong tweeted something very similar on November 8 2016. In addition to telling Trump supporters to vote on the wrong day, it also tells them to vote by text, exactly as Ricky Vaughn did.

Hey Trump Supporters! Skip poll lines at #Election2016 and TEXT in your vote! Text votes are legit. Or vote tomorrow on Super Wednesday!

– Kristina Wong, Nov 8 2016 (https://twitter.com/mskristinawong/status/79599905998717337)

Needless to day, Ms. Wong would never be charged with a crime. But Douglas Mackey would not be so lucky, being convicted in March of 2023.

> *Douglas Mackey, also known as "Ricky Vaughn," was convicted today by a federal jury in Brooklyn of the charge of Conspiracy Against Rights stemming from his scheme to deprive individuals of their constitutional right to vote. The verdict followed a one-week trial before United States District Judge Ann M. Donnelly. When sentenced, Mackey faces a maximum of 10 years in prison.*
>
> **– Office of Public Affairs, Mar 31 2023, US Dept of Justice, (https://www.justice.gov/opa/pr/social-media-influencer-charged-election-interference-stemming-voter-disinformation-campaign)**

There was even a purge of the military:

> *Last month's attack on Capitol Hill intensified concerns about extremism within the United States military. Though the number of current or former members of the armed forces who participated in the deadly MAGA riot is unknown, an NPR analysis in late January found that as many as one in five of those charged in the wake of the insurrection had a record of military service.*
>
> *During his confirmation hearing for the role of Joe Biden's secretary of Defense, Lloyd Austin vowed to root out white supremacy and right-wing radicalism in the ranks, though he provided little detail as to how that would be accomplished. "The job of the Department of Defense is to keep America safe from our enemics," he said. "But we can't do that if some of those enemies lie within our own ranks."*
>
> **– Vanity Fair, Feb 4 2021, "Biden's Secretary of Defense Is Moving to Purge the Military of White Supremacists", (https://12ft.io/proxy? q=https%3A%2F%2Fwww.vanityfair.com%2Fnews %2F2021%2F02%2Fbiden-secretary-of-defense-moving-to-purge-the-military-of-white-supremacists)**

The Biden administration has told 11 officials appointed to military service academy advisory boards by former President Donald Trump to resign or be dismissed, a source familiar with the situation tells CNN's KFile.

The officials asked to resign include prominent former Trump officials like former White House press secretary Sean Spicer, former senior counselor to the President Kellyanne Conway and former national security adviser H.R. McMaster. They were appointed to the advisory boards of the Naval Academy, Air Force Academy and West Point respectively.

– CNN, Sep 9 2021, "Biden administration tells ex-Trump officials to resign from military academy advisory boards or be dismissed"(https://www.cnn.com/2021/09/08/politics/trump-appointees-biden-boards/index.html)

The legal repercussions of J6 are ongoing. In 2023, Enrique Tarrio, former chairman of the Proud Boys, would be sentenced to 22 years in prison for seditious conspiracy, in spite of never having set foot in the capitol and not even having been in Washington DC on that day. And of course, Trump himself was indicted in August 2023, previously having been posthumously impeached for the incident on January 13, 2021.

Like Charlottesville, the immediate aftermath of J6 was a shock to the Dissident Right and caused serious damage. However, unlike Charlottesville, the damage was not permanent. Unlike the Charlottesville marchers, the J6 rioters would slowly become seen as martyrs by the entire MAGA movement, both dissident and mainstream alike.

In 2016, the Great Meme War was about trolling Hillary Clinton with edgy Pepe memes. It was all just a big joke. Now, it was suddenly very real. This might be compared to the days after the Manson murders and the Weather Underground during the 1960s counter-culture, a dark foil to the earlier epic wins of the Summer of Love and Woodstock. In the 1970s and 1980s, there was a reaction against the Left Wing counter-culture as well, perhaps best personified in the person of Richard Nixon. In spite of this reaction, the ripple effect of the hippies would not be stopped in its tracks in the 1970s and

1980s, but it would instead survive this era. It could not be undone. It was an inevitable part of the dialectical flow of history.

J6 led to a chilling effect on the Dissident Right. Real life protesting would again be discouraged. "Fed mania" would sweep over both the dissident and normie Right. Every person who ever suggested doing anything above and beyond traditional picketing, and sometimes all IRL activism whatsoever, would be met with accusations of "fed." Boomers in particular would latch onto this meme. From the moment J6 happened, Boomers would swear that the entire thing was a "set up" and claim that Antifa had been in the crowd as agent provocateurs, leading people into the capitol building. I never bought into this theory, having been there at the Million MAGA March. People entered the Capitol because they were angry that the election was stolen, not because Antifa "tricked" them into doing so. It just seemed like convenient Boomer cope, and the inability of normie Republicans to accept their new role as an insurgent, dissident movement, as the hippie counter-culture had once been. It is true that the Right values law and order. But as long as the Right Wing is against the status quo and the establishment, and as long as law enforcement serves as the enforcers of the status quo on behalf of the establishment, they are necessarily at odds with law enforcement for the time being. Even today, this is a fact that more traditional conservatives are loath to accept.

Whatever was left of the wignats online would basically become totally irrelevant after this time, feeling vindicated that J6 proved the futility of IRL activism and that there "was no political solution." But remnants of them would remain on Gab and the Fediverse instance "poast" until poast was hacked on May 25th 2023 and began to become unpopular.

Meanwhile, what was left of the Dissident Right on Twitter become more and more mild. "Frog Twitter," a small contingent of accounts that somehow managed to not be banned after the many ban waves, including Scott Greer, Mystery Grove, fans of Bronze Age Pervert, and NRx or Peter Thiel-associated accounts, began to talk to less and less about third rail issues that might see their accounts suspended. While sometimes taking mildly racial jabs at black people, they mostly tended to focus on moderate and generic critiques of the Left, bodybuilding and gym culture, eating wholefoods or vaguely masculine "based" fad diets such as eating raw eggs, mocking pit bull owners, esoteric Right Wing philosophy such as Julius Evola or Carl Schmidt, and other topics seen as safe.

With the wignats barely worth mentioning anymore, and the other factions of the online Dissident Right self-censoring their views, Nick Fuentes's America First faction, once seen as a moderate alternative to the Alt Right, now became one of the most extreme wings of the Dissident Right.

Cozy.tv: Nick Fuentes, the Banned Man

One of the main figures who was almost destroyed by the fallout of J6 was Nick Fuentes. Fuentes, unlike some of his fans, did not enter the capitol, instead giving a speech to his followers nearby. Nonetheless, he would be investigated by the FBI, his ability to make a living would be utterly destroyed, and he would be betrayed by his close friends.

Having been previously banned from YouTube during the Groyper Wars, he had moved to DLive. DLive was an independent streaming platform, similar to Twitch, where content creators were paid in "lemons," a digital cryptocurrency. DLive rose to prominence mostly due to PewDiePie, who was the most-subscribed-to YouTuber in the world. After almost becoming a victim of cancel culture due to his own edgy content (including saying the N Word on stream and making an anti-Semitic joke) PewDiePie signed an exclusive deal to only stream on DLive, given its much laxer moderation guidelines.

Many gaming and dissident politics streamers followed PewDiePie to DLive, including Fuentes. After moving to DLive, Fuentes soon rose to become to the platform's largest streamer. Other America First-aligned or Dissident Right streamers including Patrick Casey, Jaden McNeil, Vincent James, Baked Alaska, Steve Franssen, Jake Lloyd, Ethan Ralph, Woozuh, Loulz, Shallit, and Beardson Beardly also used the platform, creating a tight knit community that would later serve as the inspiration for Cozy.tv. PewDiePie even once "raided" Beardson Beardly's stream.

After J6, Nick Fuentes, along with most of the streamers just mentioned, were instantly suspended from DLive for "inciting violent and illegal activities." Their "lemons" that had not yet been withdrawn were frozen by the platform. Some tried to find new platforms to stream on, such as Trovo (another site similar to DLive) but Fuentes feared that if he moved to another platform that not only would he instantly be re-banned, but he would take down all of his fellow streamers with him, as had been the case with DLive.

Fuentes was also put on a "no-fly" list shortly after J6, which he claims was in connection with the event, although others dispute this claim, saying that he was put on the list for an unrelated incident in which he was thrown off of a plane for refusing to wear a mask.

In addition to having nowhere to stream, Fuentes had his bank account frozen as part of an investigation by law enforcement, and he was banned from all payment processors (including some crypto platforms) making it impossible for him to receive money through superchats.

Many began to compare his rise after the Groyper Wars and fall after January 6 with that of Richard Spencer's rise during the Alt Right and fall after Charlottesville. But unlike Spencer, Fuentes would persevere through the process and arrive on the other end relatively unscathed, and in fact go on to even greater heights.

Using a small group of volunteer developers, Fuentes developed his own site, AmericaFirst.live, which was little more than an iFrame in which the livestream was embedded. This led to only a week or so of down time, in which Fuentes was not able to stream. The developers used many ingenious ways of getting the stream to work, such as mirroring it from burner YouTube accounts. Meanwhile, Fuentes and his developers started on his own streaming platform, Cozy.tv.

In late 2021, Cozy.tv was launched. The first three channels were Nick Fuentes, Vincent James, and Jaden McNeil. New streamers were gradually invited onto the platform by Fuentes, eventually leading to an impressive roster of over 50 diverse streamers (although a few would never stream a single time after joining the platform). Some notable streamers on the site include: proto-Alt Right YouTuber AltHype, TikTok Right Wing comedian wurzelroot, Ethan Ralph, Baked Alaska, Beardson Beardly, Paul Town, Milo Yiannopoulos (never streamed), Jewish free speech activist Laura Loomer (never streamed), liberal streamer Destiny (never streamed), "MAGA communist" streamers InfraredHaz and Jackson Hinkle (never streamed), Alex Jones, conspiracy theorist Stew Peters, Anthony Cumia of *Opie and Anthony*, misogynist comedian Dick Masterson, anime and e-drama streamer Flamenco, Roger Stone, "Stop the Steal" organizer Ali Alexander, Gab founder Andrew Torba, anti-Judaism Catholic writer E Michael Jones, MAGA rapper Bryson Gray, pastor and politically incorrect talk show host Jessie Lee Peterson, Twitter personality Book Cat of the "old book club" Dissident Right faction, conspiracy theorist Ryan Dawson, musician and creator of "incelcore" Negative XP, Republican politician and activist Lauren Witzke, and Right Wing philosophy YouTuber and Irish nationalist Keith Woods. The platform was intended to eventually be opened up to the public, but as of December 2023 this has not occurred, largely due to the cost such an operation would incur.

Fuentes also announced that he intended to continue planning for AFPAC 2, against the advice of many of his allies, including Darren Beattie of *Revolver*

News, Patrick Casey, and Scott Greer. Patrick Casey, organizer of the previous AFPAC, reacted to this on his livestream, *Restoring Order* (streamed right before *America First* as a lead-in to the show) in an episode called "Why I'm Not Going to AFPAC." In it, Casey revealed that Nick Fuentes's bank account had been frozen, he was under FBI investigation and that he had been put on a no-fly list and was driving from Chicago to the event in Orlando, Florida. Fuentes had not previously revealed any of this information to his followers. Casey, who had previously been involved in Charlottesville, said that in all his years in the Dissident Right, he had never heard of someone being subject to this level of government scrutiny, usually reserved only for drug dealers and terrorists. He also painted a picture of America First as a cult, where one wrong word against the leader would be severely punished and total obedience to Fuentes was the rule (accusations that have been repeated by many America First defectors in years since, such as Jaden McNeil). He ended the stream by announcing his retirement from America First and threatening to leak DMs if Fuentes retaliated. Many of Fuentes's other allies, including Jake Lloyd (who was once a guest host of *America First)*, Scott Greer, and Steve Franssen also skipped the event.

In spite of this, AFPAC 2 would be a success, an act of defiance in the midst of the uncertainty of a governmental crackdown on dissent. The speakers were Vincent James, Michelle Malkin, Jon Miller of Glenn Beck's network *BlazeTV*, former representative Steve King, and featuring sitting congressman Paul Gosar of Arizona as its keynote speaker.

Fuentes himself also gave a speech during the conference:

> *"White people founded this country. This country wouldn't exist without white people, and white people are done being bullied,"*
>
> **– Nick Fuentes (https://www.newsweek.com/paul-gosar-defends-speaking-afpac-white-nationalist-organizer-1572607)**

An interesting note is that at the time of the conference, speaking out against anti-white racism was still considered a taboo topic, and Paul Gosar had to disavow it.

> *Gosar, appearing on a panel at CPAC several hours after his appearance at AFPAC, stated, "I denounce when we talk about white racism. That's not appropriate."*
>
> **– ABC News, Feb 27 2021, "GOP congressman headlines conference where organizers push white nationalist rhetoric" (https://abcnews.go.com/US/gop-congressman-headlines-conference-organizers-push-white-nationalist/story?id=76152780)**

At about the same time as the end of the Censorship Era, this would no longer be the case. As of 2023, even Charlie Kirk, once the main target of the Groyper Wars, frequently addresses anti-white racism on Twitter.

AFPAC 2 was one of the most successful Dissident Right events of all time, rivaling the likes of Jared Taylor's *American Renaissance* convention. AFPAC 3 would be held on February 25, 2022, also in Orlando. Fuentes claimed it was attended by 1,200 attendees, making it one of the largest Right Wing conferences, dissident or mainstream, in the country. It featured four elected officials, including Marjorie Taylor Greene, a rising star in the Republican party who portrayed herself as a "MAGA mom."

> *The conference featured four elected officials as speakers: Georgia Representative Marjorie Taylor Greene, Arizona Representative Paul Gosar, Arizona Senator Wendy Rogers, and Lieutenant Governor of Idaho Janice McGeachin.*
>
> ...

> *The conference additionally hosted a variety of far-right media personalities, including Gavin McInnes, Milo Yiannopoulos, and Jesse Lee Peterson, as well as white supremacists Jared Taylor and Peter Brimelow. Fuentes claimed that Yiannopoulos was responsible for connecting him with Rep. Marjorie Taylor Greene. – **Wikipedia (https://en.wikipedia.org/wiki/America_First_Political_Action_Confer ence)** **It says here Jared Taylor and Peter Brimelow are "white supremacists," but this is disputed and I would not consider them to be.**

The Vax Mandate

Since the announcement of the vaccine in 2020, many Dissident Right "conspiracy theorists" predicted that it would be mandated, and then used as justification to crack down on political dissent.

This prediction appeared to be fulfilled in 2021, when vaccine mandates were announced for the military, government workers and for companies with 100 or more employees. Thousands of people were fired from their jobs for refusing to get the jab.

Meanwhile, fake Covid vaccination cards began to proliferate on the Internet, eventually leading to forging a vaccine card becoming a felony. In some places, such as Los Angeles and New York City, establishments such as restaurants started banning entry to patrons if they did not provide proof of vaccination.

Many conservatives warned that this was only the beginning. Soon, the government would enact a digital vaccine passport system and make the vaccine passports mandatory in order to get a job, conduct business, or utilize public transportation. They would also use Bluetooth to track your interaction with everyone around you in the guise of "contact tracing" and penalize you for contact with anyone else who refused to comply.

This system would then be abused to crack down on political dissent. Political dissenters would have their vaccine passports terminated, thus effectively making political dissent impossible to organize. This Bluetooth "contact tracing" functionality was indeed added to the operating system of all iPhones and Androids. However, the rest of the vaccine passport system was not implemented in Western countries, though it was in China. In China, exactly what was predicted did come to pass in June of 2022.

Over the past two months, thousands of depositors like Liu have been fighting to recover their savings from at least four rural banks in Henan – in a case that involves billions of dollars. In late May, hundreds of them traveled to Zhengzhou from across China and staged a protest outside the office of the Henan banking regulator to demand their money back – to no avail.

Another protest was planned for Monday. But as the depositors arrived in Zhengzhou, they were stunned to find that their health codes – which were green upon departure – had turned red, according to six who spoke with CNN and social media posts.

– CNN, Jun 15 2022, "China's bank run victims planned to protest. Then their Covid health codes turned red" (https://www.cnn.com/2022/06/15/china/china-zhengzhou-bank-fraud-health-code-protest-intl-hnk/index.html)

During 2020-2021, opposition to Covid restrictions (such as mask and vaccine mandates) grew to a fever pitch among conservatives. Provocateur and IRL livestreamer Baked Alaska was especially notorious for harassing employees trying vainly to enforce these restrictions.

Anti-mask streamer Baked Alaska asks employee for mask, throws it on the ground, then refuses to leave until police arrive

–- r/PublicFreakOut, Oct 11 2020 (https://www.reddit.com/r/PublicFreakout/comments/j9duzd/antimask_streamer_bakedalaska_asks_employee_for/)

During 2020, in the midst of the COVID-19 pandemic, [Baked Alaska] would film himself trespassing on privately owned establishments that require the wearing of face coverings, while refusing to wear one. He would mock and insult employees of these establishments for wearing masks, and refuse to leave when told to do so **– Wikipedia (https://en.wikipedia.org/wiki/Baked_Alaska_(livestreamer))**

In November 2021, Fuentes visited New York City to attend a number of anti-vaccine mandate protests. The first of these were mostly unsuccessful. One, in front of Staten Island University Hospital, resulted in Fuentes and his followers being heckled with chants of "fag, fag, fag" (this chant was apparently from Jovi Val, a person I know nothing about but who appears to be a wignat of some sort). Another, outside of Pfizer HQ, was held beside another, New York-based group of protesters, who accused Fuentes and America First of being saboteurs.

"Today organizers completely disavow infiltrators and trolls attempting to link medical freedom with extremist ideologies, namely Nick Fuentes and 'Vax Watch,'" the local group posted to their Telegram channel. The outright rebuke apparently left a sour taste in the young white nationalist's mouth, because he quickly tried to sic followers on the rival protesters.

"It's unfortunate that we had to separate from this crowd over there," Fuentes stated before joining in with fellow white nationalist "groypers" chanting "boo." "We were supposed to rally alongside those people over there," he continued, referring to the local anti-vaxxer crowd that had assembled nearby.

"It's very troubling because it seems like the people over there, like a lot of people in the city, they hate us more than they hate the vaccine," the college dropout continued. Fuentes concluded by declaring "shame on you" in the direction of the local anti-vaxxers before partaking in yelling "shame, shame, shame." **– The Daily Beast, Nov 13 2021, "NYC Anti-Vax Protest Implodes as White Nationalists War With Locals" (https://www.thedailybeast.com/white-nationalist-nick-fuentes-followers-clash-with-anti-vaxxers-in-new-york-city)**

However, the final protest was a success, becoming a memorable part of the America First saga. Fuentes and his fans assembled in front of Gracie

Mansion, where he began to give a speech through a megaphone denouncing vaccines. Meanwhile, Antifa began to gather around the group, clashing with the Groypers. The two groups shouted each other down. *"Nazi Scum! Nazi Scum!"* chanted Antifa, while the Groypers chanted *"Fuck Antifa! Fuck Antifa! Fuck BLM! Fuck BLM!"* The police, ostensibly there to protect the protesters and de-escalate any conflict, instead did nothing. Fuentes then turned to chastise the police for not doing their job of protecting the protesters, even though many in the NYPD themselves had been fired due to their failure to comply with the mandates. *"Do! Your! Job! Do! Your! Job!"* chanted the Groypers. Finally, the police moved in between Antifa and the Groypers. What could have been another Charlottesville, with violent clashes between protesters and counter-protesters, was narrowly avoided. *"This is Groyper country!"* cried Fuentes at the counter-protesters. *"These are our streets."*

Resistance to the vaccine mandate culminated in the trucker protests of early 2022, which were supported by America First, and its Canadian copycat movement, Canada First (led by Cozy.tv streamer Tyler Russell). During these protests, trucker convoys blockaded several entry points to Canada from the United States. They also camped out in their trucks in downtown Ottawa, in a sort of "Occupy Wall Street" with trucks.

The trucks in Ottawa would honk throughout the day and night as a form of nonviolent disruption. On the Internet, these protests thus became known as "The Honkening."

The first meme to emerge from the Freedom Convoy discourse was on Reddit. Complaints were voiced on the platform from Ottawa residents regarding the honking within their towns being obnoxious and detrimental to their well-being. This started most notably on January 29th, 2022, in the comment sections of multiple "Convoy Megathreads." One example was posted beneath a /r/ottawa post from Redditor EVEolutionary who said, "Our kitty fear pooped in our bed, among other places. She NEVER has accidents outside of the box. I'm livid. My poor little girl. I feel so terrible for the pets of downtown," earning over 170 upvotes

...

On the same day, the honking complaint comments surfaced on 4chan's /pol/ messageboard, where anonymous users started to post memes about honking and honks. For instance, an anon started a thread on the 29th, leading it with, "THE WORLDWIDE HONKENING BEGINS TODAY." The meme they attached used the likeness of the Clown Pepe / Honk Honk meme. Subsequent 4chan users added to this thread, one of them referencing a screenshot of Redditor EVEolutionary's comment **– Know Your Meme (https://knowyourmeme.com/memes/events/canadian-freedom-convoy-convoi-de-la-liberte)**

Elon Musk also tweeted support for The Honkening.

On January 27th, 2022, Tesla and SpaceX CEO Elon Musk tweeted,"Canadian truckers rule," receiving roughly 433,700 likes over the course of four days **– Know Your Meme (https://knowyourmeme.com/memes/events/canadian-freedom-convoy-convoi-de-la-liberte)**

The protests were eventually put to an end by force. Justin Trudeau invoked the "Emergencies Act" and police forcibly removed protesters. This included Mounties trampling an elderly woman with horses, dislocating her shoulder (https://thenationaltelegraph.com/national/ottawa-police-are-lying-about-an-elderly-woman-being-trampled-by-a-police-horse).

The main blockade cited as evidence for the invocation was one that occurred on the Ambassador Bridge, a supply route that connects Michigan and Ontario. It was reported that the week-long blockade disrupted $390 million in trade each day. This blockade, and others, caused the act to be invoked, allowing the Canadian government to freeze bank accounts of citizens suspected of sending financial aid to the Freedom Convoy movement. Other measures of the act include limiting civilian travel, the use or disposing of citizen property, policing, fining or imprisoning people, as well as the deployment of the military to halt the protests that Trudeau has described as a "last resort."

– Know Your Meme
(https://knowyourmeme.com/memes/events/canadian-freedom-convoy-convoi-de-la-liberte)

Shortly thereafter, especially when it became clear that the vaccines did nothing to stop the spread of the virus, Covid restrictions finally began to be rolled back. Tyler Russell fled to the United States and joined America First, as new Canadian anti-"hate speech" laws passed shortly after the trucker protests effectively made his political opinions illegal.

The Trumpism Without Trump Moment Pt 1 - DeSantis

After J6, Trump receded a bit into the background. Several factions of the Right competed over what the GOP would look like now that Trump was no longer in power.

America First and the Groypers stressed the need for the Republican party not to backslide into what they had been before Trump and "return to business as usual." Instead, Fuentes said, "we must institutionalize the Trump revolution." He attempted to support "America First" congressional candidates and primary those not seen as sufficiently based. Paul Ryan and Mitch McConnell, meanwhile, did the exact opposite, funding primary opponents to as many MAGA-aligned candidates as possible. None of these America First congressman ever materialized, or if they did, they have never been publicly endorsed by the movement.

On the opposite side, Rick Grenell, anti-SJW content creator Karlyn Borysenko, and a small faction on the Right tried to use the opportunity to move away from social conservatism, and create a GOP that was LGBT-friendly and less strident on issues such as abortion. This faction was supported by gay married "ex-"liberal Dave Rubin and trans "conservative" Blaire White. They argued, somewhat accurately, that Trump had represented a break from the earlier "Religious Right" and social conservatism, towards a more "big tent" coalition. However, critics argued that if it was a "big tent" movement that included LGBT "conservatives," then it must also include far-right figures such as Nick Fuentes, Peter Brimelow and Jared Taylor, who were officially banned from CPAC, Fox News, and other conservative organizations. Steve Bannon took a similar position, but with race instead of sexuality. His vision was for a populist version of the GOP which he called "multiracial working class populism," inspired by record turn-out for Trump among black and Hispanic voters in 2020. Both the Rick Grenell and Steve Bannon factions were fiercely attacked by Nick Fuentes, and some of his allies such as Lauren Witzke, seeing the retreat from social conservatism as

276

perhaps the worst possible outcome for a post-Trump GOP, and claiming it was impossible to be a conservative who promoted LGBT.

> In March 2021, Witzke responded to a tweet from Richard Grenell about a trans woman who had attended CPAC by claiming that transgender people are "mentally ill" and "demonic"
>
> **– Wikipedia(https://en.wikipedia.org/wiki/Lauren_Witzke)**

They also pointed out that while there was a jump in hispanic and black voters for Trump, the overwhelming majority of them still voted for liberals and always would. According to Fuentes, they saw the Democrat party as a non-white party that best represented them for racial and cultural reasons, rather than policy.

Another faction was "Trumpism without Trump," represented by Ron DeSantis. This was seen as perhaps the greatest threat to Trump at the time. Copying many of Trump's mannerisms, Ron DeSantis adopted the persona of a "strongman," fighting back against Covid restrictions and "wokeism." At press conferences and interviews, he took an aggressive posture against the mass media and their attempts to attack him.

When it came to Covid, Ron DeSantis opened the state earlier and with fewer restrictions than others. While receiving criticism in the media at the time, this proved to be extremely popular in the long run. However, while his Covid policy was more moderate than other states, it was not absolute.

> "I was the leader in this country in fighting back against Fauci," DeSantis said in an interview on "The Ben Shapiro Show." "We bucked him every step of the way."

...

DeSantis declared a state of emergency on COVID in Florida before the U.S. had declared its state of emergency. He closed schools in the early weeks of the pandemic just as all 49 other states did; in fact, Florida schools closed to in-person instruction a couple of days before New York schools did.

...

On mask mandates, DeSantis was in the minority as one of 11 state chief executives who resisted imposing the strategy at any point during the COVID pandemic after the CDC started recommending that people wear masks outside their houses in April 2020.

...

DeSantis wasn't the first governor to risk reopening businesses, but he was one of the Republican governors who moved more quickly to do so than health experts recommended at the time.

By April 16, 2020, the Trump administration had released a reopening plan for states that advocated unwinding mitigation measures in stages as cases and deaths decreased — a so-called "gating" strategy.

Shortly afterward, Georgia, Alaska and Oklahoma attracted criticism from health officials and then-President Trump for partially reopening businesses in their states.

...

A week later, DeSantis kicked off Florida's reopening process, allowing restaurants and other businesses to open their doors to a limited capacity. He defended that decision with appeals to the public health strategy of the Centers for Disease Control and Prevention (CDC) at the time.

– CBS News, Jun 15 2023, "Ron DeSantis wasn't always a COVID rebel: Looking back at the Florida governor's initial pandemic respons" (https://www.cbsnews.com/news/ron-desantis-2024-campaign-florida-governor-covid/#:~:text=DeSantis%20declared %20a%20state%20of,before%20New%20York%20schools%20did.)

DeSantis was also popular with many conservatives for attacking "wokeism" in Florida. One example of this was passing the so-called "Don't Say Gay" law.

> *In February 2022, DeSantis voiced support for the Florida Parental Rights in Education Act (HB1557), commonly known as the "Don't Say Gay" law, which prohibits discussion of sexual orientation or gender identity in school classrooms from kindergarten to grade 3. He said it was "entirely inappropriate" for teachers and school administrators to talk to students about their gender identity. **– Wikipedia (https://en.wikipedia.org/wiki/Ron_DeSantis)***

The Walt Disney Company called for the law's repeal, worked behind the scenes with lobbyists to fight the law, and paused political donations to Florida. *(https://www.forbes.com/sites/alisondurkee/2022/03/28/disney-says-striking-down-dont-say-gay-law-is-companys-goal-after-desantis-signs-bill/?sh=4fffe78355c0).*

> *Three lawmakers, two Republicans and one Democrat, spoke to the Times/Herald on Friday about their role in Disney's efforts as the company's stance spilled into public view. Disney lobbyists set up a series of calls with Senate Education Committee Chairman Joe Gruters, R-Sarasota, before the bill received a hearing.*
>
> **– Tampa Bay Times, Mar 12 2022, "How Disney worked behind the scenes against the 'don't say gay' bill" (https://www.tampabay.com/news/florida-politics/2022/03/12/how-disney-worked-behind-the-scenes-against-the-dont-say-gay-bill/)**

In response, DeSantis fought back, rolling back special privileges given by the state government to Walt Disney World.

The Walt Disney Company, owner of Walt Disney World in Florida, called for the law's repeal, beginning a dispute between Disney and the state government. In April 2022, DeSantis signed a bill eliminating the company's special independent district and replacing its Disney-appointed board of overseers.He also threatened during a press conference to build a new state prison near the Disney World complex. On April 26, 2023, Disney filed suit against DeSantis and several others, accusing them of retaliating against protected speech. – Wikipedia (https://en.wikipedia.org/wiki/Ron_DeSantis)

Supporters painted him as a "caudillo" (a strongman type of leader typical of Latin American countries) and a Trump without the baggage of Trump (such as J6 or Trump's legal problems) who could "get things done."

This faction had the support of many former Trump supporters such as Ann Coulter, Mike Cernovich and some of "Frog Twitter." But the attitude towards DeSantis on the Dissident Right was mixed. DeSantis was attacked by Nick Fuentes, Scott Greer, and others. Fuentes argued that, unlike Trump, DeSantis was a career politician and not an outsider, who did not represent a clear challenge to the establishment in the way that Trump did. He also was not sufficiently "America First," supporting policies that put "Israel First" such as laws that targeted speech criticizing the Israeli government, thus placing priority on a foreign country rather than the free speech rights of American citizens. Greer argued that Ron DeSantis was a "nerd" who lacked the charisma of Trump, and was "not as based as you might think," saying that there was no issue on which DeSantis was further to the right than Trump, thus making Trump the clear choice for nominee, whatever faults he may have.

Many predicted that Ron DeSantis would pose a serious threat to Trump as the Republican nominee in 2023. However, after both candidates announced, and especially after the famous "Trump mugshot," Trump obliterated Ron DeSantis in political polls, leading DeSantis by 34 points. Even other non-Trump candidates, such as Vivek Ramaswamy, began to surpass DeSantis.

The Trumpism Without Trump Moment Pt 2 – Peter Thiel

Perhaps the most interesting faction was the faction of tech entrepreneur Peter Thiel. Peter Thiel was a homosexual Right Wing billionaire and a "Straussian." Like the other factions, he picked and chose the parts he liked of Trump and the Alt Right explosion of 2016, while putting his own spin on it. A deliberately opaque ideology, Straussianism believes politicians should have a "private and public position," or, as Straussians put it, an "exoteric" outward position, and an "esoteric" position intelligible only to those intelligent enough to pick up on it intuitively (similar to "meta-irony," where the "exoteric" irony hides an "esoteric" sincerity). My interpretation of *The Straussian Moment*, written by Thiel, is that he wants a small elite of secretly based and redpilled illiberal people running the country and being aware of facts such as race realism, while hiding these heterodox views from the populace in order to preserve the liberal thesis while allowing society to function smoothly (since the people running it will not be basing their decisions on the contradictions of liberalism). Of course, perhaps I am misinterpreting the "esoteric" message of the text.

> And then one encounters Schmitt's troubling challenge. A side in which everyone, like Hobbes, values this earthly life more than death is a side where everyone will run away from fighting and confrontation; but when one runs away from an enemy that continues to fight, one is ultimately going to lose—no matter how great the numerical or technological superiority may appear at the outset. Schmitt's solution to this impending defeat demands an affirmation of the political in the West. Here, however, one must confront an alternative and perhaps even more troubling conclusion. For let us assume that it is possible, somehow, to turn back the clock and set aside our uncertainties; that we can return to the faith of Cromwell and Urban II; that we understand Islam as the providential enemy of the West; and that we can then respond to Islam with the same ferocity with which it is now attacking the West. This would be a Pyrthic victory, for it would come at the price of doing away with everything that fundamentally distinguishes the modern West from Islam.
>
> ...

If one agrees with Schmitt's starting assumptions, then the West must lose the war or lose its identity. One way or the other, the persistence of the political spells the doom of the modern West; but for the sake of completeness, we must consider also the inverse possibility, indirectly hinted at in the margins of Schmitt's own writings. For while it may well be that the political guarantees the seriousness of life and that, so long as the political exists, the world will remain divided, there is no guarantee that the political itself will survive.

...

We are at an impasse. On the one hand, we have the newer project of the Enlightenment, which never became comprehensive on a global scale, and perhaps always came at too high a price of self-stultification. On the other hand, we have a return to the older tradition, but that return is fraught with far too much violence. The incredibly drastic solutions favored by Schmitt in his dark musings have become impossible after 1945, in a world of nuclear weapons and limitless destruction through technology. What sort of coherent intellectual or practical synthesis is then possible at all? The political philosopher Leo Strauss attempted to solve this central paradox of the postmodern world. The challenge of that task is reflected in the difficulty of Strauss's own writings, which are prohibitively obscurantist to the uninitiated.

...

Let us recapitulate. The modern West has lost faith in itself. In the Enlightenment and post-Enlightenment period, this loss of faith liberated enormous commercial and creative forces. At the same time, this loss has rendered the West vulnerable. Is there a way to fortify the modern West without destroying it altogether, a way of not throwing the baby out with the bathwater?

...

That is how things used to work. But we now live in a world where the cat is out of the bag, at least to the extent that we know that the scapegoat really is not as guilty as the persecuting community claims. Because the smooth functioning of human culture depended on a lack of understanding of this truth of human culture, the archaic rituals will no longer work for the modern world,

...

The world of the Enlightsenment may have been based on certain misconceptions about the nature of humanity, but the full knowledge of these misconceptions can remain the province of a philosophical elite.

– Peter Thiel, the Straussian Moment (https://wiki.chadnet.org/files/the-straussian-moment-by-peter-thiel.pdf)

Thiel is also aligned with Curtis Yarvin, better know by his *nom de plume* "Mencius Moldbug," the anti-liberal writer of *Unqualified Reservations.* In the early 2000s, *Unqualified Reservations* had been influential in the early Dissident Right, especially within the so-called "neoreactionary" or "NRx" faction.

In the 2000s, the failures of US-led nation building in Iraq and Afghanistan strengthened Yarvin's anti-democratic views, the federal response to the 2008 financial crisis strengthened his libertarian convictions, and Barack Obama's election as US president later that year reinforced his belief that history inevitably progresses toward left-leaning societies.

...

Yarvin believes that real political power in the United States is held by something he calls "the Cathedral", an amalgam of universities and the mainstream press. According to him, a so-called "Brahmin" social class dominates American society, preaching progressive values to the masses. Yarvin and the Dark Enlightenment (sometimes abbreviated to "NRx") movement assert that the Cathedral's commitment to equality and justice erodes social order. Drawing on computer metaphors, Yarvin contends that society needs a "hard reset" or a "rebooting", not a series of gradual political reforms. Instead of activism, he advocates passivism, claiming that progressivism would fail without right-wing opposition. According to him, NRx adherents should rather design "new architectures of exit" than engage in ineffective political activism.

*Yarvin argues for a "neo-cameralist" philosophy based on Frederick the
Great of Prussia's cameralism. In Yarvin's view, democratic governments
are inefficient and wasteful and should be replaced with sovereign joint-
stock corporations whose "shareholders" (large owners) elect an
executive with total power, but who must serve at their pleasure. The
executive, unencumbered by liberal-democratic procedures, could rule
efficiently much like a CEO-monarch. Yarvin admires Chinese leader
Deng Xiaoping for his pragmatic and market-oriented authoritarianism,
and the city-state of Singapore as an example of a successful
authoritarian regime. He sees the US as soft on crime, dominated by
economic and democratic delusions.*

*Yarvin supports authoritarianism on right-libertarian grounds, claiming that
the division of political sovereignty expands the scope of the state,
whereas strong governments with clear hierarchies remain minimal and
narrowly focused. According to scholar Joshua Tait, "Moldbug imagines a
radical libertarian utopia with maximum freedom in all things except
politics." He has favored same-sex marriage, freedom of religion, private
use of drugs, and written against race- or gender-based discriminatory
laws, although, according to Tait, "he self-consciously proposed private
welfare and prison reforms that resembled slavery". Tait describes
Yarvin's writing as contradictory, saying: "He advocates hierarchy, yet
deeply resents cultural elites. His political vision is futuristic and
libertarian, yet expressed in the language of monarchy and reaction. He is
irreligious and socially liberal on many issues but angrily anti-progressive.
He presents himself as a thinker in search of truth but admits to lying to
his readers, saturating his arguments with jokes and irony. These tensions
indicate broader fissures among the online Right. – **Wikipedia
(https://en.wikipedia.org/wiki/Curtis_Yarvin)***

Thiel was a shrewd political actor, who also had the financial means to put
his ideology into action. In addition to financing congressional candidates
such as JD Vance and Blake Masters, Thiel also understood the role of
technology and its role in shaping culture and politics.

Thiel used some of the remnants of the Alt Right, such as the handful of
Dissident Right Twitter accounts that had not yet been banned, to push his
message and shape Dissident Right culture. Curtis Yarvin, along with
Dissident Right Twitter influencers Zero HP Lovecraft, Benjamin Braddock,
and Gio Pennacchietti began a literary journal of Dissident Right short

stories, artwork, poetry and essays known as the *Passage Prize* in 2021 (https://www.passage.press/store/p/prizeone).

Thiel also financed underground music and art shows in New York City, featuring artists such as Paul Town and associates of Sam Hyde, such as BicFlame. In this way, he seemed to be attempting to astroturf the Dissident Right, following a long history of astroturfing artists in order to promote certain politics (such as the Congress for Cultural Freedom).

Most of Thiel's politicians, with the exception of JD Vance, failed to be elected in 2022. Thus, Thiel's influence was initially thought to have run out of steam. However, it may be too premature to call this, as he does seem to be having an effect on the new "Dime's Square" synthesis between the Dirtbag Left and the Thiel Right in New York City which has recently begun taking form. This faction has sometimes been called the "Post Left."

As of 2023, the atmosphere has changed, and Trump is once again at the center of the party, making these alternative visions of the GOP mostly a moot point for now. The aftermath of the 2024 election will most likely determine its ultimate fate.

The Post Left

Starting in 2020, those on the Left, especially in the "Dirtbag Left," began to appropriate some aspects of Dissident Right culture. The "Dirtbag Left" was a small faction of the Left based around Brooklyn, and known for the *Chapo Trap House, Red Scare* and *Cum Town* podcasts. The Dirtbag Left were democratic socialists, and agreed with the mainstream Left on nearly all social issues, such as feminism, homosexuality, transgenderism, use of drugs and sexual promiscuity, and so forth, but they were more moderate when it came to political correctness. They did not engage in aggressive cancel culture in the same way that "SJWs" did (although they agreed with most of their political opinions). They were also much more savvy and familiar with Internet culture, including the Alt Right, thus they did not make the same types of mistakes as Hillary Clinton did when she, for example, attacked Pepe the Frog. There was some crossover between fans of this scene and fans of *Million Dollar Extreme* or Thiel-sponsored (and thus on the safer side) Dissident Right artists.

During the Covid lockdown, a small area around the intersection of Ludlow and Canal on the Lower East Side in Manhattan (on the other side of the bridge from Brooklyn) known as "Dimes Square" became a popular neighborhood in New York City for outdoor dining (since there were Covid restrictions on most indoor dining). Here the "Dirtbag Left" and Thiel-aligned right started to cross-pollinate, creating what is now known as the "Post Left."

> In the last few months, the micro-neighborhood has spawned a cottage industry of hot-takery, from breathless tweetstorms to scatterbrained sociological wanderings to investigations into what's described as Peter Thiel–backed political machinations to admin reveals of anonymous local podcasters to articles in British weeklies about the neighborhood's anti-woke schisms.
>
> **— Vanity Fair, Jun 13 2022, " What Was Dimes Square?"**
> **https://www.vanityfair.com/style/2022/06/what-was-dimes-square**

> First of all, Dimes Square isn't a square, it's a triangle. Technically, the infamous headquarters of a hyper-specific, hyper-online scene of overeducated young tastemakers (Artists? Influencers? Rich kids? Whatever) falls at the intersection of Ludlow Street and Canal on New York's Lower East Side, but metaphorically, Dimes Square occupies both a number of adjacent city blocks and the minds of New York City media professionals, few of whom have yet grown tired of talking about the place.

In the past few weeks alone, the trend pieces and analyses have continued to stack up. On Aug. 9, The New York Times weighed in on the burgeoning Catholicism trend: young Dimes Square acolytes like Wet Brain podcaster Honor Levy are acknowledging their mortal sins and embracing religious ritual, apparently.

…

"Anna and Dasha really helped push the term Dimes Square into the mainstream, more as a joke about dilettantes and fashion vultures than as a sacrosanct political ethos"

…

Phillips-Horst is referring to Anna Khachiyan and Dasha Nekrasova, co-hosts of Red Scare, a cultural commentary podcast that's either hilariously subversive or blatantly fascist, depending on who you ask; either way, the podcast has become an indelible cultural touchstone of "the dirtbag left" and the perils of Trolling While Hot.

— The Daily Beast, Aug 11 2022, "How Dimes Square Became the New York City Neighborhood We Love to Hate" (https://www.thedailybeast.com/how-dimes-square-be

Red Scare was the epitome of this "Post Left" faction/subculture. *Red Scare* was a Dirtbag Left podcast founded in 2018, and hosted by Dasha Nekrasova and Anna Khachiyan. Although supporters of Bernie Sanders in 2020, they were fascinated with the excitement and controversial, subversive appeal of the Dissident Right, and began to feature more Right Wing figures on their podcast, especially those in Thiel's circle such as Curtis Yarvin. In fact, Thiel's tentacles may be at work here, too.

In a 2022 Vanity Fair article, conservative filmmaker Amanda Milius described Red Scare's laissez-faire attitude as a "premier example" of the "live-and-let-live place" occupied by the "new right", and reported that Khachiyan had met with billionaire venture capitalist Peter Thiel and U.S. Senate candidate Blake Masters. Nekrasova and Khachiyan have rejected this characterisation and denied receiving any funding from Thiel.

-- Wikipedia (https://en.wikipedia.org/wiki/Red_Scare_(podcast))

The crossover between the far-Left and far-Right here is interesting. It seems to be a small niche that liberals can latch onto, having mostly been gatekept out of the Left Wing and not sharing the values of the Right Wing. The *Red Scare* girls seem to fall into this niche. It allows a space for New York hipsters to enjoy the fun of the Dissident Right from a safe distance, while still allowing themselves to practice a hedonistic, bohemian, liberal lifestyle. They attempt to repackage what is essentially pre-Great Awokening liberalism in "tradcath" aesthetics. While attending a Latin Mass because

Anna Khachiyan ✓
@annakhachiyan

I'm not "promoting" her, I am friends with her irl and so my loyalty to her is more important than political signaling on the internet to strangers.

Why do you keep RTing a guy who's probably dysphoric himself and has confused his mysterious social vendetta for a political crusade?

> 🔵 **Anna Khachiyan** ✓ @annakhachiyan · 33m
> The "troon" in question happens to be a dear friend of mine who I love because she's a kind and caring person with principles irl. I don't care about the identity or "aesthetic" aspect of it. And my position on alternate lifestyles is that they are ma...

4:12 PM · 2024-05-13 From Earth · **3.9K** Views

1 Repost **2** Quotes **13** Likes **1** Bookmark

Novus Ordo is "boomer capitalist Catholicism" (a pretentious way of saying "cringe") Anna is pro-abortion, defends transgenderism and stands for no discernible conservative views, merely seeing it as a quaint curiosity which she can add to her repertoire of shallow hipster subversion (https://www.theamericanconservative.com/red-scare-and-postmodern-politics/). It is as if they are instinctively attracted to what is true and good and virtuous, and yet still choose to do what they know is bad for them.

Still, it is an interesting development and I will have to look into this further, as I have not really set foot on the Left side of the culture since my brief time as a Bernie Bro in 2016. Perhaps these initial impressions are incorrect or incomplete, as I have never listened to *Red Scare* and am unfamiliar with this scene, aside from Nick Mullen.

Nick Mullen's podcast, *Cum Town,* while associated with the Dirtbag Left and often featuring guests from the more explicitly socialist podcast *Chapo Trap House,* is not a political podcast at all. Although the hosts clearly are on the Left, it is strictly a comedy show, in the style of the "vulgar wave" such as *South Park* and *MadTV* (which is said to be the show's biggest inspiration). The show often features racist, sexist, anti-Semitic or otherwise politically incorrect humor. But unlike the humor of the Alt Right, it is entirely ironic, and in no way reflects the host's true political views. Nick Mullen is a fan of Sam Hyde, recognizing his talent as a comedian, and defending *World Peace* on the grounds that the offensive humor of the show was no worse than *MadTV, South Park,* or other offensive comedy of the past. (https://youtu.be/2DBWnyd8VDY?si=pxTq0MKSDYgYrg8S)

Sam Hyde Returns

After the cancellation of *World Peace* and dissolution of *Million Dollar Extreme*, Sam Hyde continued to create content apart from MDE. Although banned from Patreon and other platforms, he was still able to sell merch and subscriptions to new content on the platform Gumroad. During this period, Sam would continue to occasionally collaborate with controversial personalities such as Nick Fuentes and incel rapper Egg White (or "Eggy") as well as create videos featuring some "based" opinions. At the same time, he distanced himself somewhat from politics and was not as outspoken about his views. He also began to discourage his followers from expressing heterodox political opinions, and instead encouraged them to worry about making money and achieving success in their own lives.

Those outside of the Dissident Right also started to become more accepting of Sam, especially in the Dirtbag Left/Post Left faction, and he began to gain some Left Wing fans.

Starting in 2022, Sam Hyde finally began to make his comeback, arguably reaching a new peak in his career. It was the video "The Truth About iDubbbz" on January 8 2022 that would mark Sam's rebirth.

iDubbbz was a popular YouTuber during the pre-censorship "golden age" of the platform. Like most of the Internet, this age of YouTube was highly influenced by 4chan humor and the "vulgar wave" of comedy. iDubbbz was no different. One of his popular early clips revolved around the use of the N Word.

Tana Mongeau — a YouTuber you've probably never heard of unless you traffic in the world of vegan social media — is no stranger to the classic Internet cultural form of Vegan YouTube Drama.

...

*This year, Mongeau is feuding with another YouTuber, iDubbbz, who called out Mongeau for using the word "n- - - - -," a call-out accomplished by attending a meet-and-greet with her at the end of January and shouting "say n- - - - -!" as the two posed for a photo. He later posted a video of the interaction on YouTube, where it has been viewed over 2 million times. – **Intelligencer, Feb 9 2017 (https://nymag.com/intelligencer/2017/02/YouTuber-shames-other-YouTuber-for-n-word-also-uses-n-word.html)***

However, by 2019, iDubbbz was moving away from this type of shock humor to more serious content, in the form of documentaries. In 2020, iDubbbz became the center of controversy when his wife Anisa Jomha created an OnlyFans account, and tweeted that iDubbbz was "very supportive." This caused an uproar on the Internet, with fans accusing iDubbbz of being a "cuck." In response, iDubbbz posted a video defending Anisa and sex workers in general. This of course only made him look like even more of a cuck.

Sam Hyde speculates that it was this video that led to iDubbbz choosing him as the subject of his next documentary. According to Hyde, he could sense that iDubbbz had some sort of ill intent in making the documentary, and wanted to "expose" Hyde, figuring that if he could take down a prominent figure of the Alt Right this would redeem him from his reputation as a cuck. In response, Hyde trolled iDubbbz by inviting him to film the documentary, but creating an elaborate fake life. Hyde hired an actress to shave her head and pretend to be Hyde's insane, junkie girlfriend. He rented a dentist's office to be his "studio," consisting of a single cramped room that opened directly onto the street, which was still decorated with medical diagrams on the walls. He gave his crew various other bizarre instructions, such as working on drill rap songs, gathering around a computer screen to watch Hyde's old vertical videos, dumping supplies directly on the floor of the office in a gigantic mess, leading a chant of *"Think it! Dream it! Do it!"* in a team meeting at the start of each work day, and other bizarre antics. After days of these shenanigans, Hyde eventually revealed to iDubbbz that he had been trolled, on the very last day of shooting.

iDubbbz never released his documentary. However, Hyde had had his crew filming a "counter-documentary" throughout the entire production. Reasoning that they had spent too much time and energy on the troll to let it go to waste, Sam decided to release his version of the documentary. The video gained over one million views in six days and received overwhelmingly positive feedback from the Internet, calling it his best work since *World Peace*. It also came at a time when many viewers had not seen Sam's content for a while and felt nostalgic for the old days of the Great Meme War. Additionally, by now, the Alt Right was firmly in the past, and people were more willing to accept Sam without being deterred by his political opinions (which were not even a part of the documentary anyways).

IDubbbz eventually released his version of the documentary, "Getting Away With It," one month later. It took a more serious approach, explaining Sam Hyde's background and his pioneering use of "meta-irony." The iDubbbz documentary gained over 5.6 million views in a years, continuing to raise Hyde's profile.

However, the feud between iDubbbz and Sam Hyde did not end there. It would play out throughout the year, raising Hyde's popularity and establishing his new identity as a now universally beloved "Internet folk hero" while reinforcing iDubbbz's reputation as a cuck. Part of "The Truth about iDubbbz" contained a scene in which Sam Hyde, who had at some point taken up boxing, forces iDubbbz to fight him in a boxing match underneath a graffiti-covered bridge in an undisclosed location. This would foreshadow the next turn in the Sam Hyde versus iDubbbz saga.

On May 14 2022, iDubbbz and Anisa launched the inaugural *Creator Clash*, a boxing event between several famous content creators. One of them was Harley Morenstein of "Epic Meal Time." Originally, Harley had wanted to fight Sam Hyde, but iDubbbz and Anisa shut down the idea during a livestream, saying Sam was "a difficult guy" and fearing he might troll the event. So, instead Sam decided to train Harley.

In an April appearance on the PKA Podcast, Harley would divulge the early stages of the training process. He discusses flying out to Rhode Island half-expecting to become the victim of a practical joke. Fortunately for him, he would be greeted by a very different Sam than what was showcased in the documentary. Harley was promised training, and Sam delivered.

For two weeks, Harley was put through boxing boot camp. He would later post some of the footage to the EpicMealTime channel, showing just how grueling the training was at times. After a parking-lot sparring match, Harley was left physically exhausted. The footage also revealed a side of Sam that few had seen before. He was diligent, accommodating and candid – a significant departure from his prevailing persona. It was clear that for Sam, this training was no joke.

– Downward.News, May 31 2021 (https://downward.news/boxed-out-why-was-sam-hyde-banned-from-creator-clash/)

Apparently the training was successful, with Harley easily defeating his opponent. However, Harley's trainer was not allowed to attend. iDubbbz and Anisa banned Sam from the event, after he had already purchased $10k front row tickets. Not only was Sam himself banned, but staff even began harassing fans seen with his merch.

During the second *Creator Clash* in April 2022, Sam claimed he was going to sneak into the event "dressed in drag." As a result, several guests were denied entry to the event out of fears that they might be Sam in disguise.

According to YouTuber Jet Neptune, a group dressed in Garfield outfits were denied entry to Creator Clash 2 over the fear that one of them was Sam Hyde in disguise — despite claiming none of them even knew who the Internet prankster was.

...

Furthermore, YouTuber Brandon Buckingham also claimed that the Creator Clash organizers banned the use of face masks at the event — once more due to the fear of Sam Hyde being in disguise. **– Dexerto** **(https://www.dexerto.com/entertainment/YouTuber-claims-fans-were-banned-from-creator-clash-over-fear-of-being-sam-hyde-in-disguise-2115673/)**

Another content creator who was supposed to be featured in *Creator Clash 2*, Froggy Fresh, was removed from the event after posting content with Sam Hyde.

Leading up to Creator Clash 2, Froggy Fresh, who was meant to fight in the competition against Chris Ray Gun, was removed from the event. This resulted in significant backlash against iDubbbz and Jomha, the co-founder of the event, increasing the spread of the idea that Jomha had "ruined" iDubbbz by changing his views. People also criticized him for suggesting they could take legal action against Froggy Fresh.

Following the fight, iDubbbz posted a video explaining that Froggy Fresh was removed for training with and posting content with Sam Hyde leading up to the fight, while also insulting iDubbbz's wife numerous times online, something Hyde was also doing **– Know Your Meme** **(https://knowyourmeme.com/memes/people/idubbbz)**

These decisions further tarnished iDubbbz and Anisa's reputation, being criticized by other members of the YouTube community such as Keemstar (a prominent YouTuber and owner of a similar influencer boxing company, "Happy Punch Promotions").

Keemstar's company would sign Sam as a boxer in August 2022. While training seriously, Sam Hyde developed an alter ego, "The Candyman" for promotional interviews about the event. With a thick Irish accent and a green, supervillain-like mask, Sam Hyde would give surrealist, nonsensical responses to reporters, and read Riddler-esque candy-themed poems about beating up his opponents.

I'm fine lad don't worry about me, worry about my opponent August 27th! What's going to happen you're going to see something, you're going to see a reckoning that's been in the works since black 47, when the Irish famine hit and killed millions of people and the English sat back and did nothing! And their cornmeal owners and their sausage factory tycoons did nothing to help the Irish people! I'm going to get revenge!

– The Candyman (https://youtu.be/UUBIFVPwzgs? si=QFTgoois6GBr12hM)

The Candyman: This is what all Irish people wear every day because it's cold up in Ireland! Don't you know anything about Ireland lad? Have you ever been there?

Interviewer: I've been to Belfast.

The Candyman: Have you seen the suffering? No candy anywhere in the streets! Nobody has any candy in Ireland! That's what I aim to change with this fight! I'll be bringing candy to all the poor children of Ireland, so they can all dress like me!

Interviewer: Why candy?

*The Candyman: Because lad, what else is the purpose of life, except to eat candy? **– The Candyman (https://youtu.be/Nwn2ch0_ICE? si=tSmKO-tpoJCJ-gPo)***

Sweet sugary adversaries are perfect for the munching

With a hankering for confectioneries my fists are hungry for punching

I weave my cotton candy web and you fall into my trap

Procure my bib and dessert fork so that I may begin to snack

Should i quench him now or shall I savor every lick

I could punish him slowly or dip and sprinkle him quick

First I'll gingerly ginger snap his candy-coated pretzel arms in half

Then I'll buttery pop gumdrop smack him to the chocolatey canvas with a slap

In the marshmallow ring the ropes look like twizzlers

Body shots to my jelly belly merely give me a snicker

Cookie cups and candy canes sugar plums galore

The candyman with sour patch fists will knock you clean to the floor

I'll pumpkin crumb cream crunch punch his powder donut head until the juniper

Belly jelly jam comes tumble bumble squeezing out of his neck

– The Candyman, "Sam Hyde Puts On An Irish Persona For Press Conference Before IAmThmpsn Fight"
(https://www.youtube.com/watch?v=pusfkF7RIXk)

After defeating his opponent, iamthmpsn, Sam Hyde switched back into the character of the Candyman to give his victory speech, calling out Leftist streamer Hasan Parker and threatening to kill him.

Interviewer: You got anyone you want to call out in the heavyweight division?

The Candyman: oh you know its lad! You know that Hasan Piker: I'm coming to kill you! In Los Angeles! at your house!

Interviewer: In the ring?

The Candyman: No! In real life! I'm going to stalk him, and become obsessed with him, and wear his makeup and his dresses, and wear his skin as a coat! Like the ancient Irish did!

– Sam Hyde Calls Out Hasan Piker After His Fight Victory (https://youtu.be/p1vsNu05-v8?si=4mgbsDx2YUW1rug5)

The Candyman's victory speech went viral on Twitter and became his latest legendary Internet meme, and a piece of Internet history. The meme became a symbol of Sam's new status as universally beloved Internet folk hero.

Sam Hyde is a national treasure.

— Tipster (@JustSoTippy) August 26, 2022

In 2023, Sam launched "Fishtank Live," an interactive reality web series created by himself and Jet Neptune. The series was aired on the site fishtank.live that allowed users to switch between multiple cameras and interact with contestants in various ways.

*Fishtank Live is a reality web series by Sam Hyde and Jet Neptune where eight contestants live in a fully monitored smart house that is livestreamed 24/7 to viewers for six weeks at fishtank.live with viewers able to prank contestants and determine what happens to them via donations, similar to Control My Room livestreams. A cash prize of $30,000 is awarded to the winner. – **Know Your Meme** (https://knowyourmeme.com/memes/subcultures/sam-hydes-fishtank-live)*

While "The Truth about iDubbbz," "The Candyman," and "Fishtank Live" did occasionally contain references to Dissident Right memes or Internet culture in general, this was a minor part of the comedy. It did not employ the Alt Right inspired, politically incorrect shock humor of Hyde's earlier era. Although the original *Million Dollar Extreme* YouTube channel was lost during the ban waves of the Censorship Era, subsequent channels have remained, and Hyde has avoided actions that will cause him additional censorship problems. In addition to support from Left Wing content creators such as Nick Mullen, he also received support from other, more mainstream Internet figures such as Keemstar (he would become co-owner of Keemstar's influencer boxing company, "Happy Punch Productions").

As a grand finale of Sam Hyde's resurrection, *World Peace 2* received independent funding in December 2022, and Sam announced that Nick Rochefort would also be returning. After a few back and forth response videos to each other's streams, Charls eventually reconciled with Sam, and announced that he too would be returning to the show. And so *Million Dollar Extreme* reformed after seven years, and *World Peace 2* was produced with all original members. As of 2023, production of the series has been completed, though a release date has not been announced.

While it is unlikely to have an effect on politics in the 2024 election, given Hyde's decision to distance himself from politics, this is still an important part of the historical dialectic. The successful return of Sam Hyde and widespread acceptance of him on both the Left and the Right proves that the antithesis is continuing to be absorbed by mainstream culture, institutionalizing the Dissident Right movement. It is similar to the mainstream Right's eventual adoption of counter-culture artists and rock and roll.

Choice of Words Pt.2

In the next section, we will be discussing some anti-Semitic comments by Nick Fuentes and Kanye West. However, they claim that they are not anti-Semitic and do not hate all Jews, but are simply criticizing what they call "Jewish power." This term "Jewish power" basically describes the same phenomenon as what Leftists call "white supremacy" or "white privilege," in which Leftists claim white people are over-represented in areas of power and influence in society and use this power towards their own racial interest. The only difference is instead of whites, they apply this same argument to Jews.

In this text, I refer to this issue as "criticism of Jewish influence in society." I chose this term because I feel it more specifically describes the issue they are talking about.

I have no problem calling them anti-Semites, because that is what they would be called by an ordinary person, but I also feel this is not an honest or objective description of their views, which are a bit different from a blind, emotional hatred of all Jews (which is a real thing, especially among some "wignats").

The term "Jewish power," which they use to describe their own views, has the opposite problem. It is a little too Nazi for my taste. Like "anti-Semitic," it is not specific, and it is also not an objective term, but implies that I affirm their opinions.

My choice of words is also more factual. There do exist Jewish groups such as AIPAC, ADL, ZOA, etc. and they do influence society, through lobbying and activism. Whether this is a good or bad thing is entirely a matter of opinion. You can believe it is a good thing, depending on your politics. If you believe these groups are necessary to protect the rights of Jews in society, then you would probably believe that it is a good thing. If they try to create a society more aligned with Jewish values, and you agree with Jewish values, then you would probably believe that it is a good thing. Fuentes and others believe it is a bad thing, in part because they disagree with Jewish values, and thus they are criticizing it. Therefore, I think this is the most straightforward way of describing what is going on, taken at face value.

Of course, you may also believe Fuentes is using this as a pretense simply because he hates Jews. Some might say the fact that, since his association with Kanye West, he no longer shies away from Nazi imagery as much as in the past, that this is "proof" that he has been hiding his true views from the beginning. That is possible, but it relies on speculation about Fuentes's true motives, which cannot be known for certain. So, for now I will take his statements at face value.

In short, if someone wants to call them or their statements anti-Semitic, I think this is reasonable, and outright refusing to do so would be splitting hairs to the point of dishonesty. But I prefer the term "criticism of Jewish influence" because it is a better and more specific, and therefore more honest and descriptive, term. Therefore, this is the language I will be using when this issue is addressed.

The main purpose of this text is to present the views of the Dissident Right, even those that are the most extreme, in a fair way, so that people can understand that perspective accurately. I do not necessarily advocate for any particular view in this text, and leave it to the reader to decide what they may or may not agree with.

Ye the Wignat Pt.1: Death Con 3

Kanye West needs no introduction. He is one of the most influential celebrities, designers, and musicians of this century, and one of the richest black men in America.

In a way, Kanye fulfills a similar role as The Beatles did in the 1960s counter-culture. Both have a reputation as musical geniuses who changed and experimented over time, leaving an indelible mark on a rising new musical genre. Both were also the products of the larger dialectical movement of their time, in political, aesthetic, cultural, and various other ways. It is no coincidence that Kanye is a Christian politically incorrect conservative, while John Lennon was an idealistic left-leaning liberal and George Harrison embraced Eastern mysticism.

Kanye came out as a Trump supporter after the election in November of 2016 (although he did not vote for him in the election). In April of 2018, he posted a selfie of himself in a MAGA hat and tweeted support for the President.

"You don't have to agree with trump but the mob can't make me not love him. We are both dragon energy. He is my brother. I love everyone. I don't agree with everything anyone does. That's what makes us individuals. And we have the right to independent thought," West said in a tweet on Wednesday.

*The President responded three hours later, quoting the tweet and calling his comments "very cool." – **TIME, Apr 25 2018** (https://time.com/5254664/kanye-west-supports-donald-trump-Twitter/). Trump's reply would become a meme.*

He would appear in the MAGA hat several more times, including during an appearance on *Saturday Night Live*. He even recorded a song defending his pro-Trump stance, "Ye vs. The People."

Nick Fuentes, like Kanye a Chicago native, was a life-long fan, even before Kanye's support of Trump or other political statements. Before being redpilled or involved in politics, Nick grew up with his music in high school. He considered him, along with Trump and Sam Hyde, one of his heroes. He admired his bombastic, provocative personality and his visionary ability to create new things that no one else had ever even thought of before.

In October 2022, Kanye (who had now changed his name to just "Ye") appeared with fellow black conservative Candace Owens at a Paris fashion show wearing a "White Lives Matter" t-shirt, drawing criticism by the media.

> *After Monday's fashion show, Owens posted photos of her outfit on her Instagram story. One post appeared to be a screenshot of a story from West's account, which read: "Everyone know that Black Lives Matter was a scam now it's over you're welcome."*
>
> *...*
>
> *Hannah Gais, senior research analyst at Southern Poverty Law Center, which tracks hate groups, said in a statement to CBS News both West and Owens "have a proclivity for high-profile stunts designed to troll liberals." and that their "use of rhetoric popular among some on the racist fringe goes to show that these slogans can become normalized and part of the broader right-wing vernacular through repetition."* – **CBS News, Oct 4 2022, "Kanye West faces backlash for wearing shirt with "White Lives Matter" slogan" (https://www.cbsnews.com/news/kanye-west-white-lives-matter-shirt-candace-owens-fashion-show-backlash/)**

In the following weeks, he would appear on conservative programs such as Tucker Carlson, and became an overnight sensation in the conservative media.

Suddenly, this all changed. On October 8 2022, Ye posted his infamous "death con" tweet on Twitter:

I'm a bit sleepy tonight but when I wake up I'm going death con 3 On JEWISH PEOPLE. The funny thing is I actually can't be Anti Semitic because black people are actually Jew also You guys have toyed with me and tried to black ball anyone whoever opposes your agenda. – Ye (https://www.ajc.org/news/5-of-kanye-wests-antisemitic-remarks-explained)

As a result of the tweet, Ye would lose hundreds of millions of dollars. It was also reported at the time that JPMorgan Chase banned Ye from their bank as a result of the tweet, but it appears this may have been due to an unrelated dispute with the artist.

In response to his antisemitic statements, Vogue, CAA, Balenciaga, Gap, and Adidas terminated their collaborations, sponsorships, and relationships with West. Foot Locker and TJ Maxx removed West's products from their shelves. With the termination of his business relationships, West lost his billionaire status; Forbes estimated his reduced worth at $400 million, coming from his "real estate, cash, his music catalog, and a 5% stake in ex-wife Kim Kardashian's shapewear firm, Skims". – Wikipedia (https://en.wikipedia.org/wiki/Views_of_Kanye_West)

Tucker immediately canceled any future planned interviews with Kanye, and conservatives began deleting their earlier tweets praising him.

Since October, a Twitter account run by Republicans on the House of Representatives' judiciary committee has contained a cryptic post that said: "Kanye. Elon. Trump" – apparently claiming Ye, billionaire entrepreneur Elon Musk and former president Donald Trump as their own.

– The Guardian, Dec 1 2022, "Republicans delete tweet that appears to support Kanye West after he praises Nazis' (https://www.theguardian.com/music/2022/dec/01/kanye-west-ye-republican-tweet-deleted)

Ye explained that the tweets were in response to unfair Jewish "business contracts" that he said took advantage of black artists. He also posted screenshots of his Jewish former personal trainer Harley Pasternak, who seemed to threaten Ye with drugging him or sending him to a mental institution due to his support of Donald Trump and conservative politics, going so far as to invoke Ye's children in his threat.

> *I'm going to help you one of a couple ways... First, you and I sit down and have an loving and open conversation, but you don't use cuss words, and everything that is discussed is based in fact, and not some crazy stuff that dumb friend of yours told you, or you saw in a tweet*
>
> *Second option, I have you institutionalized again where they medicate the crap out of you, and you go back to Zombieland forever. Play date with the kids just won't be the same.* **– Harley Pasternak (https://www.marca.com/en/lifestyle/celebrities/2022/11/04/6364fb1ae 2704ed3928b45b3.html)**

"*What should be obvious by now is that I was raised to stand for my truth regardless of the consequences. So I will say this again I was mentally misdiagnosed and nearly drugged out of my mind to make me a manageable well behaved celebrity*" said Ye in the same tweet containing the screenshot of Pasternak's message. Note the effect of Internet technology here, automatically creating a paper trail of Pasternak's message and allowing Ye to easily circumvent the media and tell his side of the story.

While Ye was almost universally condemned, black comedian Dave Chappelle appeared to partially defend Ye, and Jewish comedian Jon Stewart gave a more nuanced take on the controversy.

> *Chappelle began the show by reading a statement which said "I denounce antisemitism in all its forms and I stand with my friends in the Jewish community."*
>
> *"And that, Kanye, is how you buy yourself some time," Chappelle joked.*
>
> *He went on to say that Ye had broken "the show business rules" which are "the rules of perception."*
>
> *"If they're Black, then it's a gang. If they're Italian, it's a mob," Chappelle said. "But if they're Jewish, it's a coincidence and you should never speak about it."*

Chappelle went on to talk about the abundance of Jewish people in Hollywood.

"But that doesn't mean anything," he said. "There's a lot of Black people in Ferguson, Missouri. Doesn't mean they run the place."

Chappelle said he could see "if you had some kind of issue, you might go out to Hollywood and start connecting some kind of lines and you could maybe adopt the illusion that Jews run show business."

*"It's not a crazy thing to think," he said. "But it's a crazy thing to say out loud." – **CNN, Nov 14 2022, "Dave Chappelle's 'SNL' monologue sparks backlash as being antisemitic"** (https://www.cnn.com/2022/11/14/entertainment/dave-chappelle-adl-antisemitic/index.html). This came at a time when another black man, Kyrie Irving, was also being suspended from the Brooklyn Nets after tweeting about a Black Nationalist film which the ADL called anti-Semitic.*

Stewart, who is of Jewish heritage, rejected the idea that Chappelle "normalized antisemitism," and said: "I don't know if you've been on comments sections on most news articles, but it's pretty fucking normal … I don't believe that censorship and penalties are the way to end antisemitism or to not gain understanding. I don't believe in that. I think it's the wrong way to approach it."

He referenced Brooklyn Nets star Kyrie Irving's suspension due to promoting an anti-Jewish film on Twitter. "Penalizing somebody for having a thought, I don't think is the way to change their minds or gain understanding," he said. "This is a grown-ass man and to say, 'We're going to put you in a time out, you're going to sit in a corner and stare at the wall until you no longer believe the Jews control the international banking system.' We have to get past this in the country. People think Jews control Hollywood. People think Jews control the banks. And to pretend that they don't and to not deal with it in a straightforward manner, we'll never gain any kind of understanding with each other."

...

Stewart explained wounds such as racial divides and antisemitism need to be exposed, yet the "general tenor of conversation in this country is to cover it up. Look at it from a Black perspective. It's a culture that feels its wealth has been extracted by different groups — whites, Jews. Whether it's true or not isn't the issue, that's the feeling in that community. And if you don't understand that's where it's coming from, then you can't sit down and explain that being in an industry isn't the same as having a nefarious and controlling interest in that industry.

*"Dave said something in the SNL monologue that I thought was constructive as well, which is: 'It shouldn't be this hard to talk about things,'" he added. "And that is what we're talking about. I can't believe there aren't a shit ton of people who believe that the Jews have an unreasonable amount of control over the systems and they wield them as puppet masters. I'm called antisemitic because I'm against Israel's treatment of Palestinians … those [terms] shut down debate. They're used as a cudgel. And whether it's comedy or discussion or anything else, if we don't have the wherewithal to meet each other with reality, then how do we move forward?" – **The Hollywood Reporter, Nov 16 2022, "Jon Stewart Says Censorship Not the Way to End Antisemitism After Chappelle, Kanye Scandals"** (https://www.hollywoodreporter.com/tv/tv-news/jon-stewart-antisemitism-chappelle-kanye-colbert-1235263238/)*

Needless to say, Fuentes was elated by the news, covering it on his show and praising the fact that such a high profile figure was drawing attention to one of Fuentes's most controversial views. He also chastised conservatives for suddenly pretending to be fans of Ye, something that Fuentes actually was for his entire life. He also pointed out that conservatives welcomed criticism of every other group (such as black people) and condoned every other type of controversial statement (such as saying "white lives matter") as "free speech," but drew the line at any "free speech" that criticized Jews.

Some have interpreted "death con 3," with its violent choice of words, as a real call to violence against Jews. Obviously, any calls to anti-Semitic violence should be condemned unequivocally. But, other parts of the incident are more ambiguous.

Fuentes is correct that there is a double standard regarding such statements. If Ye had said that white business people in the music industry were taking advantage of black artists with unfair business practices, and wrote "death con 3" against white people, his comments would not be condemned but instead praised. The mere fact that saying "white lives matter" was considered hate speech is proof of this. So it appears that there are some groups of people that can be criticized freely, but some that cannot, and that Jews are one group that cannot. That having been said, it is understandable why Jewish people are more sensitive than white people about this sort of talk, given the history of the two groups. I do not think that they are necessarily wrong for having this sensitivity. It is reasonable. However, it's simply worth noting that the double standard exists.

Jews criticize non-Jews frequently, particularly Christians. For example, Jewish comedian Sarah Silverman, joked on her 2005 comedy special *Jesus is Magic* that *"I hope the Jews did kill Christ. I'd do it again in a second."(https://www.YouTube.com/watch?v=GSrhJGGDqx0)*

In 2021, Silverman and another Jewish comedian, Seth Rogan, would go on to produce *Santa Inc,* an 8-episode series on HBO Max mocking Christmas with scatological humor. Here are some of the top comments on Reddit regarding this series:

> *I was raised Jewish. I also can see where people are coming from on this. If the roles were reversed, and two white Christians were making a show mocking Jewish traditions these two would call it it out. I watched the first episode, and the "jokes" were just lazy. It's basically the same garbage that has been repeated so often lately. Comedy is getting pretty bland when you can only "joke" about people that look just like you or white people. – **Unknown Redditor. This comment was later deleted (https://www.reddit.com/r/HBOMAX/comments/r844pu/seth_rogen_insults_everyone_who_criticized_santa/)**

This isn't even roast humour, Dave Chapelle making fun of white people is roast humour and he does it brilliantly and it's hilarious. Santa Inc is just Seth's self professed anti-white activism cloaked in a christmas themed TV series which is why none of the jokes land with an everyman white audience which is the primary demographic of the US and Europe. – **Unknown Redditor. This comment was later deleted (https://www.reddit.com/r/HBOMAX/comments/r844pu/seth_rogen_in sults_everyone_who_criticized_santa/)**

It's even worse when it comes from someone who doesn't actually follow the religion, too.

Can you imagine a movie, directed by someone who wasn't Jewish, critiquing Hanukkah? People generally don't like their Holy Traditions attacked. I said it in another post, too, because there was a complaint about Santa being white: What other color would he be?

It's a European tradition, from European countries about a white European. o.o I don't identify as white, but that's from white culture, and white people are allowed to have their own culture. His surprise only shows how little he understands what he did. – **Unknown Redditor. This comment was later deleted (https://www.reddit.com/r/HBOMAX/comments/r844pu/seth_rogen_in sults_everyone_who_criticized_santa/)**

Critics of the series were denounced by Seth Rogan as "white supremacists." (https://movieweb.com/seth-rogen-white-supremacists-review-bombing-santa-inc/) *(Author's note: although, to be fair, 4chan raided the comments section on promotions for this series with anti-Semitic jokes, so this is not entirely inaccurate. However, the series was also criticized for other reasons, such as being painfully unfunny)*

I did not watch the series personally, so I do not know if the Reddit comments above are accurate or justified. I could not find Silverman and Rogan, for example, specifically making fun of Jesus in this film, but rather Santa (although she did do so in her earlier comments). In any case, it actually is not necessary for making my point whether or not people being offended was "justified." My point is simply that the offense goes both ways.

Likewise, I do not criticize Jews simply for being offended at the comments
of Ye. I am only offering a few cursory instances of Jews critiquing
Christians and Gentiles, and their culture and traditions. Obviously, there is a
plethora of examples and one does not have to look very far. It is a common
theme of Jews to criticize white and Christian culture from the perspective of
"the outsider," as is the main theme of *Santa Inc.* But if Christians or Gentiles
criticize Hanukkah, or other aspects of Jewish culture, this is considered
"anti-Semitism."

Of course, Jews are free under the 1st Amendment to criticize Christians and
whites as much as they please, especially in a comedic work. But this same
protection also protects Ye and Nick Fuentes, and even Mr. Bond and
Moonman (whose work is also intended to be "satire"). While both Ye and
Nick Fuentes were banned, Seth Rogan and Sarah Silverman's comments are
promoted on major media platforms. While Ye and Nick Fuentes were
financially punished for their comments, Silverman and Rogan are free to
monetize their comments.

The Talmud, the book that Rabbis study in order to correctly interpret the
laws of the Torah, also criticizes Gentiles. For example, here are some
controversial passages from the Talmud:

*Onkelos said to him: What is the punishment of that man, a euphemism
for Jesus himself, in the next world? Jesus said to him: He is punished
with boiling excrement. As the Master said: Anyone who mocks the words
of the Sages will be sentenced to boiling excrement.* **– Gittin 57a. In
other words, according to Jews, Jesus is burning in hell in boiling
excrement (https://www.sefaria.org/Gittin.57a.4?
lang=bi&with=all&lang2=en)**

*Scoundrel! Aren't Gentiles called donkeys? As it is written: "Whose flesh is
as the flesh of donkeys"* **– Berakhot 58a:15. This appears to compare
Gentiles to animals. Similar to how an anti-Semite might compare
Jews to animals**

As it is written: "And you My sheep, the sheep of My pasture, are people [adam]" (Ezekiel 34:31), from which it is derived that you, the Jewish people, are called adam, but Gentiles are not called adam **– Keritot 6b:20**

And you, My sheep, the sheep of My pasture, are man" (Ezekiel 34:31), which teaches that you, i.e., the Jewish people, are called "man", but Gentiles are not called "man". **– Bava Metzia 114b:2**

In these verses, the Talmud seemingly implies Gentiles are not fully human. Or, at the very least, are an inferior type of human to Jews. Isn't that called racism? Isn't that the inverse of anti-Semitism, which one might call anti-Gentilism? While all Jews may not interpret this verse in this way, the point is simply that it is an inflammatory passage.

The verse about Jesus burning in hell was taken from the Talmud directly, and I know it is legitimate. The others are from WikiQuote (https://en.wikiquote.org/wiki/Talmud/On_Gentiles). Some might argue that these quotes are taken out of context. That very well may be the case. I encourage anyone truly interested in Jewish teachings to consult with a Rabbi so he may understand the quote properly, with its full context and nuance of meaning. However, a Jewish organization like the ADL, as we have seen, is never interested in the full context and nuance of meaning when evaluating the statements of those it claims to be anti-Semites, white supremacists, and racists, so I will hold the Talmud to the same standard.

For a more fair and complete opinion on these controversial verses, as well as others in a similar vein, I suggest watching the video "Religious Jews are asked about the Talmud" on the channel Corey Gil-Shuster. In it, he interviews several religious and non-religious Jews in Israel, as well as Rabbis, concerning what these and similar verses that are purportedly in the Talmud, mean. (https://youtu.be/M60FUPVtq9k?si=YdJWMN1det_kHKyO)

Most non-religious Jews in the video thought the verses were ridiculous, while some religious Jews defended them to varying degrees.

At the end of the video, Rabbi Yiztkah Brietowitz, an Israeli Hassidic Rabbi, is interviewed about verses such as these.

Rabbi Yitzchak Breitowitz is a world-renowned lecturer and rabbinic authority, who is the Rav of Kehillas Ohr Somayach, at Ohr Somayach in Jerusalem. Rabbi Breitowitz's scope of knowledge, brilliance, as well as a unique ability to grasp complicated material and communicate it clearly to others is legendary. He has lectured extensively throughout the US and Israel on medical, business, and family ethics. He has published numerous articles on bankruptcy, commercial law, medical ethics, & Jewish law. **– Torah Anytime, "Rabbi Yitzchak Breitowitz" (https://www.torahanytime.com/#/speaker?l=414)**

The Rabbi confirms some verses, such as a verse that says "to eat with a goy [Gentile] is the same as eating with a dog," explaining that the verse was meant to warn Jews against associating with immoral people. Others, such as a verse by Rabbi Rashi that compares Gentiles to dogs, he argues apply only to non-monotheistic pagans. He also says that these verses reflect that some Jews "have a chip on their shoulder towards the non-Jewish world" due to being "tortured and killed," such as in the holocaust, by non-Jews. He says he disagrees with this sentiment "philosophically" but it was "understandable." He also says that there is "certainly a belief in Judaism that the soul of the Jew comes from a higher level of holiness" and that Jews had a "higher spiritual potential" than non-Jews, while qualifying this by saying that any particular non-Jew might be more "righteous" than any particular Jew. He unequivocally denies alleged verses that purportedly claimed that Jews could cheat and even murder non-Jews, saying these actions are strictly forbidden.

I include these verses only to demonstrate that there are controversial and potentially offensive statements and attitudes in the Talmud. This is not exclusive to Judaism. Both the New Testament and Koran also contain controversial verses, including verses Jews would consider anti-Semitic.

Jews also frequently make dehumanizing and even genocidal comments towards Palestinians. During the conflict between Hamas and Israel in

October 2023, many Jews, including large accounts like @Yakovolf, Joel Pollak (editor-in-cheif of *Breitbart News)*, Avi Yemini of *Rebel News*, Daniel Bordman of *The National Telegraph* and others called for violence or in some cases genocide.

A full list of 74 public statements by Jews advocating for ethnic cleansing, torture, crimes against civilians, and the genocide of Palestinians can be found at "Law4Palestine.org" (https://law4palestine.org/wp-content/uploads/2024/01/Database-of-Israeli-Incitement-to-Genocide-LEGISLATORS.pdf)

None of these tweets were taken down or censored in any way by Twitter. Unlike Kanye, the Jews who posted these did not face any financial consequences. In fact, Twitter added a note under some tweets specifically saying that although they violated twitter guidelines, they would still remain up!

> This Post violated the X Rules. However, X has determined that it may be in the public's interest for the Post to remain accessible.   **View**
> Learn more

The point I am trying to make is this. If I am a Gentile who is offended by the Jewish religion due to these statements, am I free to cancel my business contracts with Jews? If you believe in "free speech," then no. Jews are free to say and believe whatever they please about Gentiles, and Gentiles such as Ye are free to say and believe whatever they please about Jews. But, if you believe in "hate speech," then it's only fair that Jews be held accountable for their own "hate speech."

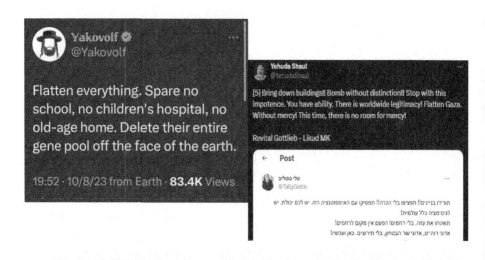

Yakovolf ✓
@Yakovolf

Flatten everything. Spare no school, no children's hospital, no old-age home. Delete their entire gene pool off the face of the earth.

19:52 · 10/8/23 from Earth · **83.4K** Views

Yehuda Shaul
@YehudaShaul

[5] Bring down buildings!! Bomb without distinction!! Stop with this impotence. You have ability. There is worldwide legitimacy! Flatten Gaza. Without mercy! This time, there is no room for mercy!

Revital Gottlieb - Likud MK

← Post

טלי גוטליב
@TallyGotliv

תורידו בניינים!! תפוצצו בלי הברה!! תפסיקו עם האימפוטנציה הזו. יש לנם יכולת. יש
לגיטימציה כלל עולמית!
תשטחו את עזה. בלי רחמים! הפעם אין מקום לרחמים!
אדוני רוה"מ, אדוני שר הבטחון, בלי תירוצים. כאן ועכשיו!!

Joel Pollak ✓
@joelpollak   Follow

I have broken the Sabbath and Jewish holiday to deliver this message: Israel should wipe out Gaza. Allow 48 hours to evacuate women, children and the elderly. Destroy everything that remains, plow it under, and annex it to Israel. This is the end for Hamas and Palestinian terror.

14:32 · 07 Oct 23 · **167K** Views

Avi Yemini ✓ ▪
@OzraeliAvi   Follow

This is Israel's chance to finally finish the job

2:46 · 07 Oct 23 · **429K** Views

Daniel Bordman ✓ @Ranting... · 6h
You want to end the violence? You don't like war? You want "deescalation"? Hamas must be DESTROYED. There is no peace for anyone until they are wiped out

💬 45   🔁 278   ❤ 1,130   📊 15.1K   ⬚

Bryan E. Leib ✓ @BryanLeibFL · 17h
It's time to carpet bomb Gaza Strip. Kill them all.

Go ahead - call me a war monger and racist. I will show you videos like this.

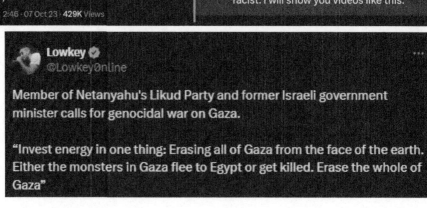

Lowkey ✓
@LowkeyOnline

Member of Netanyahu's Likud Party and former Israeli government minister calls for genocidal war on Gaza.

"Invest energy in one thing: Erasing all of Gaza from the face of the earth. Either the monsters in Gaza flee to Egypt or get killed. Erase the whole of Gaza"

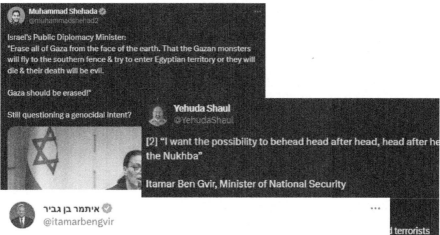

שיהיה ברור, כשאומרים שצריך לחסל את חמאס, זה גם את אלו ששרים, את אלו
שתומכים ואת אלו שמחלקים סוכריות, כל אלו מחבלים. וגם אותם צריך לחסל!

Translated from Hebrew by Google

To be clear, when they say that Hamas needs to be eliminated, it also
means those who sing, those who support and those who distribute
candy, all of these are terrorists. And they should be eliminated!

Ye the Wignat Pt.2: Christian Futurism

Meanwhile, Trump would make his extremely disappointing 2024 announcement speech. In it, Trump seemed subdued, old, and out of touch. He repeated basic Fox News conservative talking points and whined about past persecution by the deep state, including the raid on Mar-a-Lago. Fuentes, perhaps Trump's greatest advocate on the Dissident Right, called the speech, "worse than I expected. A huge disappointment, both in style and substance."

A few days later, Milo Yiannopoulos was spotted with Ye, and it was announced that he would be Ye's campaign manager for a 2024 Presidential run. At the time, Milo had become a close ally of Fuentes. Since his days in the Alt Right, Milo had converted to Catholicism and claimed to have "stopped being gay," thus eliminating any potential conflict of interest and convincing Fuentes that he could be trusted. Nick asked Milo if there was any way that he could arrange a meeting between himself and the rapper.

On Thanksgiving Day, 2022 at Mar-a-Lago, Fuentes would find himself seated between his two heroes.

> On Tuesday, November 22, 2022, former President Donald Trump hosted white supremacist and Holocaust denier Nick Fuentes and rapper Ye, formerly known as Kanye West, at his Mar-a-Lago home. Trump's willingness to associate with figures who have repeatedly spread antisemitic and white supremacist tropes is deeply concerning and has not gone unnoticed by extremists.

> Fuentes, a white supremacist and rabid misogynist who attended the 2017 "Unite the Right" rally in Charlottesville, has repeatedly spread racist and antisemitic conspiracy theories. Despite his history of antisemitism, he has forged alliances with a variety of far-right figures, including some GOP officials.

> *Ye, who announced his bid for the presidency two days after having dinner with Trump, has been embroiled in controversy for weeks after making numerous antisemitic and other inflammatory remarks.*
>
> *He was briefly locked out of his social media accounts and lost his partnerships with Gap, Adidas and Balenciaga. – **ADL, Nov 29 2022, (https://www.adl.org/resources/blog/extremists-react-trump-dinner-ye-and-nick-fuentes)***

There are multiple versions of how the meeting progressed. Some depicted the meeting as set-up by Milo to make Trump look bad, after Milo had made anti-Trump comments in the past. Many establishment conservatives went with this narrative, perhaps in an attempt to run damage control for Trump and distance the MAGA movement from Fuentes.

> *But Trump may have been walking into a trap in Mar-a-Lago's gilded halls — one that leveraged his own penchant for spectacle and showmanship against him. Ye arrived with three guests, including white nationalist and antisemite Nick Fuentes. – **NBC News, Nov 29 2022, "The inside story of Trump's explosive dinner with Ye and Nick Fuentes" (https://www.nbcnews.com/politics/donald-trump/story-trumps-explosive-dinner-ye-nick-fuentes-rcna59010)***

Later, Milo himself supported this version of the story.

> *As fallout from Donald Trump's meeting with the white supremacist Nick Fuentes continues, a far-right activist has claimed the meeting was a set-up, meant to "make Trump's life miserable".*
>
> *...*
>
> *Speaking to NBC, Yiannopoulos said he came up with a plan for Fuentes to travel with Ye and hopefully gain access to the former president.*
>
> *"I wanted to show Trump the kind of talent that he's missing out on by allowing his terrible handlers to dictate who he can and can't hang out with," Yiannopoulos said.*

"I also wanted to send a message to Trump that he has systematically repeatedly neglected, ignored, abused the people who love him the most, the people who put him in office, and that kind of behavior comes back to bite you in the end."

– The Guardian, Nov 30 2022, "Milo Yiannopoulos claims he set up Fuentes dinner 'to make Trump's life miserable'" (https://www.theguardian.com/us-news/2022/nov/30/milo-yiannopoulos-nick-fuentes-donald-trump-dinner)

Wignats also supported this narrative:

Some white supremacist leaders argued the dinner was a "hit job" arranged to damage Trump's reputation. "My brief take on the Trump, Kanye dinner fiasco is that Milo [Yiannopoulos, Ye's campaign manager], likely working on behalf of big GOP donors, got into Kanye's ear and used him as a mechanism to get Fuentes and Trump into the same room, thereby sinking Trump's 2024 run, making Ron DeSantis the uncontested GOP favorite, and making everyone involved look stupid and ridiculous," wrote Mike Peinovich [AKA Mike Enoch], a leader of the white supremacist National Justice Party, wrote on Telegram. "Trump would likely never have taken the dinner if not for some Jew donor telling him to. He was set up." – ADL, November 29 2022, (https://www.adl.org/resources/blog/extremists-react-trump-dinner-ye-and-nick-fuentes)

Fuentes denies this version of events. He insisted that it was not a setup, that Ye met with Trump in order to ask Trump if he wanted to be Ye's running mate (as Ye himself tweeted) and simply asked Fuentes to tag along at the last minute. He also said Trump took a liking to him, exclaiming, *"this kid's smart, he really gets me"* after Nick told him to attack DeSantis, take a tougher approach towards other Republicans, and to "let Trump be Trump." Other journalists support this version of the dinner.

One source who spoke with NBC News told the outlet Trump was taken by Fuentes who: 'presented as statistician'. They added: 'He was very knowledgeable of polls and Trump's campaign. Trump was very impressed but Trump didn't know who he was.

...

On Friday, Ye also confirmed that Trump was 'impressed' with Fuentes in a video posted to Twitter.

'So Trump is really impressed with Nick Fuentes, and Nick Fuentes, unlike so many of the lawyers, and so many of the people that he was left with on his 2020 campaign, he's actually a loyalist' Ye said.

– Daily Mail, Nov 25 2022, "Trump was 'very taken' with Holocaust denier Nick Fuentes and they fawned over each other during Mar-a-Lago dinner with Kanye West - but former President claims he had no idea he was a white supremacist"
(https://www.dailymail.co.uk/news/article-11470903/Trump-taken-Holocaust-denier-Nick-Fuentes-Mar-Lago-dinner-Ye.html)

Trump partially, but not fully, disavowed Fuentes, in a series of tweets.

In the days following the dinner, Trump attempted to distance himself from Ye and Fuentes, writing on Truth Social, "This past week, Kanye West called me to have dinner at Mar-a-Lago. Shortly thereafter, he unexpectedly showed up with three of his friends, whom I knew nothing about...The dinner was quick and uneventful." In a follow-up post, Trump said, "We got along great, he [Ye] expressed no anti-Semitism, & I appreciated all of the nice things he said about me on "Tucker Carlson." Why wouldn't I agree to meet? Also, I didn't know Nick Fuentes."

– ADL(https://www.adl.org/resources/blog/extremists-react-trump-dinner-ye-and-nick-fuentes)

One-time AFPAC speaker Marjorie Taylor Greene also began to condemn Fuentes around the same time, a detail that will become important later.

Rep. Marjorie Taylor Greene (R-Ga.) is condemning white nationalist Nick Fuentes and defending former President Trump after a dinner he had with the rapper Kanye West, who now goes by Ye; Fuentes and provocateur Milo Yiannopoulos.

...

In a conversation with reporters on Tuesday, Greene said that she agreed with House Minority Leader Kevin McCarthy's (R-Calif.) statement on Friday that Fuentes's views have "no place in the Republican Party."

She said she spoke with Trump and talked with people on his staff after news of the dinner broke.

"President Trump had no idea he [Fuentes] was even coming. So that's unfortunate," Greene said.

...

Greene said that knowing what she knows now about Fuentes, she would not have spoken at his conference — but does not regret her message to those in the audience.

...

Also present at the dinner with Trump was Yiannopoulos, a former Breitbart editor who was banned from Twitter in 2016 in connection with a campaign of racist harassment against actress Leslie Jones. Yiannopoulos was an unpaid intern in Greene's congressional office earlier this year.

"I talk to him [Yiannopoulos] occasionally because he actually lives in Rome [Ga.] in the same town I live in," Greene said. "I had no idea they were going down there [to Mar-a-Lago]. And I found out about it, basically, like everybody else did on Twitter."

– The Hill, Nov 30 2022, "Marjorie Taylor Greene condemns Fuentes, remarks on Trump, Yiannopoulos"
(https://thehill.com/homenews/house/3756423-marjorie-taylor-greene-condemns-fuentes-remarks-on-trump-yiannopoulos/)

Fuentes was appointed "communications director" by Ye, and also brought some of his allies, such as Ali Alexander and YouTuber Sneako, into the campaign. He announced on his show that AFPAC 4 would be postponed and *America First* put on indefinite hiatus. He, Milo, and Ye then began conducting various news interviews, including Tim Pool and, of course, the infamous *InfoWars* appearance.

In his appearance on *InfoWars*, Ye appeared next to Fuentes and Ali in a BDSM-like mask that covered his entire face, and an ostentatious racing jacket covered in logos. Alex Jones attempted to do damage control as Ye performed manic prop comedy mocking Israeli President Benjamin Netanyahu and praised Adolf Hitler, saying "I love Hitler" and "we're gonna stop dissing the Nazis."

> *Alex Jones stated that people who are not Nazis should not be called "Nazi" and be demonized, which caused Kanye to interject when he said Hitler had some "good things" to him*
>
> *...*
>
> *"Well, I see good things about Hitler, also. Every human being has value that they brought to the table, especially Hitler"*
>
> *...*
>
> *"I see good things about Hitler. I love everyone and Jewish people are not going to tell me. You can love us and you can love what we're doing to you with the contracts, and you can love what we're pushing with the pornography. But this guy [Hitler] that invented highways and invented the very microphone that I use as a musician, you can't say out loud that this person ever did anything good. I'm done with that. Every human being has something of value that they brought to the table, especially Hitler."*
>
> *...*
>
> *Continuing on with the topic of Nazis and Hitler, Alex Jones then went on to say that demonizing people by calling them "Nazis" or being against those who said they "didn't hate the Nazis" wasn't right, referencing Arnold Schwarzenegger who reportedly said he liked Hitler and still won acting awards, which prompted Kanye to say "I like Hitler" right before the cut to a commercial break.*
>
> *...*

In another moment from the episode, some online speculated that Jones was attempting to give Kanye an out or further explain his controversial statements when he related Kanye's history with fashion as a reason for his admiration of Hitler and Nazis — particularly noting the brand Hugo Boss and its ties to Nazi Germany at one point. However, after Jones said, "I get the Hugo Boss uniforms … but just because you're in love with the design, you're a designer, can we just kinda say you like the uniforms but that's about it?" Kanye responded, "No. There's a lot of that I love about Hitler. A lot of things"

…

Later on in the show after his comments on Hitler, Kanye then decided to bring out props, including a fishing net and a bottle of YooHoo, as a bit against the former Prime Minister of Israel Benjamin Netanyahu. The segment involved him holding up the net and talking as though it were Netanyahu. **— Know Your Meme (https://knowyourmeme.com/memes/events/kanye-west-on-InfoWars)**

* Ye reaches under the table and produces a neon orange fishing net and a bottle of YooHoo *

Jones: I'm in the Twilight Zone right now

Ye: Netanyahu, what do you have to say?

Ye (as Net N Yoohoo): It was bad. It was bad for Trump to meet with Nick and Ye! Ok!

— Ye does an impression of "Net N Yoohoo" (Netanyahu) during the Alex Jones interview (https://www.youtube.com/watch?v=xzyR0uKfTKs)

So much for optics. The interview was so controversial that Fuentes would be banned from Alex Jones's streaming platform, Banned.video.

Fuentes had taken a major risk. Ye, like many who become newly redpilled, had become a total wignat, thereby throwing away a brand that Fuentes had built up strategically over many years. However, from his perspective, it is easy to see why Fuentes took this risk. There was a massive upside to this gamble: the ability to work with his hero on a national presidential campaign, on top of massive exposure for himself and his views. Unfortunately for him, after the *InfoWars* appearance, things began to breakdown.

Thus began one of the strangest feuds in political history. On one side was Nick Fuentes, Ali Alexander, Candace Owens, Sneako, and Laura Loomer. On the other side was Kanye West, Milo Yiannopoulos, Tucker Carlson, and Marjorie Taylor Greene.

The conflict started as a rift began to develop between Milo and Fuentes. According to Fuentes, Milo had lied about being an "ex-gay." He tried so sleep in the same bed as Fuentes and offered Fuentes drugs, saying that he took the drugs himself in order to suppress his urge to have gay sex. Fuentes painted a picture of Milo as an out-of-control con artist, flying out with his (supposedly ex) husband to Disneyland, staying with him in a hotel room, and going on unpredictable drug benders. According to Fuentes, Jewish free-speech activist and Fuentes ally Laura Loomer (who might be considered a former member of the Alt Lite), as well as Candace Owens, were constantly warning Fuentes to keep Ye away from Milo. However, this put Nick in an uncomfortable position, as Milo was responsible for bringing Nick aboard, and was known for retaliating mercilessly against those who got on his bad side. Milo apparently also had a beef with Fuentes ally Ali Alexander. Eventually, Fuentes was able to squeeze Milo out of the campaign, and he was fired by Ye.

Milo struck back by attacking Ali Alexander. Milo released evidence that Ali had preyed on young boys, including soliciting nude photos from America First online personality "Smiley," which Smiley personally confirmed. Milo said that Nick had long been aware of the behavior and turned a blind eye in order to take advantage of Ali's many political connections. Nick cut ties with Ali over the allegations and removed his Cozy.tv channel, but also defended himself, saying the soliciting of nudes from Smiley happened before Nick was even involved in politics and was still a senior in high school. He also said that, while he had heard about the allegations regarding Ali, he had never seen any definitive proof. According to him, when Milo told him about Ali initially, he said that if he had to cut ties with people over every allegation, he would also have to cut ties with Milo.

Based on the allegations that Fuentes knew about Ali's solicitation of minors, enemies of Fuentes would accuse him of being a "pedophile" for months after the revelation. As further "proof" of these allegations, they used other controversial comments by Fuentes where he claimed that wanting to marry a 16 year old was not pedophilia and that he wanted a 16 year old wife when he was 30. Fuentes defended himself on the basis that the age of consent was 16 in much of the world, that people should get married when they were teenagers instead of having promiscuous sex for 10 years before getting married, and that younger women were hotter. By now his list of enemies had grown to include a slew of defectors from America First including Jaden McNeil, former interns of Fuentes, and former Cozy.tv streamers Michael Alberto, Big Tech and Ethan Ralph. According to rumors from Michelle Malkin, Tucker Carlson had also been looking into Fuentes, considering painting him as a "fed," as *Revolver News* had done to Ray Epps, and blaming him for Ye's comments.

Ye, for unknown reasons, but probably due to the fallout over Ali, distanced himself from Fuentes and re-hired Milo as campaign manager. Milo then banned Fuentes and all of his people from the campaign. Ye became distracted from politics, refocusing on music and marrying architect Bianca Censori, who allegedly began to act as a handler for Ye. As of December 2023, the YE24 campaign has not been heard from again and has become a flash in the pan.

Fuentes, undeterred, rebranded America First with a new, even more explicitly Christian vision. In it, the influence of Ye can clearly be seen.

Fuentes appeared on March 4 2023 at a "Fuentes rally" in a puffy Ye-inspired jacket and sunglasses, with images of crosses, skulls, rosaries, and bombs projected behind him. During the rally, he unveiled his new vision: "Christian Futurism."

Fuentes said that he had been inspired by Ye to change his approach to politics. Instead of critiquing, he wanted to create. Instead of focusing on problems, he wanted to focus on solutions. Instead of the conservative perspective of looking towards the past and despairing at how far society had fallen due to the corrosive effects of liberalism, Fuentes wanted to look towards the future, and create a "post-Liberal" Christian society.

> In the next five years, it is unequivocal, the message goes from "America First" to "Christ Is King." That has gotta be the new vision. And the reason why is because you could implement all the other things, and it wouldn't be good enough. You could have an immigration moratorium. You could have free speech on social media. They are now even giving out some concessions to the white people, you see this all the time now.
>
> ...
>
> Insofar as you have non-Christians running the institutions, that does not solve the problem. That has gotta be the main mission.
>
> ...
>
> Here's the other thing. So often we as conservatives, I would say even Christians, the message is always something like 'we gotta go back!', 'It used to be so different', 'Remember when.' I don't call myself a conservative anymore. I don't call myself even a traditionalist. Because history doesn't repeat. We can't go back to the past.
>
> ...
>
> We're never going back. It's done. All of that is gone. But I would call myself something like a "Christian Futurist" instead. Because Jesus Christ was our past. Before any of us were born or conceived. Jesus Christ is our present now. And Jesus Christ is our future, after we die on Earth.

...

We want this century to be the most Christian century in the history of planet earth.

...

We don't want to talk about Constantinople, we will build new cities.

– Nick Fuentes, Fuentes Rally 1 (*https://Cozy.tv/aff/replays/2023-03-05*)

"Liberalism already happened" Fuentes would explain in an episode of *America First* that year. According to Fuentes, the good part of liberalism was the compassion, but the error in liberalism was in the accommodation. What we could learn from liberalism was to be compassionate towards homosexuals, transsexuals, immigrants, and so forth, while still condemning sexual deviancy as sinful and protecting our borders and demographics.

Thus, while relaxing his stance on the incorporation of fascist imagery somewhat, and criticizing Jewish political influence more often than in the past, even at its most extreme moment America First was still a more mature movement than the Alt Right, with a complex, nuanced political vision. It continued to employ politically incorrect rhetoric to some degree, while explicitly denouncing race-based violence or cruelty. It criticized Zionism and Jewish influence in society, while at the same time allying with Jews such as Darren Beattie and Laura Loomer (and, before their falling out, Milo). While fighting for the rights of white people and for retaining a white majority in America, it included Mexicans (such as Fuentes himself), black people (such as Cozy.tv streamer Tenryo, Jon Miller and Bryson Gray), and even non-religious Jews. Its most important legacy of all, however, would ultimately be bringing God back to the table in American politics.

Fuentes would go on to endorse Trump for the 2024 election.

Elon the Redditor saves the Internet

The real end of Big Tech censorship was instigated by the banning of Donald Trump on Twitter, which finally caused mainstream conservatives to take an active role in fighting it. From that point on, many "Twitter clones" including Gettr, and Trump's own Truth Social began to become popular.

Even before the Censorship Era, some attempts to circumvent censorship had been created. Parler, a Twitter clone created in August 2018, became very popular with Boomers, who wanted to talk about Q-Anon or Covid without being censored. However, it was essentially torpedoed after J6.

> *After reports that Parler was used to coordinate the 2021 storming of the U.S. Capitol, several companies denied it their services. Apple and Google removed Parler's mobile app from their app stores, and Parler went offline on January 10, 2021, when Amazon Web Services canceled its hosting services. Before it went offline in January 2021, according to Parler, the service had about 15 million users.*

> **– Wikipedia (https://en.wikipedia.org/wiki/Parler)**

Another platform worth mentioning is Gab. Gab was founded by Andrew Torba all the way back in 2016. Its mascot and icon are a green frog (an obvious allusion to Pepe). It exploded in popularity after Charlottesville, which had led to a ban wave of many Alt Right accounts. Almost immediately after Alt Right accounts began to flock to Gab, it became a target of censorship.

> *In early September 2017, Gab faced pressure from its domain registrar Asia Registry to take down a post by The Daily Stormer founder Andrew Anglin, giving Gab 48 hours to do so. Gab later removed the post.*

> *...*

> *Robert Gregory Bowers, the suspected shooter in the attack against a Pittsburgh synagogue on October 27, 2018, maintained an active, verified Gab account*

...

After Bowers was arrested, Gab suspended his profile, gathered all user data for the account, and contacted the Federal Bureau of Investigation (FBI). On October 27, 2018, the day of the shooting, PayPal, GoDaddy, and Medium terminated their relationship with Gab, and PayPal released a statement that it had it done so based on its review of accounts that may engage in the "perpetuation of hate, violence or discriminatory intolerance". Later on the same day, Gab announced on Twitter that Joyent, Gab's hosting provider, would terminate their service on October 29 at 9:00 am ET. The tweet said that the site expected to be down for weeks.Stripe and Backblaze also terminated their services with Gab after the shooting.

...

Gab returned online on November 4, 2018, after Epik agreed to register the domain

...

Gab turned to cryptocurrency payment processing services after being rejected from PayPal and Stripe in the aftermath of the 2018 Pittsburgh synagogue shooting. In January 2019, Coinbase and Square, Inc.'s Cash App closed the accounts held by Gab and Andrew Torba.

...

*On July 4, Gab switched its software infrastructure to run on a forked version of Mastodon, a free and open-source decentralized social network platform. The change attempted to circumvent the rejection of Gab's mobile app from the Google Play Store and the Apple App Store, as Gab users gained access to the social network through third-party Mastodon apps that did not subsequently block Gab. – **Wikipedia (https://en.wikipedia.org/wiki/Gab_(social_network))**

Gab is notable for having the most permissive terms of service of almost any tech platform (with the possible exception of the Fediverse) allowing all legal speech protected under the 1st amendment, except for pornography.

Restrictions on content on Gab include illegal activity, credible threats of violence, promotion of terrorism, obscenity, pornography, spamming, selling weapons or drugs, child exploitation, impersonation, and doxing.

– Wikipedia (https://en.wikipedia.org/wiki/ Gab (social network)#Violence and terrorism policy)

In spite (or perhaps because) of this, the user experience on Gab can be fairly poor. When your community consists solely of people who were banned from everywhere else, it creates a filter bubble of extremist and low quality content. It tends to be full of wignats and unironic neo-Nazis spamming anti-Semitic slurs at each other, with little point to them aside from gratuitous obscenity. Andrew Torba, a self-described "Christian Nationalist" and member of the Dissident Right himself, makes the site even more repellent to the mainstream by often personally making anti-Semitic comments. He advocates for Christians to withdraw from the system as much as possible and create a "parallel society." Because Gab has been able to successfully circumvent so many attempts to cancel it, still being fully operational as of September 2023, it has served as an important pinoneer of Alt Tech.

Another Twitter alternative is "the Fediverse."

*The Fediverse (a portmanteau of "federation" and "universe") is an ensemble of social networks, which, while independently hosted, can communicate with each other. ActivityPub, a W3C standard, is the most widely used protocol that powers the Fediverse. Users on different websites can send and receive updates from others across the network. Noted Fediverse platforms include Mastodon, Lemmy, PeerTube, and Pixelfed. Nearly all Fediverse platforms are free and open-source software. – **Wikipedia (https://en.wikipedia.org/wiki/Fediverse)***

The Fediverse can be thought of as a technology with a decentralized structure similar to email. It is a protocol, not a platform. Just as many email services exist that can all send email to each other (Gmail, Yahoo mail, Protonmail, etc.) so too can each Fediverse "instance" see the posts from other Fediverse "instances," with each "instance" being its own Twitter clone. In theory it is impossible to censor, since if a user gets banned on one instance, they can simply move to another instance (in the same way, if I get banned from Gmail, I can make a Yahoo account and continue to send email). In reality, the ecosystem is not as decentralized as it is in theory. Instances can "opt-in" to sharing information with other instances (called "federating" with the instance) and thus control which instances they share information with. If an instance becomes unpopular, other instances can simply "defederate" with it. This creates a "ghettoizing" effect and cuts one's potential audience exponentially. The Fediverse became popular with wignats, especially on the instance "poast" (until it was hacked in 2023). Recently, the Fediverse has also became popular with Leftists, who have flocked there in protest to Elon Musks's acquisition of Twitter.

Some of these "free speech" platforms were in fact not much more "free speech" than Twitter. For example, all platforms, except for Gab and Rumble, either banned Nick Fuentes from the platform or hid some of his content.

Rumble was one of the most successful Alt Tech platforms. It was a "free speech" alternative to YouTube. Although going all the way back to 2013, Rumble especially became popular in 2021, as a response to YouTube's censorship of content related to Covid. Rumble also caught the eye of Peter Thiel, who seemingly uses it as another chess piece in his strategy of manipulating online culture in order to influence the political.

Rise of viewership in 2020 has been attributed to Representative Devin Nunes, who accused YouTube of overly censoring his channel. Nunes began posting content on the platform with other prominent conservatives, such as Dinesh D'Souza, Dan Bongino, Sean Hannity, and Representative Jim Jordan, following soon after.

...

*Rumble received investment from venture capitalists Peter Thiel and J. D. Vance in May 2021, with that round of funding valuing Rumble at around $500 million. A month later, US President Donald Trump joined Rumble in preparation for recording his Ohio campaign rally. In October 2021, Rumble acquired Locals. On December 14, 2021, Trump Media & Technology Group (TMTG) announced that it entered a "wide-ranging technology and cloud services agreement" with Rumble in a statement which also stated that Rumble would operate part of Truth Social as well as TMTG. Also in December 2021, Rumble challenged a New York law prohibiting hate speech on social media. – **Wikipedia (https://en.wikipedia.org/wiki/Rumble_(company))**

It is interesting also to note this last line. As we have seen, Thiel seems to be orchestrating a two-pronged attack on political correctness and so called "hate speech" laws by uniting the Dissident Right and anti-woke Dissident Left.

While the rise of Alt Tech was an important factor in ending the Censorship Era, the official end came on April 4, 2022, when Elon Musk bought Twitter.

On the Internet, Elon Musk was once seen as being a personification of Reddit, appropriating popular memes from Internet culture, such as "doge" and making them cringe. Telsa made him associated with the Leftist crusade against "climate change." These, and other factors, made him popular on Reddit, and loathed on 4chan.

u/WhimsicalFletcher:

Why is Elon Musk so popular on Reddit?

I don't really understand it. According to various articles I read, to me, the guy looks like a standard businessman, but for some reason most people on Reddit keep gobbling up his self-aggrandizing bullshit. He's constantly presented as the smartest, brightest person ever who will save the world, lead humanity to Mars, blahblahblah. A new Isaac Newton, Einstein or something like that. At the moment, the hive mind thinks of him as of an ultimate authority on all things technology. Anything slightly critical of Elon Musk usually gets heavily downvoted.

So why does he have such a high status among Redditors? I don't see many reasons for it. Does he appear a lot on American TV / Printed newspaper? I feel like I'm missing a part of the picture.

u/beanfiddler:

Technology CEO = stem circlejerk

Electric cars banned by government = libertarian / smug consumerist circlerjerk with shades of underdog circlejerk

Rich dude who has interesting personality = lick Tony Stark's balls circlejerk

SpaceX = space circlejerk

Private space exploration = libertarian circlejerk / "I could be an astronaut too!" circlejerk

Company literally named Tesla = Nikola Telsa circlejerk

Seems to be a nerd = nerds are literally oppressed, nerdface circlejerk

**– /r/circlebroke, October 27 2014
(https://www.reddit.com/r/circlebroke/comments/2kgvjn/why_is_elon_musk_so_popular_on_Reddit/)**

On 4chan, he was regarded in the same vein as other "pop science" figures as Neil DeGrasse Tyson. 4chan considered "pop science" to be enjoyed primarily by "midwits." Midwits were Leftists who over-estimated their own intelligence. They were the type of people who claimed to "love science" while not having a deep understanding of it, bastardizing complex scientific concepts and mixing it with new-agey "live laugh love" style self-affirmation through sentimentalist statements such as "we are all heckin' star dust!"

However "cringe" Elon may have been considered by 4chan at one time, he has done more for Internet freedom than perhaps any other figure in recent history. Like the rise in Alt Tech after the banning of Trump, this really was the result of overzealousness by the censorship regime.

Immediately after the acquisition, Musk fired several top Twitter executives including CEO Parag Agrawal; Musk became the CEO instead. He instituted a $7.99 monthly subscription for a "blue check",and laid off a significant portion of the company's staff. Musk lessened content moderation, and in December, Musk released internal documents relating to Twitter's moderation of Hunter Biden's laptop controversy in the leadup to the 2020 presidential election.

...

*In April 2022, The Washington Post reported that Musk privately claimed that supposed censorship on the platform, including the banning of accounts such as The Babylon Bee, had prompted him to begin the acquisition. The New York Post revealed that Musk's ex-wife Talulah Riley had encouraged Musk to purchase Twitter, specifically citing the Bee's ban. Following the acquisition, he made reinstatement of accounts like the Bee an immediate priority. – **Wikipedia (https://en.wikipedia.org/wiki/Elon_Musk#Twitter)***

*On April 11, after publishing several tweets critical of the company, Musk decided not to join the board. Instead, he informed Twitter that he intended to make an offer to take the company private. – **Wikipedia (https://en.wikipedia.org/wiki/Acquisition_of_Twitter_by_Elon_Musk)***

While having previously voted for Hillary Clinton in 2016, and Joe Biden in 2020, Elon began to drift towards conservatism around the same time as the acquisition.

In 2022, Musk said that he could "no longer support" the Democrats because they are the "party of division & hate", and wrote a tweet encouraging "independent-minded voters" to vote Republican in the 2022 U.S. elections, which was an outlier among social media executives who typically avoid partisan political advocacy.He has supported Republican Ron DeSantis for the 2024 U.S. presidential election, and Twitter hosted DeSantis's campaign announcement on a Twitter Spaces event.

– Wikipedia (https://en.wikipedia.org/wiki/Elon_Musk#Politics)

Elon Musk also began to make posts decrying so called "gender-affirming care" ("transgender" child sex change operations).

Any parent or doctor who sterilizes a child before they are a consenting adult should go to prison for life

– Elon Musk, Twitter post from April 14 2023 (https://krcrtv.com/amp/news/nation-world/elon-musk-says-any-parent-or-doctor-who-sterilizes-children-should-go-to-prison-for-life-ron-desantis-msnbc-michael-cohen-sex-change-gender-affirming-care)

He also began promoting prominent Right Wing Twitter accounts in the algorithm (on the "for you" Twitter tab that showed curated content) such as Ian Miles Cheong (although he also promotes Left Wing accounts, particularly the Krassenstein brothers). He also announced his intentions to make Twitter a "free speech" platform, and to avoid permanent suspensions in favor of temporary ones.

Twitter brought back a number of banned accounts, including Keith Woods, Marjorie Taylor Greene, Chief Trumpster (a Cozy.tv streamer), The Babylon Bee, Dick Masterson, anti-SJW professor Jordan Peterson, misogynist influencer Andrew Tate, Right Wing investigative journalists Project Veritas,

Patrick Casey (who since leaving America First has greatly moderated his views), and of course, Donald Trump himself. Nick Fuentes was also brought back for 24 hours before being re-banned for an unknown reason. Andrew Anglin was unbanned for a while before being banned again. However some accounts were never brought back or were banned by Elon, in particular Alex Jones, Jared Taylor, and many users who have expressed views considered anti-Semitic or critical of Israel, such as evolutionary biologist Kevin MacDonald and National Justice Party chairman Mike Enoch.

Aside from the already monumental, history-bending consequence of ending Big Tech censorship, Elon's apparent shift to the right and flirtation with Dissident Right figures such as Keith Woods (more on this in the next chapter) is also significant. First of all, it is yet another indication of the slow but inevitable dialectical shift to the Right in American culture, as it slowly permeates through society. Secondly, it gives the Dissident Right its first elite support.

Ever since 2020, conservatives have begun to speculate more and more on the idea of a "national divorce" or "civil war" along ideological lines. Commentators such as Scott Greer, however, have pointed out that this is impossible. In a civil war or revolution, both sides must have elite backing. Even the French revolution was not fully a top-down event. The first half of it was instigated by the nobles (resulting in a constitutional monarchy) before it descended into the truly proletarianized second half (leading to the dysfunctional French Republic and reign of terror). In the American Revolution, the founding fathers were the elites of America, but were outside of the political system of Great Britain, and had much to gain from independence (they also gained support from Great Britain's adversary, France). Likewise, the Russian Revolution was supported by the German elites and parts of the mutinous Russian armed services. In the English civil war, the revolutionaries were backed by Parliament. In the Spanish civil war, the revolutionaries were backed by the Church and parts of the military. In the American Civil War, the Confederacy pitted state against federal power.

Greer points out that in contemporary America, the Right has no elite. Conservative state governments are not interested in seceding, nor do they have the means to do so, as they depend on federal funding. Additionally, most are internally divided, consisting of blue cities within rural red areas. No major private institutions support the Dissident Right. In 2020, Wall Street donated 51.1 million dollars to Biden, and only 10 million to Trump (https://www.cnn.com/2020/09/25/business/trump-biden-wall-street-campaign-donations/index.html). In the military, while many of the rank and file have traditionally been conservative, the generals are not, such as the infamously liberal Chairman of the Joint Chiefs of Staff, General Milley. However, Musk (and even Ye to a lesser degree) may indicate a growing fracture in the elite, that would make such a revolution possible.

By 2022, with Alt Tech platforms such as Rumble becoming robust, and Musk's reversal of the trend of Big Tech censorship, the height of the Censorship Era appears to be in the rearview mirror, although it will probably never return to the same level of free speech as during the Wild West Era. This development is probably the biggest whitepill for any dissident movement. It has smoothened and accelerated the synthesis of the illiberal antithesis.

Chapter 7 - 2023 & 2024: X v ADL, Trump Or Death, TikTok, Migrants take Manhattan, The End of White America, The End of The End

The Next Generation: Andrew Tate, The Redpill Community and Keith Woods

While the last few years of the Dissident Right have been dominated by Nick Fuentes and America First, in 2022 and 2023, a "new generation of dissent" began to emerge as the Censorship Era receded.

According to the Dissident Right, their greatest strength is that they have "the truth" on their side. The contradictions of the liberal thesis have become unsustainable. Even ordinary people can now tell that there are inherent differences between the races, that the media and academia push an agenda, that feminism has ruined the relationship between men and women, and that you cannot change your gender. The only way to combat the rise of the illiberal antithesis is to totally shut down people's access to information, and have complete censorship to a level that is not even possible by a totalitarian state such as China. Even then, you cannot shut down the real world. You cannot shut down reality. And as long people are allowed to share their real experiences with one another, the redpilling will continue. After all, the failure to fully censor an obscure anime imageboard full of degenerate hentai-watching weebs is what led to the Alt Right.

In 2022, misogynist and politically incorrect Internet personality Andrew Tate exploded in popularity, especially on the social media app TikTok.

> *Tate received attention for his tweets describing his view of what qualifies as sexual harassment amid the Harvey Weinstein sexual abuse cases and for tweeting several statements about his view that sexual assault victims share responsibility for their assaults. In 2017, he was criticised for tweeting that depression "isn't real".*
>
> *...*
>
> *He became widely known in mid-2022 and was searched on Google more times than both Donald Trump and COVID-19 that July. In an interview, he described himself:*
>
> *"You can't slander me because I will state right now that I am absolutely sexist and I'm absolutely a misogynist, and I have fuck you money and you can't take that away."*
>
> *He has stated that women "belong in the home", that they "can't drive", and that they are "given to the man and belong to the man", as well as claiming that men prefer dating 18- and 19-year-olds because they are "likely to have had sex with fewer men", and that women who do not stay at home are "hoes". **– Wikipedia (https://en.wikipedia.org/wiki/Andrew_Tate)***

A number of similar channels also became popular, such as Sneako, the livestream *Fresh & Fit* and anti-feminist content creator Pearl Davis. This community, known as "the redpill community" promulgated politically incorrect and anti-feminist views, especially towards matters related to dating and the social roles of men and women.

While primarily anti-feminist, they would also touch on other politically incorrect subjects such as race. Both *Fresh & Fit* and Pearl would invite Nick Fuentes on as a guest in 2023. Sneako had become a friend of Fuentes in 2022, shortly before the YE24 campaign.

Sneako was canceled from YouTube after associating with Fuentes, moving to Rumble. In the case of *Fresh & Fit*, their channel became demonetized after featuring Fuentes, and even before airing the episode they were warned directly by YouTube that he was not allowed to be featured in the thumbnail or video title. In the case of Pearl, hosting Fuentes resulted in her having to go on an apology tour and a mutiny by some of her black staff due to comments by Fuentes that were considered anti-black (although this was not until after the staff themselves received negative backlash from the "black community." During the episode, they displayed a friendly attitude towards Fuentes and agreed with some of his points).

Another new personality on the scene in 2023 was Keith Woods. Keith Woods was an Irish content creator. I am not sure when he began creating content, but his first YouTube video is from September 2019. At first, he took a neutral stance in the "Optics Wars," siding with neither the Groypers or wignats but instead being friendly towards both groups. However, he began to be resented by the wignats, in part due to his failure to denounce Fuentes, and started to drift away from TRS and other wignat groups. He was eventually invited to stream on Cozy.tv. Later he would criticize wignats for being too blackpilled, writing *"I think Mike and the rest of TRS got burned from hanging onto Trumpism too long and now they project this onto everything."*

Keith Woods was a philosophy major in college, where he became redpilled. After graduating, he decided to become a content creator rather than pursue academia, reasoning that very few people actually read academic articles, and that he could gain a larger audience on the Internet. His specialty is "effort posting." "Effort posting" refers to making longform, well-researched content delivered in a professional, academic manner, as opposed to the irreverent trolling of the Alt Right. In addition to videos about politics, he also reviews books, and creates videos on philosophy. He hosts a podcast called "Understanding Platonism." He is an Irish nationalist who is deeply critical of mass immigration into Ireland and supports the Irish National Party, becoming involved with their activist efforts. He is also notable for taking a "third position" on economic issues, often criticizing capitalism as well as Leftist social issues.

His philosophical works create a deep and rich ideological foundation for Dissident Right ideas, reviving earlier, less liberal philosophical traditions in attempt to deal with the great philosophical problem of our age: nihilism. He recognizes, like Father Seraphim Rose and other thinkers (such as Nietzsche) that it is ultimately this nihilism that is upstream from all of our political and cultural problems. Due to his carefully worded and meticulous style, he is still on most major platforms, including YouTube. He sometimes edits the more controversial parts out of the YouTube versions of his videos and posts the full version on Rumble.

On April 1 2023, Keith Woods would regain his Twitter account, leading to several viral tweets that were promoted by major mainstream figures, including Elon Musk.

The first of Keith Wood's campaigns to go viral was a tweet drawing attention to a proposed Irish hate speech law which would criminalize possession of "hateful" material with prison time, and even made it a crime to refuse to hand over passwords or encryption keys with one year of prison time (https://gript.ie/up-to-a-year-in-prison-for-refusing-to-hand-over-passwords-under-new-hate-speech-bill/).

> *Ireland is about to pass one of the most radical hate speech bills yet. Merely possessing "hateful" material on your devices is enough to face prison time.*
>
> *Not only that, but the burden of proof is shifted to the accused, who is expected to prove they didn't intend to use the material to "spread hate".*
>
> *This clause is so radical that even the Trotskyist People Before Profit opposed it as a flagrant violation of civil liberties. Dark times.*
>
> **– Keith Woods (t.me/keith_woods/3934)**

Elon Musk responded, *"This is a massive attack against freedom of speech"* (*https://Twitter.com/elonmusk/status/1652441004312788993?s=20*). Donald Trump Jr. and Jordan Peterson retweeted the tweet (https://t.me/keith_woods/3942), reaching 11 million people and causing the hashtag *#NoHateSpeechLaws* to trend. As a result of this media attention, Irish politicians spoke out against the law. Keith would also be featured on Stew Peters and *InfoWars* to speak out against the law. Elon later said he would "file legal action" against the Irish hate speech bill.

> *Exactly.*
>
> *[Twitter] will be filing legal action to stop this. Can't wait for discovery to start!*
>
> **– Elon Musk, August 23 2023(https://Twitter.com/elonmusk/status/1694439520517624064)**

On July 2 2023, Keith Woods created a thread on Twitter concerning slavery.

> *It has become popular to blame White people for slavery, to the point that many actually believe slavery was invented by or exclusively practiced by Europeans.*
>
> *But the history of slavery outside the West is far more brutal.*
>
> **– Keith Woods (*https://threadreaderapp.com/thread/1675566139382849536.html*))**

The thread would point out that the Arab slave trade was far more brutal, that Africans had a hand in the slave trade, *"[conducting] raids on rival groups to provide slaves for sale,"* that whites were also sold into slavery by the Arabs, that the Native Americans and Chinese practiced a brutal form of slavery, and that it was whites that ultimately ended the slave trade on humanitarian grounds. This thread was also liked by Elon Musk. (https://t.me/keith_woods/4124).

In June 2023, Twitter would rebrand, taking on the name "X." A formal break with the past, and a symbol of its new life under Elon Musk.

The next month, conservative commentator Benny Johnson would bring attention to a video in which the third largest political party in South African party chanted *"Kill the Boer, kill the white farmer."* Elon (himself a white immigrant from South Africa) replied:

> *They are openly pushing for genocide of white people in South Africa. @CyrilRamaphosa, why do you say nothing?*
>
> *– Elon Musk*
> *(https://Twitter.com/elonmusk/status/1686037774510497792)*

On August 4 2023, after *The New York Times* defended the song, Musk wrote:

> *The New York Times actually has the nerve to support calls for genocide! If ever there was a time to cancel that publication, it is now.*
>
> *You can read their articles for free anyway using*
>
> *http://removepaywall.com*
>
> *– Elon Musk*
> *(https://Twitter.com/elonmusk/status/1687520435825745920?lang=en)*

Keith Woods also drew attention to the song and reposted both of these Elon Musk tweets on his telegram.

However, the greatest and most infamous collaboration between Elon Musk and Keith Woods would come in late August 2023. X would finally have a showdown against the greatest anti-speech organization of them all, The ADL.

X versus the ADL

Hey stop defaming me!

– Elon Musk replying to the ADL on Twitter, Nov 19 2022 (https://Twitter.com/elonmusk/status/1594197468970946560?lang=en)

Almost as soon as Elon Musk bought Twitter, the ADL went on the attack, and began making threats.

Whatever happens to @Twitter, new social platforms need to center trust and safety from the outset, or risk being subject to the same fate. In the meantime, @elonmusk has put Twitter on deathwatch. It didn't have to be this way.

– ADL (https://Twitter.com/ADL/status/1593714829516324869)

As well as demands.

In addition to Trump, other high-profile and dangerous individuals may be allowed to return to Twitter:

White supremacist and former Ku Klux Klan leader David Duke

White nationalist Nick Fuentes

Conspiracy theorist Alex Jones

Former Trump adviser and Steve Bannon

Misogynist Andrew Tate

Providing these individuals again with the vast megaphone of Twitter to spread hate and misinformation would lead to dire consequences.

– ADL (https://www.adl.org/resources/blog/5-things-adl-watching-following-elon-musk-buying-Twitter)

They then attempted to get Musk to bend the knee by organizing an advertiser boycott, just as they had done to Zuckerberg in 2020.

Major civil rights organizations including the NAACP and the Anti-Defamation League are calling on advertisers to boycott Twitter. In a statement released Friday afternoon, NAACP President and CEO Derrick Johnson wrote that "until [actions] are taken to make Twitter a safe space, corporations cannot in good conscience put their money behind Twitter." Johnson affirmed that "Twitter must earn its advertisers by creating a platform that safeguards our democracy and rids itself of any account that spews hate and misinformation."

– Rolling Stone, Nov 4 2022 (NAACP, ADL, Other Orgs Call for Advertisers to Boycott Twitter)

Today, we are joining dozens of other groups to ask advertisers to pause Twitter spending because we are profoundly concerned about antisemitism and hate on the platform. Here's why we're asking advertisers to #StopHateForProfit and #StopToxicTwitter

– ADL, Nov 4 2022 (https://Twitter.com/ ADL/status/1588587735711121408)

As a result, Elon Musk met with The ADL, possibly to smooth things over. However, later that year, Elon Musk decided to defy the ADL by unbanning Trump, calling his banning "divisive." The ADL responded with disapproval:

For @elonmusk to allow Donald Trump back on Twitter, ostensibly after a brief poll, shows he is not remotely serious about safeguarding the platform from hate, harassment and misinformation.

– Jonathan Greenblatt, director of the ADL, Nov 19 2022 (https://Twitter.com/JGreenblattADL/status/1594161763859431424)

When @ADL and other #StopHateforProfit leaders met with Elon Musk on 11/1, he committed to not replatform anyone, regardless of stature, until he installed a transparent, clear process that took into consideration the views of civil society.

– Jonathan Greenblatt, director of the ADL, Nov 19 2022 (https://Twitter.com/JGreenblattADL/status/1594161767432658945)

As a result, Twitter/X took a financial hit. According to Elon himself, ad revenue declined so much that it was still down 60% one year later, in August 2023. Whatever the percentage, most major media sources report at least some loss of revenue.

Twitter has struggled to maintain advertising revenue following Musk's takeover of the company in October. Several major corporations appear to have heeded the calls from the ADL and others to stop spending money on the platform. Media Matters for America, a progressive advocacy group, determined that 50 of Twitter's top 100 advertisers had either announced or appeared to stop advertising on Twitter last November, around the time that the ADL announced their call for a boycott.

Stop Toxic Twitter found that Audi, Balenciaga, Best Buy, Capital One, Chipotle, Coca-Cola, Ford, Verizon and a number of other large companies had suspended advertising on Twitter.

– Forward, Aug 1 2023 (https://forward.com/news/556095/adl-Twitter-advertising-boycott/)

In 2023, Twitter/X amended its terms of service and said it would ban users who posed a financial risk to the company. Keith Woods suggested that they ban the ADL, since it was using the platform to directly organize advertiser boycotts, thus violating the new ToS. To this effect, he created the hashtag *#BanTheADL.*

It's time for @elonmusk to ban the ADL from X. Since Musk's takeover, the ADL has been using this platform to damage his reputation and promote advertiser boycotts, which have cost the company billions.

The ADL claim that no one's legally protected right to political speech extends to private platforms like X, so why should it tolerate users working to make its business model untenable?

**– Keith Woods
(https://Twitter.com/KeithWoodsYT/status/1688338597177409536)**

Over the next few weeks, the campaign rose to #1 trending on Twitter with 250 thousand tweets in four days. Almost everyone on the Right Wing, both mainstream and dissident, shared the hashtag. Among them: Dinesh D'Souza, MMA fighter Jake Shields, Iraq War veteran Lucas Gage, LibsofTikTok, Sam Hyde, Laura Loomer, Tristan Tate (brother and collaborator of Andrew Tate), Andrew Torba, Charlie Kirk, and Matt Walsh. Charlie Kirk tweeted that the ADL was *"A mass purveyor of anti-white hate"* before deleting the tweet and retweeting one with more mild language, *"The ADL itself is America's number-one purveyor of hate speech (and the SPLC is #2)."* Kirk's former nemesis Nick Fuentes, who was banned from X, ordered his legion of Groypers to promote the hashtag.

Elon Musk responded to Keith several times over the course campaign, saying that *"ADL has tried very hard to strangle X/Twitter"* (https://twitter.com/elonmusk/status/1697655308946944257). However, instead of banning them, he threatened to sue them for defamation.

Since the acquisition, The @ADL has been trying to kill this platform by falsely accusing it & me of being anti-Semitic

...

To clear our platform's name on the matter of anti-Semitism, it looks like we have no choice but to file a defamation lawsuit against the Anti-Defamation League ... oh the irony!

– Elon Musk, Sep 4 2023(https://Twitter.com/elonmusk/status/1698828606598734225) (https://Twitter.com/elonmusk/status/1698754179148214495)

Many Jews, such as Larua Loomer, Chaya Raichik (the person behind the account LibsofTikTok), Ben Shapiro, Stephen Miller, and lawyer and first amendment advocate Ron Coleman also expressed criticism of the ADL or Jonathan Greenblatt. Loomer and Raichik supported the campaign on freedom of speech grounds, while Coleman arguied that the ADL had become an organization more dedicated to promoting Leftist causes than stopping anti-Semitism.

In a move that should surprise no one, the ADL issued a response, calling the campaign anti-Semitic.

> *"It is profoundly disturbing that Elon Musk spent the weekend engaging with a highly toxic, antisemitic campaign on his platform -- a campaign started by an unrepentant bigot that then was heavily promoted by individuals such as white supremacist Nick Fuentes, Christian nationalist Andrew Torba, conspiracy theorist Alex Jones and others.*
>
> *...*
>
> *But to be clear, the real issue is neither ADL nor the threat of a frivolous lawsuit. This urgent matter is the safety of the Jewish people in the face of increasing, intensifying antisemitism. Musk is engaging with and elevating these antisemites at a time when ADL is tracking a surge of bomb threats and swatting attacks of synagogues and Jewish institutions, dramatic levels of antisemitic propaganda being littered throughout Jewish and non-Jewish residential communities, and extremists marching openly through the streets in Nazi gear.*
>
> *– ADL (https://www.adl.org/resources/press-release/adl-statement-xtwitter). In fact, Alex Jones did not promote the hashtag, but actually condemned it.*

The hashtag was also condemned by Israeli publication *The Times of Israel*, and Israeli Prime Minister Benjamin Netanyahu.

> *Elon Musk is engaging with white nationalists and antisemites who want to ban the Anti-Defamation League from Twitter, the influential social media platform he now calls "X."*
>
> *...*
>
> *Woods' tweet came after a day after Jonathan Greenblatt, the ADL's CEO, spoke with Linda Yaccarino, the CEO of X, about users trafficking in hate on the platform. The ADL has tracked massive spikes in racist, antisemitic and homophobic content and harassment since Musk bought the platform last year and restored extremist accounts banned under the previous management.*
>
> **– The Times of Israel, Sep 4 2023, "Elon Musk amplifies call by antisemites to ban the ADL from X"(https://www.timesofisrael.com/elon-musk-amplifies-call-by-antisemites-to-ban-the-adl-from-x/)**

> *Israeli Prime Minister Benjamin Netanyahu urged Elon Musk to strike a balance between protecting free expression and fighting hate speech at a meeting on Monday after weeks of controversy over antisemitic content on Musk's social media platform X.*
>
> *...*
>
> *"I hope you find within the confines of the First Amendment, the ability to not only stop antisemitism ... but any collective hatred of a people," Netanyahu said during the meeting that was broadcast live on X from Tesla's factory in Fremont, California.*
>
> *"I know you're committed to that ... but I encourage and urge you to find a balance," Netanyahu said.*
>
> **– Reuters, Sep 18 2023, "Israel's Netanyahu urges Musk to balance free speech, fighting hate on X" (https://www.reuters.com/world/middle-east/israels-netanyahu-urges-musk-balance-free-speech-fighting-hate-x-2023-09-18/)**

Netanyahu also arranged a meeting with Musk in response to the hashtag on September 18.

> *Israel's Prime Minister Benjamin Netanyahu will be in California today meeting with tech leaders before heading to New York City for the United Nations General Assembly. Among those tech leaders is Elon Musk, whose social media platform, X, or Twitter, has been flooded with antisemitic hate in recent weeks, some of it amplified by Musk in his own tweets.*
>
> *...*
>
> *MARTÍNEZ (NPR): Now, we should stipulate that the Anti-Defamation League has been critical of Netanyahu and his government policies. What do you think, though, Jonathan, are the chances that Netanyahu would use his leverage in this meeting today?*
>
> *GREENBLATT: Well, I would hope that Prime Minister Netanyahu would use his leverage. Look; Israel's the homeland of the Jewish people, regardless of how they vote or what they value or even where they live. And so it's imperative for the prime minister to recognize that what Elon Musk has done - and his platform, even before Elon bought it - is to normalize the kind of ugly antisemitism that we used to associate with Cossacks and Nazis and white supremacists. Now you can see it 24/7 with just a click on X.*
>
> **– NPR, Sep 18 2023, "Israel's Benjamin Netanyahu to meet Elon Musk amid antisemitism controversy"**https://www.npr.org/2023/09/18/1200076853/israels-benjamin-netanyahu-to-meet-elon-musk-amid-antisemitism-controversy)

After the dust from the campaign settled, Keith had this to say in an article for Jewish conservative Ron Unz's *Unz Review:*

As much as I would like to take credit for the #BanTheADL campaign, this showdown was inevitable. Elon Musk's plan is to deliver a free and fair platform for not only political speech but entertainment, culture, and groupware-style communication and planning. His vision is fundamentally incompatible with ADL's mission to define, direct, and dictate the nature, tone, and boundaries of the political conversation in a specific direction.

...

But don't take my word for it. Borat explains why the unelected and unaccountable ADL should dictate who's allowed to speak rather than the owners of the corporations. Sacha Baron Cohen made his fame and fortune by peddling hateful and vulgar stereotypes of impoverished ethnic groups, implying that they're illiterate, incestuous, and sex-crazed rubes. But he would like you to know that his ethnic group will not tolerate equal treatment.

...

Predictably, the ADL is now defaming me as (you guessed it) a "raging antisemite". They dredged up an ancient tweet where I joked that Ben Shapiro had made me a "raging antisemite" to mock liberal claims that Ben (an Orthodox Jew) is promoting fascism. The joke was obvious in context, but the ADL isn't big on either jokes or context.

...

Now, Jonathan Greenblatt's hitting the media circuit to insist that Elon's resistance to the ADL's hostile takeover through tortious interference with its advertising budget is fueled by antisemitism. This would be comical if the ADL wasn't well-funded and well-connected enough to suck all of the comedy out of the room (and deplatform your favourite comedians).

Greenblatt began to sound like his old self on his damage control tour, insisting the ADL is not an enemy of free speech, and his only job as its leader of a "small non-profit" is to protect Jews from violence. Unfortunately, none of the interviewers asked him what promoting LGBT to children has to do with protecting Jews, or how his demand that President Trump's social media bans be permanent is not in conflict with his apparent love of free speech and opposition to cancel culture.

...

Musk is a naturalized immigrant to America who has bought in, without reservation, to the American promises of free enterprise and free speech. And literally nobody's making more money and speaking more freely than Elon. If anything, it's the ADL's attempts to shut it down in the name of the Jews that's fuelling antisemitism.

Of course, you guessed it, suggesting that the ADL is contributing to antisemitic sentiment by silencing conservatives in the name of the Jews and accusing everybody of antisemitism is also antisemitic. Asking yourself if they might be obsessively fixated on antisemitism? Antisemitic.

...

The rollout of free social media was the most revolutionary development in information dissemination since the printing press. When the regime realised just how revolutionary it was, they got to work spending years fighting for control through lobbying and financial manipulation. While much of this pressure was informal, through networks and backchannels, the ADL is the institutional, public face of this political racketeering network. In five years, they had all but destroyed the revolutionary potential afforded by these platforms.

...

If the Internet was the most revolutionary development of our age, the fight to protect it from near total control by insidious actors like the ADL may turn out to be one of the most important fights of the century. I have no idea how this will play out, it's still possible nothing will come of it, though Elon now seems committed to taking on this fight.

...

Regardless of what Musk delivers from here, millions have been shown the man behind the curtain, and they're not happy. People who believe in a free public square have actually been united and motivated to launch a pushback against these unelected tyrants like Greenblatt, a private citizen who has appointed himself the sole arbiter of what may and may not be discussed in the public square.

As far as I can tell, this is the first time there has been meaningful pushback against the censors. Instead of being on the defensive, looking to disavow the person immediately to their right, conservatives and believers in free speech of all stripes are now on the offensive, working to expose the ADL to their millions of followers.

If we lose this fight to wrestle our ability to speak from the ADL, we'll lose every other fight. The #BanTheADL campaign is diverse, bipartisan, and inclusive of everybody who believes in the power of open discussion and debate. Whether it all ends with the ADL getting banned for platform manipulation, getting bankrupted for tortious interference in several companies, catching another defamation lawsuit, or backing down in response to the popular outcry, anything is better than a future where the ADL dictates what you can and can't say. Godspeed Elon.

– Keith Woods, Sep 9 2023, "#BanTheADL: Taking the Public Square Back from the Censors" (https://www.unz.com/article/bantheadl-taking-the-public-square-back-from-the-censors/)

#BanTheADL proves why speaking of Jewish influence in society is a substantial debate to have, and not mere Jew hate. Accusations of anti-Semitism from groups such as the ADL make it impossible for the promises of the 1st amendment and freedom of speech to be realized. As discussed in an earlier chapter, they also adhere to a double standard by which Jews are free to criticize non-Jews as much as they wish, but non-Jews may never criticize Jews. By promoting a double standard that favors Jews at the expense of Gentiles, and threatening the free speech rights of Gentiles, they are only inviting anti-Semitism by antagonizing non-Jews.

Any Jew that truly values free speech, and harmony and peace between Jews and Gentiles, should combat the efforts of Jewish groups to censor Americans. Jews such as Laura Loomer and Ron Coleman are some of the greatest fighters for freedom of speech in America. This is proven by their defense of freedom of speech even for those many would consider anti-Semites, such as Nick Fuentes (publicly defended by Loomer) and The Proud Boys (defended by Coleman in court).

I would like to see a world where Jews and Gentiles can peacefully co-exist. Where Gentiles protect the civil rights of Jews against discrimination, while Jews also respect the civil rights, including freedom of speech, of Gentiles.

Perhaps my Jewish family, or Jews in general, will look poorly upon me due to playing devils advocate towards alleged anti-Semites in this text. I can see why they would feel this way. But, at the end of the day, I have to follow what I believe is true and just. Otherwise, I feel I am betraying God, for God is the Truth and God is Justice. My goal in writing this is to try my best to portray the arguments of the various personalities I have covered charitably, in order that people may understand their perspective.

Trump Or Death

After a disappointing announcement speech, and challenges by Republicans such as DeSantis, Trump's situation looked desperate. That all changed after the system started prosecuting him.

Former President Donald Trump surrendered on Thursday for a fourth time this year, with this case focusing on his efforts to overturn his 2020 general election defeat in Georgia.

...

Here's a look at some of the other top probes against Trump as he campaigns for the 2024 Republican nomination:

...

Classified documents case

In all, Trump faces 40 felonies in the classified documents case. The most serious charge carries a penalty of up to 20 years in prison.

...

Election Interference

*Smith's second case against Trump was unveiled in August when the
former president was indicted on felony charges for working to overturn
the results of the 2020 election in the run-up to the violent riot by his
supporters at the U.S. Capitol.*

...

Hush Money Scheme

*Trump became the first former U.S. president in history to face criminal
charges when he was indicted in New York in March on state charges
stemming from hush money payments made during the 2016 presidential
campaign to bury allegations of extramarital sexual encounters.*

*He pleaded not guilty to 34 felony counts of falsifying business records.
Each count is punishable by up to four years in prison, though it's not
clear if a judge would impose any prison time if Trump were convicted.*

...

New York Civil Cases

*New York Attorney General Letitia James has sued Trump and the Trump
Organization, alleging they misled banks and tax authorities about the
value of assets including golf courses and skyscrapers to get loans and
tax benefits.*

*That lawsuit could lead to civil penalties against the company if James, a
Democrat, prevails. She is seeking a $250 million fine and a ban on
Trump doing business in New York. Manhattan prosecutors investigated
the same alleged conduct but did not pursue criminal charges.*

**– AP News, Aug 24 2023, "Trump has surrendered for a fourth time
this year. Here's where all the cases against him stand"
(https://apnews.com/article/donald-trump-investigations-other-
charges-b8b064a00caad4306fb54d2f6a320468)**

While these indictments all involve varying issues, the cases dealing with the 2020 election are what have truly turned Trump into a martyr, especially since most Republicans still believe the election was stolen, and view the J6 defendants as political prisoners. The Trump mugshot, as a result of the case in Georgia, may have been meant to humiliate Trump, but it has given him a symbol as an "outlaw" fighting on behalf of the people against the establishment. This fits perfectly with Trump's own representation of himself since he first ran in 2016.

> *"I am your voice. I am with you, I will fight for you and I will win for you."*
>
> *Those words are the core message of the Trump campaign, the promises of an unlikely populist leader, a very rich man who claims to have a real affinity for carpenters, bricklayers, coal miners and the struggling common people of all races in this country who believe the system is rigged against them.*
>
> **– Los Angeles Times, July 22 2016, "With law and order his priority, Trump declares, 'I am your voice'"(https://www.latimes.com/opinion/topoftheticket/la-na-tt-trump-voice-20160722-snap-story.html)**

Trump's lead is so far ahead of all of the other candidates, that he did not even bother to show up at the Republican primary debates. Less people seemed to be interested in news of the debate than they were of the Trump mugshot. As of September 2023, the Republicans seem ready to fight and die for Trump. Not even having to run from a jail cell would dissuade them. Recently, Trump flags bearing the slogan "Trump or Death" have begun to be sighted, including during major sporting events. It seems that the 2024 election may become the final showdown between the establishment and Trump, no matter who wins the election.

If Trump does not win, will his supporters accept it, or will they assume that massive voter fraud is to blame? After all, the voting laws have not really changed since 2020. Even if the vote is not rigged, the political persecution through the justice system itself amounts to election interference and an attempt for Biden to jail his political rivals. Not to mention the rigging in the mass media, such as the 2020 suppression of *The New York Post* Hunter Biden laptop story.

On the other hand, if Trump wins, will the other side accept it? Or will they riot, as they did in 2017 and 2020? Won't the establishment fight it, knowing that when Trump gets in this time, he actually may "lock them up" for real?

> *If you insist upon placing the choice of "Trump or death" before the rest of the country, and will accept no other terms, recognize that there are high odds that the rest of country will refuse to be intimidated into electing someone they detest. The answer may well be, "Let's go with death, then."*
>
> **– National Review, "Who Embraces the Slogan, 'Trump or Death'?"July 6 2023 (https://www.nationalreview.com/the-morning-jolt/who-embraces-the-slogan-trump-or-death/)**

Migrants Take Manhattan

The election also comes at a time when the fabric of society seems to continue to be unwinding around us, a process that truly accelerated in 2020. Supply chain issues, rampant inflation, beyond unaffordable housing, record crime, homeless encampments burying every major city, and a wide open border are putting an extreme strain on American society with the establishment seemingly unwilling or unable to solve these problems.

Even liberal cities like Chicago and New York City are beginning to cry uncle from the pain that the ever-increasing hordes of migrants have inflicted on them.

On Wednesday, Desmon Yancy, the alderman representing the Hyde Park district, called a meeting to discuss the plans to turn the Chicago Lake Shore Hotel into a shelter, and told the agitated crowd he had only just learnt of the plan.

'I was absolutely livid, and you guys are so hypocritical,' one woman told the gathered aldermen, according to CBS News.

Another woman complained at the meeting that the local homeless people - the overwhelming majority of whom are black - were not being given help.

'You've got 73 percent of the people homeless in this city are black people,' she said. 'What have you done for them?'

– Daily Mail, Aug 31 2023, "Chicago residents slam 'hypocrite' lawmakers over plans to house 300 new migrants in hotels while city's majority-black homeless population is left to suffer on streets" (https://www.dailymail.co.uk/news/article-12468299/chicago-migrants-hotel-anger-protests.html)

Unable to find anywhere else to put them, migrants are now living at O'Hare Airport.

Hundreds of asylum seekers are seemingly sleeping on the floor of O'Hare International Airport with little information being offered by the city on what's next for any of these people.

The area where asylum seekers being kept is under the guise of black curtains, by the bus shuttle center, out of sight for most of the people coming through the airport. Those stationed said O'Hare has been their home for several days.

– WGNTV (local Chicago news channel), Sep 5, 2023, "Hundreds of asylum seekers temporarily living at O'Hare International Airport"(https://wgntv.com/news/chicago-news/hundreds-of-migrants-temporarily-living-at-ohare-international-airport/)

Even New York City is perhaps regretting not building the wall.

New York City Mayor Eric Adams made some of his strongest comments yet on his concerns about the unending flow of migrants coming to the city, warning it will upend neighborhoods and continue to strain resources.

"Never in my life have I had a problem that I did not see an ending to. I don't see an ending to this," Adams said Wednesday night.

Adams, a Democrat, was speaking at a town hall organized by his office on Manhattan's Upper West Side. His opening remarks lamented the financial impact of the city's efforts to house and serve more than 100,000 migrants over the last year.

"This issue will destroy New York City. ... All of us are going to be impacted by this. I said it last year when we had 15,000, and I'm telling you now at 110,000. The city we knew, we're about to lose," he continued.

– Politico, Sep 15 2023, "Adams: Cost of migrants 'will destroy New York City'"(https://www.politico.com/news/2023/09/07/eric-adams-migrants-new-york-city-00114437)

In New York City, the city has to make cuts to its own citizens to take care of these migrants.

Mayor Adams' revised $110B budget cuts sanitation, library, education and migrant services, puts NYC on track to have less than 30K cops.

...

Most of New York City's public libraries won't stay open on Sundays anymore. The city's universal pre-K program is getting curtailed. There will be fewer sidewalk trash bins and less street cleaning across the five boroughs. Various services for newly arrived migrants will be phased out, and the NYPD is on track to have less than 30,000 cops for the first time in decades.

...

In a written statement, Adams — who did not hold a briefing to take reporters' questions on the budget update — said the steep belt-tightening is necessary to offset the more than $12 billion his administration projects the city will spend by mid-2025 on sheltering and providing services for the tens of thousands of migrants who have arrived since last year.

– New York Daily News, Nov 16 2023 (https://www.nydailynews.com/)

This is a great example of why Trump was elected in 2016. The establishment, like the Chinese government during the century of humiliation, simply refuses to alter its failing liberal ideology for any reason, even after it inflicts avoidable problems onto society time and time again. So long as it resists reformers like Trump and fights the inevitable illiberal antithesis, these problems will only continue to grow in severity.

The problems are most pronounced in Democrat-controlled cities, which have become increasingly unlivable. Many have moved to the edges of America, to states that are more rural and red. However, the problems will eventually follow even to the most remote parts of America. Even in deep red states such as Idaho and Montana, the mayors are often liberal, more migrants arrive each day, and trans flags hang from the rafters. In rural America, the cities look more Mexican than white, and the whites that are there are poor farmers, not a parallel society of red elites.

The End of White America and the Future of Western Civilization

Whatever happens, and even despite any rightward swing as a result of the dialectic, white America is over forever. According to the 2020 census, Gen Z (perhaps fittingly named) was the last American generation in which white people accounted for a majority.

The following are my predictions for the West as it shall develop in the coming decades and centuries, if current trends continue.

Of course, there are always unpredictable events which can occur in the interim, such as Donald Trump winning the 2016 election, or the Covid pandemic. These unpredictable events can potentially rewrite the course of history and change or reverse its current trajectory. These aside, here are my predictions.

Gradually, native Westerners — that is, white Europeans — will continue to decline in relative and absolute population in both Europe and its colonies, and the population will be replaced with those of non-white European ancestry (non-whites). The immediate consequences of this will be as follows:

- Whites will become a minority in both their ancestral homelands and in their colonies.

- As whites become a minority, they will follow the same trajectory as other populations that have met the same historical fate. Whites will face discrimination and persecution by non-whites, just as all minority populations have throughout history.

- Minorities that feel a historical grievance against whites, such as Native Americans and blacks, will use their increased political and cultural influence to take vengeance against whites in the form of reparations, treating whites as second-class citizens, destroying and repressing white cultures, and perhaps also through violent acts such as pogroms.

- The whites that remain, and continue to identify as whites in spite of persecution, will become more radically ethnocentric. Logically, this must happen, because they will have to value their white identity to a level that makes them motivated to retain their white identity even when it is disadvantageous and it is harder to find other whites to start a family with. Probably in aesthetic and ideology they will resemble "neo-Nazis" of the present day, embracing symbols such as the Black Sun or perhaps even the Swastika. However, this will not result in any sort of Nazi takeover of the government, lacking the political capital to carry out any sort of repression of other races. It will not be considered seriously, but more along the lines of a lost cause. It will be similar to Native Americans of today speaking in extremely inflammatory language about kicking out the White Man and taking their land back, but lacking any ability to do so (thus such threats are not taken seriously either by whites or by the Native Americans themselves).

This period is in its earliest stages, and will accelerate throughout the coming 50 or so years.

At the same time, the historically majority-white nations will lose their remaining white European character and a new civilization will emerge in its place. Whether the character of this new civilization is an improvement or step backward from traditional Western Civilization is entirely up to one's personal opinion. However, it is certain that it will be different, because it will be created and perpetuated by people who culturally and genetically differ from white Europeans. Because of this, something will be lost to the world which once existed, just as something was lost in the world when the culture of the indigenous people of the Americas was lost. And what comes after will not truly be Western Civilization at all, but something as different from the West as the Roman Empire is to Italy.

Therefore, long after this initial period of vengeance has run its course, and the West has entirely become transformed and lost nearly all traces of its white European character to such an extent that it is popularly recognized to be an entirely distinct entity, a new phase will occur. During this period, the new civilization that supplants it will become nostalgic towards the old, white European civilization that preceded it, and a highly idealized myth of "the good old days" of white European civilization will emerge, just as we now have an idealized mythological idea ("the Noble Savage") of what pre-European indigenous civilization was once like.

By this time, figures such as Hitler and Martin Luther King will still be treated as mythological figures to some extent, but people will no longer have strong personal feelings about them or enforce strong taboos regarding them. The historical events of their lives will finally be far enough in the past for historians to study objectively, assuming objectivity is still valued by historians of the successor culture. (Although many cultures favored mythological over objective depictions of history, objectivity remained intact from the Greeks to their various successor civilizations, and in turn has been passed on to most modern industrialized societies, so it will most likely survive. But this cannot be guaranteed).

The various achievements and contributions of white Europeans will be recognized and appreciated at this point in time, and their historical grievances, while they may continue to be acknowledged to some degree, will be buried deep in the past, where they will lie inert. Hopefully all whites will not have been genocided by this time. However, given the wide area in which whites have settled across the globe, it is more likely than not that they will survive in some form in some part of the world, even if the backlash against them is particularly extreme, which it may not be. This second period will occur in the next few generations after the first period, roughly 100-150 years from now.

There is nothing particular about those of white European descent that will in any way exempt them from the same historical fate of all other peoples who have been in an analogous position, so it is reasonable to expect that something similar to this course of events will occur.

There may be a revanchist white period at some point in history. After all, the Reconquista took place after hundreds of years of Muslim rule. But such a thing as that is impossible to predict.

The End of The End: History Reboots

Aside from this, non-demographic reasons are leading to the demise of the West. These factors are wholly political, and a direct result of a foreign policy in which America tried to control the entire world. To add insult to injury, in areas under Western control, the West has also began pressuring the world to adopt its now totally degenerated Clown World culture, including promoting feminism, transgenderism and BLM racial grievance politics.

> *National Security Council spokesman John Kirby has been making curious pronouncements from the White House podium lately.*
>
> *"LGBTQ+ rights are … a core part of our foreign policy," Kirby said last week.*
>
> *What does that mean, exactly? Cross-sex hormones and gender surgery for your kids or you get no foreign aid? That will win hearts and minds across the globe.*
>
> *A couple of days later, Kirby warned that the US will "have to take a look" at imposing economic sanctions on predominantly Christian Uganda if an anti-LGBTQ identity law is enacted that was just passed by its parliament. This would be "really unfortunate," Kirby admitted, since most US aid to Uganda is for health care, especially for AIDS.*
>
> *Meanwhile, Samantha Power is creeping around socially conservative Hungary, stirring up trouble with intersex activists over a law banning gender studies and the portrayal of LGBTQ content to minors.*
>
> *It's one thing to fly the rainbow flag outside our embassies in Kabul and the Holy See. It's quite another to impose American social mores on traditionally Christian or Islamic countries. You know this kind of woke imperialism in our names won't end well for anyone.*
>
> **– New York Post, Mar 26 2023, "White House's push for woke foreign policy will backfire with our socially conservative allies"(https://nypost.com/2023/03/26/white-houses-push-for-woke-foreign-policy-will-backfire-with-our-conservative-allies/)**

This has resulted in the decline of American hegemony in the world, as a new, non-Western alliance, BRICS arises in its place. The cornerstone of this failure of foreign policy was the Ukraine War. As a result of this war, Russia was hit with economic sanctions, the West intending to topple the Russian economy and degrade its ability to fight. This strategy seems to have been unsuccessful. Instead, it forced Russia into the arms of China.

Russia was also removed from many aspects of the global financial system, including SWIFT. This attempt by the United States to take advantage of the financial system to attack another country for political reasons alarmed other countries. As a result, they are trying to move away from a system that relies on the United States to one that is more independent, including by moving away from the US dollar.

As of 2023, BRICS now has a larger GDP than the G7, and their military and economic power is only increasing by the day. In 2023, BRICS began to add more countries to the growing block: Saudi Arabia, Iran, Ethiopia, Egypt, Argentina and the United Arab Emirates. These countries are also expanding in both influence and economic power.

> *In deciding in favour of an expansion - the bloc's first in 13 years - BRICS leaders left the door open to future enlargement as dozens more countries voiced interest in joining a grouping they hope can level the global playing field.*
>
> *The expansion adds economic heft to BRICS, whose current members are China, the world's second largest economy, as well as Brazil, Russia, India and South Africa. It could also amplify its declared ambition to become a champion of the Global South.*
>
> *But long-standing tensions could linger between members who want to forge the grouping into a counterweight to the West - notably China, Russia and now Iran - and those that continue to nurture close ties to the United States and Europe.*

"This membership expansion is historic," Chinese President Xi Jinping, the bloc's most stalwart proponent of enlargement, said. "It shows the determination of BRICS countries for unity and cooperation with the broader developing countries."

...

The entry of oil powers Saudi Arabia and UAE highlights their drift away from the United States' orbit and ambition to become global heavyweights in their own right.

Russia and Iran have found common cause in their shared struggle against U.S.-led sanctions and diplomatic isolation, with their economic ties deepening in the wake of Moscow's invasion of Ukraine.

...

"But it's also obvious that this process of the emerging of a new world order still has fierce opponents."

Iran's President Ebrahim Raisi celebrated his country's BRICS invitation with a swipe at Washington, saying on Iranian television network Al Alam that the expansion "shows that the unilateral approach is on the way to decay".

– Reuters, Aug 24 2023, "BRICS welcomes new members in push to reshuffle world order" (https://www.reuters.com/world/brics-poised-invite-new-members-join-bloc-sources-2023-08-24/)

If BRICS manages to decisively surpass the G7, it will represent the first time in roughly 500 years that the West has not dominated the rest of the world. It is no coincidence that this is occurring at the same time that whites, the people of the West, are becoming a global minority as well as minorities within their own historical nations. We may be returning to a time like that of the ancient past, where the Islamic Empire, China, and India were the leaders of the world, while Europe was a backwater.

While the illiberal antithesis is rising in the West, this is an internal change. On a global scale, it will probably be dwarfed by this change in power from West to East. The global ideology will thus be determined by the cultural landscape of the East, in whatever form that will take (although this form will probably be less liberal than the extreme liberal society of the West today). However, the loss of status in the world will hopefully also further reinforce the failure of the liberal ideology in the West, and accelerate the process. If the illiberal antithesis can properly be synthesized and reinvigorate the West, then perhaps in time it can rise from the ashes.

Final Thoughts about the Internet

Although the Censorship Era seems to be over, it left a permanent mark on Internet culture. While Alt Tech has allowed for some circumvention of the censorship regime, we have hardly returned to the days where you could watch Mr. Bond on YouTube.

Even X, the one major platform trying to fight censorship, is in an ongoing war with groups like the ADL who are trying to prevent Elon's dream of a free speech platform. His plans of finding an alternative revenue source to ads do not sound very promising. He has suggested a few things that may actually make censorship worse: eliminating anonymity, and changing X to a subscription service. Eliminating anonymity will not only make the risk of expressing a heterodox opinion extremely high, it will actually be even higher than expressing it offline, since it will be available for everyone to see and copy verbatim, and for many years. We all have heard of people getting canceled for tweets they made 15 years ago as a teenager. Changing to a subscription service, meanwhile, will make X less of a "public square" and more of a private forum, severely limiting people's reach and ghettoizing their opinions. Again, this is almost no better than the situation was before the Internet was even invented.

Additionally, we seem be drifting further and further away from the unique "transmitter" -> "transmitter" of the Internet, and closer and closer to a "transmitter" -> "receiver" model due to the rise of apps like TikTok, which still contains user-generated content but which is curated and delivered to the user via algorithms, reintroducing a chokepoint at the infrastructure level. When someone scrolls TikTok, it is much like the behavior of a person passively flipping through cable channels. The only difference is that it is even worse, because the nature of short-form content is that the information must be presented in an extremely brief, shallow way, and it is gone and replaced by a new video almost as quickly as it appeared. The only possible advantage it retains over mass media is its user-generated nature, but this is almost entirely canceled out by the ability to hide undesirable user-generated content through the algorithm.

I feel in a way that we are reaching the beginning of the end of the Internet's lifecycle. I believe society is in the first stages of absorbing this medium totally, and its days of being a disruptive force are starting to wind down. It is perhaps appropriate that its decline coincides with the end of the Trump Era. The two will most likely be considered part of the same phenomenon in future history.

As far as legacy media goes, it seems that, while their viewership continues to decline and their paper editions are totally irrelevant, they have retained their prestige status. Elon Musk has also taken notice of this. In a reply to a *Rolling Stone* article in which X was referred to as "zombie Twitter," Musk replied:

> *This is hilarious coming from a magazine that doesn't even exist anymore. When is the last time anyone saw a copy?*
>
> *Their main purpose, and that of many other de facto defunct publications, is to manipulate public opinion by serving as a "mainstream media" source for Wikipedia, to provide probable cause for bogus government investigations and to cancel people who ignore the woke mind virus.*

– Elon Musk, Sep 20 2023
(https://Twitter.com/elonmusk/status/1704717018845397008)

This is the correct take. The mainstream media has been totally replaced by now with the Internet. It no longer serves its supposed primary purpose of informing the people at all anymore. Now, it solely serves as a naked propaganda instrument to manufacture public opinion.

Final Thoughts about Politics

This text has mostly focused on the Right Wing of the Internet, which dominated during the Trump years, especially from 2014-2021. The Left, while certainly present on the Internet, was not as historically significant or as connected to the 4chan-dominated subculture of this time, and was in some ways simply a continuation of pre-Internet forms. However, in researching for this book I have discovered some newer and more recent events on the Left, including the apparent New York-based alliance between the Thiel Right and the socialist Dirtbag Left. This is an interesting development that warrants further investigation. It seems to have only gotten started since the early 2020s. Perhaps in another text, I could cover the Left Wing on the Internet, including its activities during Occupy Wall Street, the emergence of liberal or Leftist Independent journalists such as Tim Pool, _The Young Turks, Buzzfeed_, etc. as well as this new New York-based phenomenon.

> During the Trump years, college students and struggling young professionals across the country looked to Brooklyn for the podcasts, publications and organising models of a new democratic socialism. This cultural energy soon took broad-based political form with electoral victories in major primaries for figures such as Bernie Sanders and Alexandria Ocasio-Cortez.

> ...

Then came the pandemic. The Brooklyn-based cultural scene took the pandemic seriously, and in-person parties and events largely ground to a halt. Not so across the East River in Manhattan. Filling this sudden void in the city's culture was a nascent, mostly younger, twenty-something crowd centred on a gentrifying area of Chinatown sometimes known as "Dimes Square" (a portmanteau of Times Square and the name of one of the scene's preferred restaurants). The defining ethos was scorn for the hyper-cautiousness that reigned in Brooklyn – and more generally for the sanctimony of the "woke" left.

...

Some critique the habits of the "professional-managerial class", while others toy with converting to Catholicism. There is tech money sloshing around in the Manhattan scene, too. Some use the cash from foundations attached to conservative venture-capitalist Peter Thiel to put on festivals of "transgressive" film. Supporters hail the resurgence of art that refuses to trade in its power to shock in exchange for adherence to political dogma. Critics see a scene that practices transgression for its own sake – or for mercenary ends – and warn of the consequences of flirtation with reactionary concepts such as the abandonment of ideals of social progress, Catholicism, and an admiration for the aristocratic past.

– The New Statesmen, May 22, 2022 "New York's Hipster Wars (https://12ft.io/proxy?q=https%3A%2F%2Fwww.newstatesman.com %2Fworld%2Famericas%2Fnorth-america%2Fus %2F2022%2F05%2Fnew-yorks-hipster-wars)

This seems to indicate a movement on the Left away from political correctness and cancel culture and a return to an earlier form of the Left: liberalism. It also shows that the synthesis of the Dissident Right has progressed so far that even its antagonists on the Left are beginning to absorb it, just as the Right eventually began to listen to rock and roll and synthesize parts of the 1960s Leftist counter-culture. This is further proof of my prediction that the dialectic-driven shift to the Right is an inevitable force that cannot be stopped. I still do not see any evidence that the Left will contribute any new political or cultural ideas anytime soon. This shift away from "wokeism" to liberalism will simply absorb the previous cultural

changes, such as transgenderism, without offering any alternative to
challenge them.

The Trump Era marks one last Hail Mary by the American people to fight
back the forces of liberalism with an illiberal ideology. If it is defeated, then
the ultimate zenith of liberalism will be 2024, and any remaining resistance
against the liberal thesis will be permanently crushed, leading to a "century
of humiliation"-style outcome as outlined before. Or, perhaps the country
will simply balkanize and fall apart, allowing a power vacuum in which an
entirely different nation will arise. If it succeeds, then the zenith of liberalism
will have been somewhere around 2015 or 2020, having failed to eliminate
all challenges to its power before receding. In the latter case, hopefully we
will see America live on, and take the first steps towards finally addressing
its many systematic problems that have been piling up since at least the end
of the Cold War and perhaps earlier. It may be something similar to the
rebirth of the Roman Republic as the Roman Empire.

This Hail Mary was made possible by the final great American-led
technological revolution, the Internet, at the very end of the 20th century.
Itself the ultimate manifestation of the American principle of "freedom of
speech," which had never before been realized to the degree that it was
during the Wild West Era of the Internet, reaching its peak in 2016.

There may be only one year left in the Trump Era. Or, it may live on longer
still. The political climate is similar to that of the early 2010s, in the days of
Occupy Wall Street and the proto-Alt Right. On the surface, things seem
more peaceful than in the chaos of the Covid years, but there is much tension
bubbling beneath the surface, ready to erupt at any moment. In the 2024
election, 10 years after GamerGate and the beginning of the Trump Era, it
seems destined to erupt in one way or another.

Index

Printed in Great Britain
by Amazon

42912288R00215